THE PUBLIC MIRROR

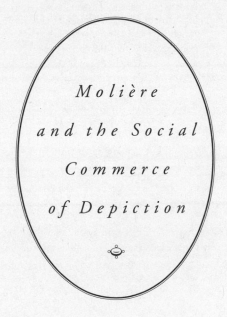

Molière

and the Social

Commerce

of Depiction

LARRY F. NORMAN

The University of Chicago Press

Chicago & London

LARRY NORMAN is assistant professor of French in the
Department of Romance Languages and Literatures at the University
of Chicago. He has written numerous articles on baroque and
neoclassical French theater, moral philosophy, and the
history of ideas.

The University of Chicago Press, Chicago 60637
The University of Chicago Press, Ltd., London
© 1999 by The University of Chicago
All rights reserved. Published 1999
Printed in the United States of America
08 07 06 05 04 03 02 01 00 99   1 2 3 4 5

ISBN: 0-226-59151-4 (cloth)
ISBN: 0-226-59152-2 (paper)

Library of Congress Cataloging-in-Publication Data

Norman, Larry F.
    The public mirror : Molière and the social commerce of
depiction / Larry F. Norman.
        p.   cm.
    Includes bibliographical references and index.
    ISBN 0-226-59151-4 (alk. paper). — ISBN 0-226-59152-2 (pbk. :
alk. paper)
    1. Molière, 1622–1673—Criticism and interpretation.   I. Title.
PQ1860.N67   1999
842′.4—dc21   99-32926
                                                                CIP

Chapter 8 is adapted from an article previously published as
"Dramatic Distance and French Classical Comedy: D'Aubignac's
Theory of the Spectacle" in *Romance Languages Annual* 8:1996.
© Purdue Research Foundation, reprinted with permission.
All rights reserved.

Contents

Acknowledgments

This book would not have been possible without the support, encouragement, and advice of Pierre Force and Antoine Compagnon. Bruce Redford's careful reading of the manuscript and suggestions were invaluable, both intellectually and stylistically. Alan Thomas shepherded this book as editor not only with rare thoughtfulness but also with inimitable grace and good humor. Among others who have offered their support, time, and counsel during the research and writing of this book are Valérie Bénéjam, Sophie Rabau, Françoise Meltzer, Robert Morrissey, Philippe Desan, Gita May, Michel Charles, Marc Fumaroli, Patrick Dandrey, Georges Forestier, Thomas Pavel, David Bevington, Kathy Eden, Michael Seidel, David Morgan, Everette Dennis, Laurence Giavarini, Chet Weiner, Olivia Rosenthal, Janet Rickershauser, Henry Alford, Nadine Kolowrat, and Jenni Fry. I thank each of them for their generous help. I am most grateful to the Lurcy Foundation, which provided funding for a year of research in France, and to Columbia University and the University of Chicago for their research support. The patience and encouragement of my friends during this project provide a model for emulation, as do the support and confidence of my parents. Above all, I am forever grateful to Frédéric for his intellectual inspiration, unfailing help, and unparalleled patience.

INTRODUCTION

Miroirs dans les logis, miroirs chez les marchands,
Miroirs aux poches des galants,
Miroirs aux ceintures des femmes.
—La Fontaine, "L'Homme et son image"

Molière has long been deified as the originator of modern satirical comedy. But the title is a vexing one. The problem for those reading or staging Molière today is this: how can a genre associated with caricature and castigation deliver believable and engaging theater? Where is the place for a credible rendering of life in the satiric ridiculing of vices? Where is the dramatic conflict if the moral lines are so clearly marked, so unambiguous? These problems understandably have led many to dismiss social satire as a foundation for Molière's theater; good drama, according to this argument, demands the kind of universal human conflicts and shifting sympathies toward complex characters that satiric ridicule would apparently preclude.

My aim in undertaking this book, on the contrary, is to take very seriously Molière's own claim to be an author of satires that are first and foremost *effective theater* and, in so doing, to uncover the aesthetic and social conditions that generated this revolution in dramatic form. Molière crafts his comedies in dialogue with his audience: he responds to the powerful craving felt by a new theater public under Louis XIV to see itself depicted on stage. By calling his comedies "public mirrors," Molière conceives of comic representation as a site of audience self-recognition. But the self-recognitions generated by his theater are necessarily volatile: spectators want a satire of their contemporaries, yet recoil from a satire of themselves. Molière thus flirts continuously with the audience's susceptibility, stirring the excitement of individual identifications while dodging the indignation of those identified. Comedy is provocative portrayal. Its moral charge arises not from a flat univocal censure, but from a dynamic process of viewer identification with characters on stage. Instead of producing a static moral denunciation, Molière's satire creates an animated surface, which like the

I

mirror, is metamorphosed by each new viewer. The play is an image in action, one that is formed by exchange and conflict with its audience, and one that provokes a second comedy in the audience viewing it.

There is of course nothing radically new in the mirror analogy itself: the playwright turns to a metaphor that has served since antiquity for mimesis, the representation of reality. The richness of Molière's theater, however, results from its exploitation of a very particular seventeenth-century mania for the mirror, one that held sway over both the aesthetic and social imagination of the period. Its timeliness springs in part from a quite literal source. Mirror technology had improved through the century, producing an explosion of reflective surfaces. The French monarchy even felt the need to promote the industrial fabrication of the device, considering it a prestigious product for the national economy. Though still precious, mirrors were no longer limited to such spectacular creations as Versailles's *Galerie des glaces,* but penetrated for the first time the interior decors of the bourgeoisie. And mirrors not only provided grandeur for walls, but also served as personal accessories, miniature mirror-jewels stylishly appended to belts and ribbons.[1] They were, as La Fontaine illustrates in his fable of a modern Narcissus, simply inescapable in the daily life of the French town and court.

But the mirror was perhaps even more omnipresent in its metaphoric appearances than in its decorative ones. It has become a critical commonplace since the publication of Michel Foucault's *The Order of Things* to label the French classical age "the age of representation." Classical usage, with its penchant for the appropriate metaphor, might prefer the appellation "the age of the mirror." The mirror has two senses here, equally powerful for the seventeenth-century mind. It is first a reproduction of reality, a copy of nature for contemplation and instruction. The century saw the proliferation of the "moral mirror" genre—works of literary portraiture that offered examples, good and bad, of human nature. But the mirror does not only reflect nature, it also reflects other mirrors. This is the second sense of the mirror: a double to artifice. French classicism, despite its emphasis on clarity, reveals here a continuing baroque taste for multiple narrative and pictorial levels, for the *mise-en-abyme,* for the play within the play.

This twin desire for reproduction—for the reproduction of reality and for the reproduction of the reproduction—defines not only the aesthetic principles of the age, but also its sense of identity.[2] The mirror is the site

1. For a history of the mirror in seventeenth-century France, see Melchior-Bonnet.

2. I follow Georges Forestier's formula here: "Ce jeu qui consiste à mettre du théâtre dans du théâtre doit sa naissance et son succès à la mentalité d'une époque, c'est-à-dire à la fois à une vision du monde qui s'exprime en termes de théâtre et à un goût exacerbé pour le dédoublement" (*Le Théâtre dans le théâtre* 15). Bernard Beugnot's "Spécularités classiques" offers perhaps the most useful short

where the beholder recognizes his or her image, thus the definition of portrait in Furetière's 1694 dictionary: "When one looks in a mirror, one sees one's portrait." Such a vision is both flattering and deflating, but it is always irresistible: whether transfixed by vanity or by indignation, the beholder is fascinated by the self-image. But the narcissism of the century is surprisingly lucid. As the definition shows, the classical mind is not fooled by the resemblance between the image and the thing. It readily distinguishes the representation from the thing represented, the copy from the original. In the mirror one sees not one's *face*, but the face's reproduction, its *portrait*. Yet, this awareness of the representation's indirectness—of its artificiality and otherness—does not spoil its moral utility. The seventeenth century celebrates the power of a reproduction, while understanding its limits, for there are realms where representation must replace immediate vision, realms where the inaccessibility of the original requires the creation of a copy.

Chief among these realms is that of self-knowledge. The mirror, after all, is necessary because one cannot see one's face without the aid of reflection: this simple corollary to "know thyself" has been a commonplace since Plato's *Alcibiades I* (132). A contemporary of Molière translates this moral precept into the painful image of a face literally contorting itself in a futile attempt to grasp its own image without the help of a mirror:

> Nous ne sçaurions pas bien nous connoistre par nous-mesme, et l'âme ressemble en cela à notre visage, qu'elle ne se peut voir que dans les miroirs non plus que luy. Si elle entreprend de se regarder autrement, la peine qu'elle a de se replier sur soy la rebute. (Cureau de la Chambre 4)

> We cannot see ourselves by ourselves, and in this the soul is like our face, in that it too cannot see itself except in a mirror. If the face tries to see itself otherwise, the pain it feels in bending over itself frustrates it.

To see oneself, the individual can turn to various mirrors, which the classical imagination endlessly catalogued: the image of one's peers who reflect one's own personal characteristics; the reaction that can be read in the eyes of one's interlocutors; and finally the portrait conveyed by the canvas—or the stage. This last arena is where Molière steps in to gratify his public's desire. In his dialogue with his audience, Molière might well echo the words of Shakespeare's Cassius to Brutus:

---

summary of the metaphorical appearances of the mirror in the French classical age. Though I will be commenting on numerous studies of the mirror metaphor, I note the following for an introductory survey: Baltrušaitis; Genette, "Narcisse"; Greenblatt 1–20; Lyons and Nichols; Marin, *Champaigne* 87–109; and Rousset, *L'Intérieur* 199–211.

[S]ince you know you cannot see yourself
So well as by reflection, I your glass
Will modestly discover to yourself
That of yourself which you yet know not of. (*JC* I.ii.67–70)

Molière, however, would no doubt proclaim "I your glass" with some-what less unctuous "modesty." For unlike the ingratiating Cassius, Molière presents to the beholder not a flattering image, but a belittling one. The satiric mirror is meant to reprove, not to assure. Such is the definition of comedy offered by Molière in his preface to *Tartuffe:*

Les plus beaux traits d'une sérieuse morale sont moins puissants, le plus souvent, que ceux de la satire; et rien ne reprend mieux la plupart des hommes que la peinture de leurs défauts.[3]

The finest strokes of high moral philosophy are less powerful, most often, than those of satire; and nothing reproaches most men more effectively than a painting of their faults.

Molière's potent proclamation of satire's aims has provoked a great deal of debate in the last three centuries. The problem concerns just how realis-tic or topical Molière's "painting of their faults" is. It is certain that Mo-lière—as well as his apologists and his critics—repeatedly refer to the time-liness of the faults portrayed: they all insist on the powerfully direct sense of recognition provoked by the comedies. Yet many twentieth-century scholars have tried to erase Molière's own claims of painting specifically the faults of his day, *de son siècle,* as he says in *La Critique de l'Ecole des femmes.* Inspired by the revitalized interest in Molière's theatricality, these critics believe that satire detracts from the comedies' universal dramatic power.[4] In short, satire is considered a kind of historical gossip sheet un-worthy of serious literary or dramaturgic appraisal. Others have accepted a satiric component in the comedies, but viewed it as a dangerous task that the playwright was forced to abandon in the face of powerful opposition,

3. All references to Molière's work (and to certain documents as noted in the bibliography) are from Couton's Pléiade edition (hereafter cited as *OC*). The authoritative Grands Ecrivains edition remains, however, an important resource, which I regularly consulted.

Although all translations of Molière are mine, Richard Wilbur's brilliant rendering in English of plays such as *Le Misanthrope, Tartuffe,* and *L'Ecole des femmes* have been most helpful to me; indeed, I have modeled some of the translations (particularly from *Le Misanthrope* and *L'Ecole des femmes*) on his work. Unfortunately, though, for reasons of textual analysis, I have had to revise these adaptations for more literal, if less elegant, word-for-word translations.

4. Led by W. G. Moore (1949) and René Bray (1954), the pronouncement of satire as a hindrance to effective drama found a scholarly continuation in the works of Jacques Guicharnaud (1963) and Marcel Gutwirth (1966).

particularly after the censorship of *Tartuffe*.[5] According to this perspective, satire is a kind of philosopher's reprimand administered to an unwilling public, which successfully resists the lesson. More recently, scholars have profited from the renewed interest in historical context and embraced the centrality of satiric representation, but with the sole purpose of mining its sociological and political significance while too often ignoring its dramatic inventiveness.[6]

But for Molière satiric portrayal is an act of tremendous complexity; it is much more than the banal means toward a meaningful end, whether that end be called ideological, political, or moral. Despite the discourse of transparency associated with the mirror, Molière was as lucid as any contemporary in understanding its intricate and often paradoxical workings. After all, the most "faithful" of comic depictions, the most "natural" or "naïve," are obviously never mere reflections; they are instead the product of an artist working within the prevailing codes of representation. And there is nothing simple about those codes. They are not fixed rules; rather, they are a dynamic set of parameters, of multiple poles of attraction, within which the portrayal oscillates and takes form. My argument is not that Molière simply engages in artless direct satire, skewering his contemporaries and resurrecting the raucous topicality of the Old Comedy of Aristophanes. My intention is rather to resituate the comedies within their original creative matrix, one characterized by a tension between direct and indirect representation. Most importantly, I want to examine how the codes governing satiric portrayal are both theatrical *and* social in origin. Molière's stage is the site where two systems of depiction dialogue, where social practices and theatrical traditions flirt, unite, and occasionally collide.

The aesthetic codes are those of French classicism in particular, and more generally of European "baroque." I take this last term in its largest sense, following the art historian John Rupert Martin in defining the obsession with verisimilar representation and the illusion of reality as the central motor of the baroque, whether in its visual, literary, or philosophical forms: "It is to this naturalism" Martin observes, "that we must turn to find the most direct link between Baroque art and thought" (13).[7] What

5. This argument has been most thoroughly and brilliantly explored by Gérard Defaux. Patrick Dandrey has since presented a serious challenge to this vision of Molière's career, arguing for a transcendental definition of *le ridicule* and its depiction, one that would be applicable to all of Molière's work (*Molière, ou l'esthétique* 8–10 and passim).

6. The last two decades have seen important studies of Molière's vision of social classes (Gaines), of absolutism (Vincent et al.), and of paternal authority (Waterson). I am indebted to these authors and would hardly suggest that their analyses are insensitive to dramatic form. Nevertheless, their goal is to determine a supposed end of representation, rather than its means.

7. While Anglo-Saxon and German critics tend to place French classicism in the larger context of European baroque, French critics still tend to oppose the baroque and the classical: the first is based

are the *conditions of depiction* that govern this "classical naturalism"? As I have suggested, the mimetic artist must negotiate between two often contradictory demands, one to portray the universal or ideal, the other to portray the particular or real. To represent the ideal, or the *ideally real,* is the aim of the higher genres, whether historical painting, epic poetry, or heroic tragedy. This ideal is not necessarily beautiful or good: there is, as Corneille knew, an ideal greatness in villains as well as in heroes. It is instead a metaphysical ideal: the higher genres aspire to depict a concentrate of human nature rather than the watery fluid of contingency. They strive toward essence rather than happenstance, toward the verisimilar rather than mere verity, toward the Aristotelian "what should be" of poetry rather than the "what is" of history. By contrast, the lower or middle genres—such as portrait and "genre" scene painting, comedy, farce, satire, and epistles—are required to represent particularities of daily life. Furthermore, by portraying the here and now, rather than a grand past or an exotic land, they must meet the test of likeness. The public can measure the actual model against the portrait. Accidental details must be seized; ephemeral fashion and momentary manners captured. And yet, even while practicing these less exalted and more realistic genres, the painter or writer desiring distinction and authority must also present something more universal in his rendering, lest it be denigrated as a mere copy. It is here that Molière tests the limits of European neoclassicism: by presenting "the greatest measure of realism" possible in the period, by being "more intent upon rendering the individual reality than the majority of the moralists of his century," it is clear, as Erich Auerbach has argued, that Molière slyly advances the subterranean evolution of Western realism at a moment of general aesthetic retrenchment (*Mimesis* 361, 365). Yet despite these experiments outside certain mimetic norms, Molière was hardly indifferent to the glorious title of poet, and in seeking the aesthetic prestige associated with ideal verisimili-

---

on imaginative conceits and self-conscious play; the second on formal simplicity and reason. When Martin declares that "seventeenth-century classicism . . . may be best understood as an integral part of the Baroque whole," he follows an established historical schema, illustrated, for example, by Arnold Hauser's notion of the "classicistic baroque" (2: 202). On the other hand, the authoritative French work on the topic, Victor Tapié's *Baroque et Classicisme,* engages a dialogue between the two tendencies only while stubbornly maintaining their mutual "autonomy" (292). In literary studies, the work of Jean Rousset has no doubt gone the furthest in revealing the baroque inside the classic, including inside Molière's work. More recently, Forestier has attempted to advance the dialogue in his *Le Théâtre dans le théâtre,* though he refuses to transcend the aesthetic dichotomy. Any such strict opposition proves, I believe, a dead end for the study of Molière. Here I join with Nicholas Hammond in his dismissal of an artificial dichotomy that has survived its usefulness (20–21). And yet while rejecting hard and fast borders between the two, I do not wish to dismiss the terms themselves. Baroque reflexivity and classical mimesis dialogue in these plays that portray social reality while dramatizing the very process of portrayal.

tude he shared the tenuous position of ambitious portrait painters and satirists. It is precisely from the shakiness of Molière's foothold, negotiating as he was between contradictory demands of universality and specificity, that he created the new comic form that was to become the authoritative model for generations to come.

These aesthetic norms are paralleled by another set of constraints that determines the playwright's creative field. These pressures come not from above, from the theoreticians of art, but from the base, from the audience. For Molière's audience is engaged in its own commerce of depiction. Mid-seventeenth-century France sees the flowering of a new kind of social dynamic: a continual exchange of peer observation and representation. In the good society of the rich bourgeoisie and aristocracy that forms Molière's Parisian audience, each participant observes the other and competes for distinction in the eyes of the other: social commerce becomes, as Norbert Elias remarks, a kind of stock exchange in which reputations swing wildly depending on the judgment of one's peers (476). Naturally enough, in this society of mutual observation and estimation, verbal satire forms one of the principal conversational sports of the town and court. Mocking others is this public's obsession, whether at an aristocratic salon, at a worldly bourgeois home, or at the theater. And yet it is needless to say that few are those who wish to see themselves mocked (though these fascinatingly perverse creatures do exist, as we will see).

This then is the playwright's dilemma: he must keep the portrait specific enough to delight audiences by satirizing their contemporaries, yet without making them realize that they themselves may be targeted. The satirist would indeed be lucky if it were really true, as Jonathan Swift remarked in his preface to *The Battle of the Books,* that "satire is a sort of glass, wherein beholders do generally discover everybody's face but their own." Molière's public was not always so complaisant. From his first effort on the Paris stage, *Les Précieuses ridicules,* he was faced with censure (and possible censorship) from those who identified themselves in his characters. His art then became one of crafting portrayals that both provoke and dodge the audience's sense of self-recognition. In order to do so, he created an armory of weapons to advance satire: indirection, disguise, ventriloquism, irony, and even the menace of public humiliation for his targets. These tools make satire a dramatic art and not a static moral commentary.

Those who argue that satire stops with opposition, defeated by an angry public and official censorship, miss then the true power of the form. Satire starts precisely with opposition—or at least that is where it starts to get interesting. Holding up a cruel mirror is no sport unless the beholder be susceptible to insult, and ready to retaliate. The game begins when the satiric ball is returned. Representation is an act designed to arouse response: "The play's the thing wherein I'll catch the conscience of the King." Like Hamlet's court performance of the dumbshow, Molière's theater is a place where the public is confronted with its own vices, and where it reacts with its own violence. Of course, Molière, unlike the impolitic Hamlet, must carefully measure all resemblances to life in such a way as to please the guilty, and hold their gaze, rather than shame them into quitting the audience. Nevertheless, Molière's performances resembled those of Elsinore's court—in a Paris where the tragedy of self-recognition is transformed into the comedy of misrecognition and narcissism.

Of course, Hamlet's dumbshow differs from Molière's comedy in one crucial way: once taken away from its originally intended spectators, Hamlet's recreation of the crime would become at best an eerie ballet of tragic mimes; Molière's satire, in contrast, continues centuries later to excite audiences for much the same reasons that it energized his contemporaries. Molière seizes on a moment of social and aesthetic history in order to craft comedies that crystallize the most brilliant and cunning rays of satire. He does so by finding formal structures that transform his audience's commerce in satiric observation into a motor for effective drama: the conversational techniques of sly indirection, irony, and caustic disguise become in Molière's hands tools to advance comic action; the daily life experiences of painful self-recognition, misrecognition, and vanity provoked by peer criticism become the engine of dramatic conflict. Molière, working in conjunction with his public's own capacities for satiric representation, injects a powerful shock of reality into mimetic comedy, too long defanged by a residual fear of direct satire, the old ghost of Aristophanes defaming Socrates. At the same time the playwright makes the necessary concessions to generality, concessions that happily prevent the kind of topicality prohibitive to the posterity of the play; and he does so again in a dialogue with his public—out of fear of offending individuals, out of respect for the codes of decorum that frame his exchange with the audience. When Molière metamorphoses this social commerce into comedy, he undertakes innovative experiments in dramatic form, the complexity of which continues to fascinate today. Paradoxically, it is in the very topicality of the plays, in their dangerous proximity to Molière's original audience, that we find the roots of Molière's timeless appeal to spectators and readers. For it is from his troubled exchange with an avid but susceptible public that Molière transformed satire into a triumph of theater.

⟡

In the first two parts of this book I examine how Molière engages in a dynamic exchange with his public, both in the creation and in the reception of his works, before turning in the third part to the dramatic structure of the plays themselves. I begin with the genesis of Molière's comedies, a subject of heated polemics from the beginning of the playwright's Paris career. During the Quarrel of *L'Ecole des femmes* Molière was accused of appropriating portrait sketches *(mémoires)* written by members of his public and then constructing his comedies solely from these amateur transcriptions of social life. I argue that he negotiates this accusation to his advantage, establishing a kind of mythic collaboration with his audience: both the playwright and his public share a talent for keen social observation that guarantees satire's likeness to life. The social genesis of the comedy permits the myth of a transparent comedy, one in which comic artifice, and the professional playwright, are cannily effaced.

However, this transparency, desired though it is by the audience, creates its own set of problems. Part 2 considers the plays' reception, examining texts by Molière and his contemporaries that depict spectators in the uneasy position of being confronted with their own unflattering portrait. These scenes of spectator indignation, narcissism, and blindness formed what Molière called a "second comedy," where the spectacle shifts from the stage action to the audience reaction. This theater of spectator recognition reveals a concept of personal identity specific to the classical age, a concept of the self that is not formed by conscious introspection, nor by metaphysics, nor even by name and title, but instead by the mirror of social commerce, by the exchange of self-representations that constitutes the main pastime of Paris's leisure classes. Personal identity is a shifting molecule of visible social traits—manners, rank, sex, morals—that one shares, more or less according to the case, with one's peers. Just as the satirist portrays a range of personal features from the universal to the particular, so too does the beholder identify the portrait's model by operating subtly among categories of genus, species, and individual. Is a woman to see herself in the *generic* satire of her sex? Or should she define herself by her *specific* moral character, and thus distinguish herself from the satire's broader target— differentiating between say a lady of virtue and women in general? Should she furthermore see herself as an autonomous *individual* within her moral or social group, a woman unlike others of her grouping? Molière undertakes a theatrical investigation of the dysfunctions of spectators' identifications, and the results for comedy are, it must be admitted, troubling. The tendency to misrecognize models and misapply reproof seriously endangers the moral purpose of comedy: if indeed the theatrical exchange between stage and audience follows the same pattern as the social commerce of representation, then there seems little hope to escape the brutal games of criticism and counter-criticism, of malicious satire and indignant riposte, games that prove brilliant material for the theater, but little help for moral reform.

The questionable utility of satiric depiction becomes a driving force in the dramaturgy of Molière's theater, and in part 3 I turn to the plays' internal structures. The conditions of comic creation and reception are reenacted in the dialogue and action of the comedies, where characters engage in exchanges of provocative personal portraits. By designating characters as portrayers and censors of their peers, Molière interrogates the social commerce of representation and identification, mercilessly exposing its intricate rules and treacherous etiquette. In particular, Molière dramatizes the techniques of verbal indirection and irony employed by characters wishing to mask their offending portraits and thus avoid affront. The act of depiction then creates the suspense of response: Will the ridiculed character recognize himself in the verbal portrait? If not, the resulting scene presents the adroit maneuvering of the mocker before the myopic, or the more brutal comic ballet of repeated punches to the incognizant. If, however, the subject identifies herself, the action produces either the absurd complacency of the narcissistic or the retaliation of the susceptible. The latter case is the most richly exploited and offers a number of variants. Characters understand that self-recognition is a tricky business: to identify one's own faults in a generalized or indirect portrait is to confess to the fault portrayed. Depending on the finesse and lucidity of the character, a number of possible scenes result: humiliating self-incrimination, direct riposte (either physical or verbal, depending on the stature of the character), and, in the most elaborate variant, an exchange of indirect counterportraits, a duel of ironic insult and concealed indignation.

Even if faith in the corrective power of the comic mirror is severely tested by Molière's unmasking of the *amour-propre,* blindness, and spite that characterize it, his comedies do not ultimately denounce their own utility. Indeed, it is precisely when satire exposes itself—and its own dysfunctions—that it best promotes the chief, perhaps sole, virtue existing in a world defined by self-presentation and peer description. That virtue is lucidity. In the following pages, I want to discover how the satiric comedy bares to its original audience its system of imagining itself and might provide for us today a key to the classical culture of representation.

Part
One

CREATION
CREATION

One

⋄

URANIE AND THE "GENERAL THESIS"

After arriving in Paris in 1658, Molière quickly embarked on a controversial career as a theatrical satirist. Beginning with his first effort, *Les Précieuses ridicules,* Molière had to defend himself against the charge of directly satirizing several powerful Parisian personalities; indeed, he may nearly have faced censorship for slander. And yet the playwright continued along his path, targeting in the next three years social types such as paternal tyrants, prudes, pedants, and with *Les Fâcheux,* the courtiers who surrounded Louis XIV himself. The success of these short satirical works led Molière to realize his ambition of producing a successful work in the grand style of a five-act verse comedy. His previous attempt at this prestigious form was the disastrous pseudo-tragedy *Dom Garcie de Navarre,* a "heroic" comedy far from the lively portrayal of current reality in which he excelled. His new *grande comédie, L'Ecole des femmes (The School for Wives),* however, built on his previous efforts at a simple ("naïve" in classical diction) depiction of contemporary manners.

The play was dangerously triumphant. His rivals and critics could not suffer the elevation of this public clown to respected playwright, to modern heir of Plautus and Terence. The aesthetic order was being subverted. Middling realism was ranking itself equal to the idealized portrayal of the heroic. Comic recognition of the audience's own world was supplanting tragic admiration of a wondrous past.

Molière replied with a polemical play, *La Critique de l'Ecole des femmes,* which cleverly masquerades its self-serving apology in the form of parodic criticism. But the true originality of the comedy lies in placing both the criticism and the defense of the author in the mouths of the theater public, gathered in a Parisian salon where they discuss Molière and, in particular,

the accuracy of his portrayal of contemporary society. In short, with Molière's new play *La Critique,* the public is depicted on stage criticizing its
own stage depiction in Molière's previous play, *L'Ecole des femmes.* It is in
this context that the playwright undertakes his self-defense—and given
the situation, it is by necessity a wily one. We have already summed up
Molière's dilemma: he must defend the pleasure of satire's immediacy while
at the same time softening the blow to those who felt immediately targeted. Molière crafts a double-pronged apology, one that paradoxically emphasizes both the delectable specificity and the comforting universality of
his plays. The following two apologies from *La Critique* perfectly expose
the tension between the approaches embraced by Molière:

> [L]orsque vous peignez les hommes, il faut peindre d'après nature. On veut
> que ces portraits ressemblent; et vous n'avez rien fait, si vous n'y faites re-
> connaître les gens de votre siècle. (1: 661; sc. vi)

> When you paint men, you must paint from life. People want these portraits
> to be lifelike; and you haven't done anything if you don't make the audience
> recognize the people of your times.

> Toutes les peintures ridicules qu'on expose sur les théâtres doivent être regar-
> dées sans chagrin de tout le monde. Ce sont miroirs publics, où il ne faut
> jamais témoigner qu'on se voie; et c'est se taxer hautement d'un défaut, que
> se scandaliser qu'on le reprenne. (1: 658; sc. vi)

> All the ridiculous portraits that are exposed on the stage ought to be seen
> by all without distress. They are public mirrors, where one should never
> admit to seeing oneself; to be offended by the reproof of a fault is to accuse
> oneself openly of it.

The contradictions are glaring. The audience must at the same time recognize the people of their time and yet never recognize themselves—a logical
dead end if the statement is to apply to the entire audience, for there would
be no one left to recognize. Furthermore the portrait is qualified as both
direct, that is to say painted from life, from individual models as in a stu-
dio, and as indirect, as a public mirror, that is, a broad reflection on society
at large. However, these contradictions, irreconcilable as they may appear,
may actually coalesce to form a certain coherent position. Though the
statements disagree on the exact nature of the comic portrait and its desired
effect, they do concur in stressing the primacy of portraiture for the comedy. Indeed the two passages have often been cited together to arrive at a
totalizing aesthetics of Molière's theater. The common conclusions can be
summarized as follows:

1) The emphasis on portraiture implies that the representation of manners and character drives the play, supplanting the traditional emphasis on plot structure. *Depiction* replaces *action* as the motor of comedy.

2) The images of the portrait from life and of the mirror both bind comedy to a mimetic program proscribing abasing deformations and flattering distortions. Both caricatural farce and heroic idealization are banned from Molière's theater.

These propositions are among the most debated in the last half century of Molière scholarship. Some critics reject these precepts as actually guiding Molière's creation; they celebrate instead the plays' energetic plots and farcical verve. Others accept the precepts, but only for part of Molière's career. Yet even if we accept the seriousness and validity of these precepts, which I do, it must be admitted that they produce more questions than answers. Just how are manners to be depicted in a dramatic form, and how can they structure that form? To what extent are the manners portrayed specific or general? Finally, where is the art in characterizations so faithful that they seem like life itself, like the reflection of a mirror rather than the creation of a poet? Is it poetic imitation or merely an artless copy?

These are the questions that will allow us to arrive at Molière's *dramaturgy of depiction*. But to answer them we must look beyond the plays themselves and toward the representational exchange between author and public. Indeed, Molière himself in no way regards his comedies as autonomous structures, detachable from the situation of their creation and reception. As we have seen, the two statements from *La Critique* concentrate primarily on the audience's reaction to these portraits—on how they "are to be seen," on what "one wants" from them—and on the playwright's efficacy in pleasing this audience; as for issues of internal dramatic structure, one must look elsewhere. The attention given here to the reception of the work seems natural: to qualify the comedy of manners as a mirror reflecting its own audience is necessarily to conceive of it as part of a dynamic exchange: the play is a spectacle that produces sense only in relation to a spectator. If we wish then to understand the aesthetics of Molière's comic mirror, we must look at the social configuration of its performance. The comedy of manners is a place where the public sees itself.[1]

1. This formula plays on two senses of the word "public"; it is a semantic double play firmly established in the seventeenth century and one that is most important to our problem. The public is (1) the audience of the literary portrait and (2) the subject matter of that portrait. This is the double sense of the word in the famous formula with which La Bruyère opens his preface to *Les Caractères:* "I render to the public what it has loaned me" [Je rends au public ce qu'il m'a prêté]. The author renders to the *public-as-audience* what the *public-as-model* has furnished his depiction. In terms of the theatrical

It is therefore most appropriate that Molière's aesthetic principles are enunciated in a dialogue with the public, couched in the fictional response by his supposed audience that constitutes the dialogue of *La Critique de l'Ecole des femmes*. If, for Molière, representation is indissociable from its reception, then in *La Critique* reception becomes in turn the subject of representation. Audience reaction is transformed into comedy. This is a central fact we cannot ignore in examining the weight of the precepts I have up to now attributed to Molière. For these reflections on the power of representation are dramatized in such a way as to transform their meaning. In particular, the dramatic exchange on public mirrors astonishingly *enacts* its own scene of depiction and recognition. Even more importantly, this scene of social representation and recognition is explicitly compared with those of Molière's comedies.

Unfortunately, scholars have for too long ignored the dramatic frame in which the mirror precept is placed, generally citing it as an autonomous statement of aesthetics, one credited to Molière (as I myself have done thus far) and not to the character speaking, Uranie. Marco Baschera has recently unmasked some of the semiotic significance of this scene;[2] I would like to further gauge the dramatic context of the precepts, with the aim of learning just how the theatrical exchange of comic depiction operates within the frame of the social commerce of peer description. A close reading of the dialogue will reveal that the reciprocity of social communication thoroughly grounds the dialogue between stage and audience.

In the scene, Uranie, cohostess of the salon and Molière's apologist, defends Molière's satire against the criticisms leveled by Climène. (Naturally Climène, being a critic of Molière, is portrayed as a ridiculous type, in this case, a hybrid of prude and *précieuse*.) Here is the passage that immediately precedes the extract on "miroirs publics":

> CLIMÈNE: [V]ous ne me persuaderez point de souffrir les immodesties de cette pièce, non plus que les satires désobligeantes qu'on y voit contre les femmes.

---

spectacle, the public's dual status can be formulated as follows: the playwright portrays the public on stage for the pleasure of the public in the audience.

2. Baschera's brilliant analysis of the scene was published (1998) after these pages were written, and I believe our readings are happily complementary. While Baschera concentrates on the significance for Molière's system of theatrical signs, considering, for example, the relationship between the "mask" and the character, I use the scene instead to uncover the social dynamic that shapes Molière's aesthetics.

Huguette Gilbert's compelling article, "Molière et la comédie polémique," also explores the dramaturgy of *La Critique* in relation to Molière's aesthetics. Gilbert does not, however, explore the dramatization of aesthetic pronouncements and precepts such as those made by Dorante.

URANIE: Pour moi, je me garderai bien de m'en offenser et de prendre rien sur mon compte de tout ce qui s'y dit. Ces sortes de satires tombent directement sur les moeurs, et ne frappent les personnes que par réflexion. N'allons point nous appliquer nous-mêmes les traits d'une censure générale; et profitons de la leçon, si nous pouvons, sans faire semblant qu'on parle à nous. Toutes les peintures ridicules qu'on expose sur les théâtres doivent être regardées sans chagrin de tout le monde. Ce sont miroirs publics, où il ne faut jamais témoigner qu'on se voie; et c'est se taxer hautement d'un défaut, que se scandaliser qu'on le reprenne.

CLIMÈNE: You will not persuade me to suffer the immodesty of this play [*L'Ecole des femmes*], nor the unkind satires it presents of women.

URANIE: As for myself, I'm careful not to be offended by them and take anything personally [to my account] that is said there. These kinds of satire target manners directly and strike people only by reflection. Let us not apply to ourselves the strokes of general censure and profit from the lesson if we can, without seeming as if we were spoken to. All the ridiculous portraits that are exposed on the stage ought to be seen by all without distress. They are public mirrors, where one should never admit to seeing oneself; to be offended by the reproof of a fault is to accuse oneself openly of it.

Climène considers Molière's comedy an affront. But it is important to note that she expresses her indignation in general, rather than personal, language. She does not say that she recognizes herself in Molière's satire, only that she views Molière's depictions of women as unbearable; she will not countenance such representations of her sex. However, if Climène's language suggests that her repugnance to Molière's satire is nothing but a disinterested defense of women, this pretense of detachment does not impress Uranie, who has no doubt that Climène actually sees herself in Molière's mirror. Thus Uranie insinuates that Climène is "offended" because she takes the portrait of women to her own "account." Uranie then proposes two responses to the kind of painful self-recognition that she has detected in Climène, two ways to soften the blow of seeing one's faults in the comic mirror. She first contends that Molière's satires are not intended to target any specific person, but instead to ridicule general social manners. "Never see yourself," Uranie seems to urge. But this proposal is difficult to support, given that Molière's satires are so lifelike. She then implicitly concedes that one may indeed be forced to recognize oneself in Molière's mirror. At this point Uranie makes a second, more sly recommendation: "always hide the fact that you see yourself." It is to confess to a fault to disapprove of its denunciation. Indignation, according to Uranie, is a sure sign of shameful self-recognition.

Uranie's argument is aimed directly at Climène, who has inculpated herself by objecting to Molière's satires. Uranie's speech thus acts as a kind of verbal satire of Climène. It provides an analysis of Climène's behavior, ridiculing her self-identification in the satiric portrait. However, Uranie prudently makes this satire a general one and never refers specifically to Climène; nor does she address Climène in particular: Uranie's remarks concern "us," the spectators, and in particular, the female spectators. Nevertheless, Climène suspects with some reason that Uranie's generalities are a camouflage for a personal attack, and that she, Climène, is specifically targeted by Uranie's argument. Climène responds accordingly:

> Pour moi, je ne parle pas de ces choses par la part que j'y puisse avoir, et je pense que je vis d'un air dans le monde à ne pas craindre d'être cherchée dans les peintures qu'on fait là des femmes qui se gouvernent mal.

> For my part, I don't speak of these things because I have any part in them, and I think my life is such that I need not fear being sought in those portraits of women of ill conduct.

Climène replies to what she feels are two closely linked accusations against her. The first comes from Molière with his satire against women. The second now comes from her hostess Uranie with her denunciation of susceptible spectators like Climène. And her response to Uranie is as damning as her response to Molière. By insisting so strongly—and with such obvious defensiveness—that she does not fit into Uranie's description of self-recognizing spectators, Climène reveals through her very indignation (a sure sign of self-recognition, as we have seen) that she has recognized herself as the target of Uranie's commentary— a commentary, appropriately enough, on the very dangers of expressing self-recognition. And the danger at hand is quite serious: Molière's satires are against "women of ill conduct." To recognize oneself in such a portrait is to admit to a serious fault. The skirmish between Uranie and Climène thus risks becoming an affair of honor and disrupting the polite exchange of salon conversation. To quiet the scandal raised by Climène, Uranie and her sister, the ironic Elise, reassure the affronted *précieuse:*

> ELISE: Assurément, Madame, on ne vous y cherchera point. Votre conduite est assez connue, et ce sont de ces sortes de choses qui ne sont contestées de personne.
> URANIE: Aussi, Madame, n'ai je rien dit qui aille à vous; et, mes paroles, comme les satires de la comédie, demeurent dans la thèse générale.
> CLIMÈNE: Je n'en doute pas, Madame. Mais enfin passons sur ce chapitre.

ELISE: Certainly, madam, you'll not be sought there [in Molière's satire of women]. Your conduct is sufficiently known and such things are contested by no one.

URANIE: So too, madam, did I say nothing that regards you; my words, like the satires of the comedy, remain in the general thesis.

CLIMÈNE: I do not doubt it, madam. But let us leave this topic.

By insisting on the impersonal nature of her remarks, Uranie explicitly compares her own depiction of her peers (about spectators' susceptibility) with Molière's satires (of women's behavior). This parallel between conversational and dramatic satire invites, I believe, a serious reconsideration of the stated principles of the comic mirror. How are we to interpret the comparison between Uranie and Molière?

First of all, we must take into account the highly precarious nature of Uranie's claim. When she asserts that her own satire of spectators is meant to be entirely general, her claim is most dubious. The sincerity of Uranie's remark is undermined first by the irony dripping from her sister Elise's defense of Climène. Climène's reputation is, says Elise, "sufficiently known"—but known for *what*? There we are invited to use our imaginations. Uranie roguishly supports her own assertion upon Elise's treacherous ambiguity; her use of the conjunction "so too" [aussi] firmly links her own claim to Elise's arch double entendre. Furthermore, Uranie's faith in her own proposition is rendered questionable by the purely conventional nature of her "apology." In order to avoid a direct insult, which would transgress the rules of polite conversation in which they are engaged, she claims not to have intended a personal attack. And Climène's response to Uranie's apology shows how well she understands the conventional nature of it. Her claim to have no doubts concerning Uranie's sincerity ("I don't doubt it, madam") is a purely formal one, designed, like Uranie's comment, to quiet hostilities and allow the conversation to continue. It is therefore naturally followed by a desire to change the subject and thus put an end to a dangerous topic, one that threatens reputations.

If we now pursue the consequences of Uranie's comparison of her own satire with Molière's satires, we can by analogy call into question the frankness of Molière's assertions concerning the generality of his "public mirrors." We know the satiric bite of Molière's plays often placed him in as difficult a position with his spectators as Uranie's comment places her with her interlocutor, Climène. Affairs of honor can be provoked by theatrical portraits as well as conversational ones. Satire is a dangerous business, and claims to a "general thesis" provide the best defense when one is faced with a hostile spectator. Peace must be maintained in the theater as well as in the salon. By placing his theorization of comic *miroirs publics* in the context of the skirmish between Uranie and Climène, Molière suggests that his remarks, like Uranie's, are to be read either as ironic or as a purely conventional apology designed to maintain good relations with his audience, to facilitate the decorous exchange between playwright and public. The dramatic context of the precept regarding public mirrors, then, acts as a sign to alert the reader to "read between the lines" and to question the literal value of the pronouncement.

I believe that the tensions exposed by the Uranie-Molière comparison—tensions between general and specific depiction, between public and private denunciation—undermine the apparent fixity of all of Molière's stated principles concerning comic portraiture, and I will pursue the consequences for the aesthetics and social function of theater throughout this book. What interests me first though—what astounds even before considering such consequences—is the simple *existence* of this comparison. The parallel between Molière and Uranie, between comedy and conversation, emphasizes the active *communication* between playwright and public; it accents its dynamic nature, one in which the audience reacts and responds, and in which the playwright takes into account this reaction in his productions. It is a parallel between two systems of representation and identification: one employing verbal portraits, and operating between social interlocutors; the other employing dramatic portraits, and operating between playwright and public.

However, Molière does more than compare the comedies' representational dynamics to that of social commerce. More than analogic, the relationship between the two is dynamic. Social representation generates comic creation. Comedy is not simply like conversation: it is in fact born of conversation. Such is the paradigm that Molière embraces at the end of his comedy. In a surprising and baroque turn of events, *La Critique* concludes with the characters deciding to transcribe the whole conversation and then to send it to Molière for staging. The dénouement enacts the very genesis of the comedy: the play ends with its creation, that is to say, with the characters writing their own play. Molière's audience is depicted attributing to itself authorship of the comedy. I will examine later the detailed terms of the contract between the audience-author and Molière, but for the moment we must ask simply, why would Molière attribute the play to his audience rather than himself? Why would he suggest his comedy is born of social interaction and thus not of his own personal genius?

It must be admitted first that on a tactical level, there is a certain logic to attributing the play to the audience. Molière is well aware of the danger that the play might appear shamelessly biased.[3] By claiming the comedy is a transcription of an actual conversation, and one undertaken freely at the initiative of the participants, Molière insists upon the authenticity of *La Critique* as a sample of public reaction. Furthermore, there is a more basic strategy no doubt at work: that of ingratiating the public—and in particular the most influential segment of the audience, the cultivated elites portrayed here—by relinquishing to it the honor of authorship. There is indeed a long tradition of such authorial transfers in dedicatory texts.[4] Molière himself embraces the tactic in his preface to *Les Fâcheux,* practicing it with the most important member of his audience, Louis XIV. Molière thanks the king for having served in two capacities: first as a spectator of the play, and then as its cocreator:

> Je le dois, sire, ce succès qui a passé mon attente, non seulement à cette glorieuse approbation dont Votre Majesté honora d'abord la pièce . . . mais encore à l'ordre qu'Elle me donna d'y ajouter un caractère de fâcheux, dont Elle eut la bonté de m'ouvrir les idées Elle-même, et qui a été trouvé partout le plus beau morceau de l'ouvrage. (1: 481)

> Sire, I owe this success, which exceeded my expectations, not only to that glorious approval with which His Majesty honored the play first . . . but also to that order His Majesty gave me to add the character of a bore, and of which He had the goodness to give me the ideas himself, and which has been found by all to be the best part of the work.

Clearly Molière's abdication of authorship in favor of the king shows that a collaboration between public and playwright is not entirely innocent of short-term political strategy. But the scene implicitly pictured of the king dictating a character sketch to the playwright is one that plays a much larger role than this apparent flourish of royal praise might suggest. Indeed, it is the kind of scene we will see repeated constantly in accounts of Molière's creative process. These attribution scenes are in fact much more than tactical; they reveal something fundamental about the conception of comic creation.

Molière is in fact radically recasting comic form in the years in which he inscribes his audience in the creative process, and these attribution scenes are two of the most vital steps in the theatrical revolution Molière

---

3. So it is that Molière recounts (in the preface of *L'Ecole des femmes*) that he rejected an earlier version of *La Critique* written by a friend because the play was "trop avantageuse" to his cause and would make it appear that he had fished for praise ("mendié les louanges") (1: 543). At the same time, by publicizing the fact that his friend, "une personne de qualité," wrote what we can call this *Ur-Critique,* Molière already suggests the strategy of public composition that he will use in *La Critique.*

4. See Chartier, *Forms and Meanings* ("Princely Patronage and the Economy of Dedication").

undertakes after his arrival in Paris. The 1661 *Les Fâcheux* and the 1663 *La Critique* survey the territory on which Molière will finally construct his definitive comedy of manners, *Le Misanthrope* (1666). *Les Fâcheux* presents the first series of realistic portraits of an elite public—indeed the court itself—that Molière undertook. Written just two years after *Les Précieuses,* Molière moves from a burlesque parody of the Parisian elites, one that disguises itself in a farce of bourgeois provincials, to a much more direct and thoroughly undisguised portrait gallery of courtiers in *Les Fâcheux.* It is precisely this move from farce to "classical naturalism" that the fabulist La Fontaine remarked upon soon after the performance. The poet evokes the image of a new Terence and opposes the farcical actor Jodelet, who appeared in *Les Précieuses,* to a new fidelity in comic depicting. Molière has created an aesthetic revolution:

> Nous avons changé de méthode:
> Jodelet n'est plus à la mode,
> Et maintenant, il ne faut pas
> Quitter la nature d'un pas. (*OC* 1: 478)

> We have changed method:
> Jodelet is no longer the fashion,
> And now one cannot
> Quit nature by even a step.

Even more critical than *Les Fâcheux,* though, is *La Critique.* For while the play acts as a defense of Molière's satiric comedy of manners, it also enacts the dramaturgy of that comic form: the play is both an apology for and incarnation of Molière's poetics. The polemical dialogue transforms itself into an experiment in dramatic form. And the experiment is radical. *La Critique* is Molière's first portrayal of an aristocratic salon; as such, it represents an important movement from the burlesque frame of *Les Précieuses* to the elegant realism of *Le Misanthrope:* Climène is a Parisian "précieuse" and not a provincial copy; Lysidas a respected poet and not a valet in his master's clothes; Dorante is arguably Molière's first credible moral spokesperson or *raisonneur,* a characterization that moves beyond the reactionary Gorgibus and the complacent Chrysalde toward the credibility of *Tartuffe*'s Cléante or *Le Misanthrope*'s Philinte. Furthermore, the play develops a dramaturgy of debate (or "dispute," as Uranie says) that will be developed on religious turf in *Tartuffe,* in the field of manners with *Le Misanthrope,* and in the realm of learning and feminism with *Les Femmes savantes.*

It is particularly apt, then, that with *La Critique* Molière ostentatiously embraces the concept of public collaboration in comic creation. The new comedy has a new genesis. But in crediting the play to his public, Molière is not inventing a new paradigm of public self-portraiture; he is in fact responding to a paradigm already in existence, and a polemical one at that. When, at the end of the play, the characters promise to write up an account of their own dialogue, their language allows Molière to reply explicitly to what was certainly the most original charge made against him: that he was no author at all, but simply a compiler of his audience's own little writings, their *mémoires.* According to this polemical vision, Molière does nothing but stitch together character sketches and social reports written by his own audience. The charge allows critics to claim in one fell swoop that (1) Molière is not a poet worthy of the name but simply a plagiarist and that (2) the public's approval of the comedies is aesthetically null and void: their favorable prejudice toward Molière is solely the effect of a self-interested desire to see their own portrayal on stage, as conceived by their own hand.

The irony of this accusation is that it presents a model of comic creation and reception that is in fact perfectly suited to Molière's project of seducing his audience with public mirrors. What could provide a more faithful portrait of the public than the firsthand accounts of the public made by that public itself? So it is that Molière not only refuses to deny the accusation at hand, but furthermore actually appropriates this model of comic creation via public self-portraiture. Though we have noted the appropriateness of this model for *La Critique,* it is a paradigm whose applicability extends well beyond this one play, and even beyond Molière's theater. In fact, this model, which insists upon the proximity, even the unity, of portraitist and model, is one that is at work in the very polemics of Molière's critics. It is a model of comic creation that informs the classical notion of the representation of manners.

In arguing this point, I want to push beyond certain paradigms of audience collaboration with the author that have long been applied to the French classical age. On the most fundamental level, critics have fully recognized the implications that the classical imperative of "pleasing the public" holds for the creative act. Paul Valéry, for example, has defined classical texts as "works that are, as it were, created by their public (whose expectations they meet and are thus almost determined by the knowledge of these expectations)" [oeuvres qui sont comme créées par leur public (dont elles remplissent l'attente et sont ainsi presque déterminées par la connaissance de celle-ci)].[5] The model of public creation we have seen operate in *La Critique,* however, pushes this conception of public participation in literary production beyond the level of such comparative speculation ("it is *as though* the work was created by its public") to that of material reality (the work *is* created by its public). It is no longer a question of the public's influence on the author, but instead of the public's assumption of the author's role.

More recently, scholars have examined a number of concrete forms of this kind of collaboration, and I will return to these models of intersecting social and literary practices. But above all I want to suggest how radical is Molière's conflation of these two practices. I want to challenge the image of a literarily conservative, even reactionary, Molière. According to this established perspective, the playwright, by mocking literary affectation in salon conversation, intends to ridicule the creative—and depictive— capacities of his audience. In attacking, for example, the attempts at portraiture and playwrighting among the amateur *précieuses,* Molière would seem to suppress the literary license of the nonprofessional public and award it only to trained poets.

This argument has been given a gendered reading by Joan DeJean, whose *Tender Geographies* offers a brilliant analysis of the collaborative tendencies of women novelists in the mid seventeenth century. DeJean shows how salon writing seeks its aesthetic justification in the art of conversation; the "author" becomes the director of a collaborative workshop of amateurs known as a "salon" instead of an autonomous creator who places pen to paper. This harnessing of social commerce as literary genesis is, according to DeJean, fundamentally feminine: "salon writing was always women's writing" (73). In contrast, "male writers like Molière" (22) suppress this literary engagement of an anonymous nonprofessional public in order to shore up the authority of the Author, so necessary for the growing literary marketplace and the incipient foundations of the French literary canon.

But it will become quite clear that Molière can in no way be placed in this reactionary role. We have seen how willingly he relinquishes authorship to a nonprofessional public in *La Critique;* it now remains to be seen

5. In "L'enseignement de la poétique au Collège de France" (*Oeuvres* 1: 1442). Jacques Scherer applies this paradigm to the classical theater, equating the influence of the public with an imaginary role as author: "On serait . . . tenté de dire que le véritable auteur de la dramaturgie classique, c'est le public, n'était que les réactions de ce public ont dû être interprétées par des auteurs dramatiques et des théoriciens qui tentaient de dégager les lois du théâtre de leurs temps" (*Dramaturgie* 426). This general perspective informs Bray's chapter "Au Service du public" in *Molière* 169–90.

just how far this abdication is pushed in the narratives of Molière's career. Furthermore, Molière's collaborative creation is not without implications for issues of gender. The playwright does not hesitate to compare his satiric words with that of a witty woman in a salon; indeed, it is Uranie herself who proposes that the transcription of the play be handed over to Molière to be staged. Molière is staging a play generated largely by women's conversation. Uranie and Elise, the hostesses of *La Critique*'s salon, are thus in more than one way self-portraits that Molière creates for himself. Like these two *salonnières,* his creative genius is in presiding over and exploiting a social interchange of observations, estimations, and representations. Molière deeply identifies his art with that of the social commerce of depiction as practiced by women. This is not to deny that this identification is profoundly problematic, as my reading of the satiric Célimène in *Le Misanthrope* will later show. But as vexatious as this collaboration is, it is a founding principle of Molière's comic mirror.

It is also an unorthodox principle. Audience authorship radically breaks, as DeJean suggests, with the predominating models of literary creation—even if, it might be added, the author is male. Could such an act of audience authorship be considered credible? Do amateurs really have that much talent? If so, what are the powers of depiction that authorize the public to share, if not entirely assume, the playwright's function? And what then is the role of Molière? Has he not abandoned his prized position of poet, of *le nouveau Térence,* in abandoning authorship to the audience? If Molière wrote *La Critique* to justify his art, how can he profit from renouncing his title of author? It is the last question I examine first, for literary collaboration must necessarily operate within a certain conception of authorship.

T w o

※

"MOLIÈRE AUTHOR!"

As an author, Molière's reputation has always been oddly precarious. Few
literary figures have found themselves so thoroughly canonized and yet so
sharply challenged in their very function as author. Since the publication
in 1954 of René Bray's *Molière, homme de théâtre,* the playwright's status as
writer has been at the center of much critical debate. By suggesting a negative response to the question "Does Molière think?" [Molière pense-t-il?],
Bray finds Molière "essentially a comedian and not a writer" (34). What
does it mean to say that Molière is not essentially a writer? Though Bray
attacks the figure of "Molière, author," he in no way denies the playwright's
legal or practical authorship of the plays. Instead Bray deprives Molière of
what he, as well as an entire critical tradition, considers to be the essential
points of the author's status. Molière did not create his plays as literary
works, meant to be read as autonomous products, but instead considered
the plays as simple "notations" for performance (40). As such, Molière did
not take true creative responsibility for "la valeur littéraire" of the work
(38). The proof? Molière did not take the time to oversee the publication
of his collected works (unlike Corneille or Racine), nor did he bother to
reread or correct his individual plays before publication (38–40). Furthermore, far from being inspired by a coherent literary project, Molière did
not seek to construct a unified *oeuvre* (172). These statements annul Molière's very status as author, as a source responsible for the quality and unity
of a body of writing. This kind of thinking—which crowns the *theatrical*
genius by dethroning his *literary* authority—existed well before Bray's
summa of the critical tradition. It leads to phrasing that denies—in letter
if not in spirit—that Molière truly *wrote* the plays. We might quote out of
context Sainte-Beuve's remark about Molière's work, "he did not write

them" [il ne les écrit pas]. Of course, the critic placed that daring statement in a frame that flatters the great playwright, lauding his creativity as a living art rather than literary recording.[1] Despite their adoration of Molière, Sainte-Beuve and Bray, as well as the entire "Molière, man of theater" tradition, call into question the value of the body of writing organized under Molière's name, and thus the figure responsible for it.

The last two decades of Molière scholarship have seen a rebirth of Molière as author, in the sense of a "conscious" literary artist.[2] Nevertheless, on the outskirts of critical respectability there are certain voices in the past half century that have moved in a radically different direction. They do not simply deny that Molière is an "author" of the highly conscious literary type, they deny he is an author in any sense at all, and indeed that he could even spell. Pierre Louÿs was the first to claim that Molière did not write the plays of Molière, or at least not the masterpieces of Molière, but that instead these plays were the work of Pierre Corneille. This theory has been developed in the last decades by critics who draw on the biography of Molière the actor in order to erase Molière the author.[3] How could anyone who spent so much time organizing a troupe and performing on stage have time to write these masterpieces? Could someone who wandered the provinces for fifteen years without printing a word suddenly compose such accomplished poetry on his arrival in Paris? Could a man with such a small library know so much? Given the impossibility of responding affirmatively to these questions, these critics grant the authorship of the plays to a poet, Corneille, whose own biography happily attests to the personal cultivation and literary authority so necessary to a great author.

Such debates, of course, reveal a great deal about various twentieth-century concepts of the authorial function, but my mission is to explore the social and literary configuration in which Molière's plays operated. Yet when returning to this context, it is surprising the degree to which these modern literary deflators of Molière echo seventeenth-century polemics. Indeed, certain of Molière's contemporaries considered the very conjunc-

1. "Vrai poète du drame, ses ouvrages sont en scène, en action; il ne les écrit pas, pour ainsi dire, il les joue" (qtd. in Bray, *Molière* 34).

2. In 1980, Defaux presented his *Molière, ou Les Métamorphoses du comique* as a response to "cette tendance à priver Molière de sa liberté, à réduire, dans la création, la part de la conscience créatrice," and answered Bray's famous question with the formula, "Molière est un artiste qui pense" (27). Major works in recent years by Dandrey *(Molière, ou l'esthétique du ridicule)* and Andrew Calder *(Molière: The Theory and Practice of Comedy)* treat Molière as a highly conscious artist who molded his own aesthetic of comedy and with it a coherent body of work.

3. First by Henry Poulaille (*Corneille sous le masque de Molière*, 1957) and most recently by François Vergnaud, whose research has been summarized and presented in *Molière, ou l'auteur imaginaire?*, a 1990 paperback polemic penned by two lawyers (Wouters and de Goyet).

tion of the words "Molière" and "author" as an oxymoron that could only provoke astonishment:

> Molière Autheur! Il n'y a que de la superficie et du Jeu; Sa présomption est insupportable, il se méconnoist depuis qu'on court à quatre ou cinq Farces qu'il a dérobées de tous costés. (*La Guerre comique,* "Dispute dernière" 2: 455)

> Molière Author! There is nothing but show and acting; his presumption is unbearable, he no longer knows who he is since everyone is running to four or five farces he stole from every which way.

Such is the reaction of one of the audience members portrayed in a polemical play during the quarrel over *L'Ecole des femmes.* Several strategies are operating in this critique. First, "Molière, author" is placed in opposition to "Molière, actor." He acts well but writes badly. However, there is no argument made here—or elsewhere at the time—that a good actor cannot by definition also be a good author. The union of the two talents did not violate the theatrical expectations of the time. The contention here is simply that the *author's* poor plays succeed because of the *actor's* crowd-pleasing performances. More dangerous is the charge that Molière is the author of nothing but farces, a comic genre of dubious rank. Tragedy and Comedy are the works of poets; their status is guaranteed by their place in the poetic treatises of Aristotle, Horace, and "modern" theoreticians. Farce, on the other hand, is associated with a number of elements—actors' improvisation, physical action rather than dialogue, and the recycling of popular tales (or in the case of *commedia dell'arte,* standard plot lines)—all of which leave little place for an author's invention.[4]

Nothing so damages Molière's literary authority, however, as the accusation of plagiarism. Indeed, the charge that Molière "has stolen from every which way" is one repeated throughout his career, and particularly during the Quarrel of *L'Ecole des femmes.* According to his critics, Molière is nothing more than a "rhapsode," that is, a reciter of collected bits and pieces, one who simply stitches together morsels of existing texts. Molière himself puts the accusation in the mouth of his opponent Climène in *La Critique:* "I have just seen, for my sins, this bad rhapsody of *L'Ecole des femmes.*" [Je viens de voir, pour mes péchés, cette méchante rapsodie de *L'Ecole des femmes*] (1: 647; sc. 3). It is in fact this accusation, and this accusation alone,

---

4. The question of Molière's relation to farce has been a central one since Gustave Lanson's seminal article "Molière et la farce" in 1901. An important synthesis of critical perspectives on this problem is provided by Roger Guichemerre with his article "Molière et la farce" in 1981 and more recently by Bernadette Rey-Flaud; Dandrey seeks to attenuate the role of farce in Molière's work in his chapter "Le Malentendu farcesque et satirique" (*Molière* 56–68). On the related problem of Molière and the *commedia dell'arte,* see Philip Wadsworth's book on the subject, and Peter Nurse's *Molière and the Comic Spirit* 35–43.

that undercuts Molière's *status as author,* rather than simply his literary talents. The question is no longer: "Is Molière a good author?" It is now: "Is Molière an author?" It is a matter of definition of terms. "Rapsodie" is defined in Furetière's 1694 dictionary in the following manner:

> Recueil de plusieurs passages, pensées et autorités qu'on rassemble pour en composer quelque ouvrage ... [Q]uand on veut mespriser l'ouvrage d'un Auteur, on dit que ce n'est qu'une rapsodie, qu'il n'y a rien de son invention.

> a collection of certain passages, thoughts and authoritative citations amassed to compose a work ... When one wants to disdain an author's work, one says it is a rhapsody and has nothing of his invention.

Now according to Furetière's definition of "author," an author of a "rapsodie" is in reality no author at all:

> L'Auteur est celui qui n'a pas pris son ouvrage d'un autre; c'est lui qui l'a produit.[5]

> The Author is one who has not taken his work from another; it is the one who has produced it.

Molière's critics often use the charge of mechanical imitation against him. After citing some of Molière's thefts (from Cervantes and Rabelais),

5. This definition well reflects the attitudes of the period. Sorel, for example, in his *De la connaissance des bons livres* also insists that only those who do not steal from others (Sorel uses the same term—"dérober"—that has been applied to Molière) are "véritablement des autheurs, étant créateurs de leurs ouvrages" (17–18). Furthermore the coherence of the work is always credited to the singleness of the author. Aesthetic unity and authorial unity are indissoluble. Descartes states the case most strikingly in 1636: "Il n'y a pas tant de perfection dans les ouvrages composés de plusieurs pièces et faits de la main de divers maîtres, qu'en ceux auxquels un seul a travaillé" (*Discours de la méthode* pt. 2; see Jaouën's commentary [142]). Descartes follows Montaigne here, who adamantly refuses the status of author to those who compile others' writings. Speaking of a scholarly rhapsode—an author who has done nothing but collect a heap of others' phrases (his book is a "fagot de provisions incogneuës" that has been "empilé par son industrie")—Montaigne comments, "Cela c'est en conscience achetter ou emprunter un livre, non pas le faire" (III, 12, p. 267).

It must be added that the very term rhapsody entered another important polemic of the classical age. Not long after Molière saw *L'Ecole* labeled a "méchante rapsodie," the abbé d'Aubignac brought the same charge to the *Iliad* in his *Conjectures académiques, ou Dissertation sur l'Iliade.* D'Aubignac's logic is the following: His critical examination of the poem finds it lacking in any coherent artistic design, and thus lacking a single source. The absence of unity "fait bien connaître que cet ouvrage n'a point été entrepris par un poète qui ait envisagé un sujet pour le traiter" (124). Only a multiple, hence bastardized, paternity could explain the poem's numerous infractions of classical standards of decorum and order: d'Aubignac cites inconsistencies in character, in style, and in genre as well as a general lack of narrative economy. The *Iliad* merits its title of "Rhapsodie," "car ce terme ne veut dire autre chose qu'un recueil de chansons cousues, un amas de plusieurs pièces auparavant dispersées, et depuis jointes ensemble." These are the same terms ("amas," "cousu") we have seen applied by Donneau de Visé to Molière's disorderly copyings. Of course, an essential difference distinguishes the two criticisms: unlike d'Aubignac's analysis of the epic, no one denies the existence of a biographical Molière. But Molière's artistic or authorial "existence" is discredited nevertheless. If the playwright is a simple rhapsode, then the expression "Molière Autheur!" is indeed an oxymoron.

one of Molière's rivals asserts that Molière is not "a running spring, but instead simply a basin that receives water from elsewhere" [une Source vive, mais seulement un Bassin qui reçoit ses eaux d'ailleurs] (Robinet, 1: 210; sc. 5). And the basin seems inexhaustible in its capacity to receive. One of Molière's critics lays out the case admirably in *La Guerre comique*:

> Il lit tous les Livres satiriques, il pille dans l'Italien, il pille dans l'Espagnol, et il n'y a point de bouquin qui se sauve de ses mains.[6]

> He reads every satiric book, he pillages in Italian, he pillages in Spanish, no book can escape his hands.

An interesting paradox appears here. If for modern critics it is Molière's unliterary quality, his theatricality, that makes him less an "author" and more a "man of theater," in contrast, for his contemporaries, it is precisely his literary erudition, and his ruthless use of it, that makes Molière less an "author" and more a simple scribe or copier.

It is in the context of this running accusation against Molière's originality that the issue of the public's *mémoires* is first raised. It seems that the indictment is leveled in order to add some zest to these rather banal charges of literary theft. After all, there were no laws at the time against plagiarism, and though the activity was widely disapproved, it was also widely practiced.[7] Even if the classical age, as Foucault argued, is the period in which the author function asserted itself as a powerful organizing force in literary mentalities, and even if it was the period in which individual "invention" determined the author's status,[8] it still must be admitted that the aesthetics of imitation granted a great deal of leeway for recycling the texts of others. Indeed, Corneille even loudly vaunted his powers of "pillaging" comic material written by other hands.[9] One of Molière's defenders made it clear

6. "Quatrième Dispute" 2: 452. Ironically enough, La Croix's formulation of the accusation of plagiarism is itself an almost identical copy of certain lines found in an earlier play by another polemicist. Donneau de Visé in his *Zélinde* comments on how a playwright should emulate Molière: "vous devez . . . lire comme lui tous les livres Satiriques, prendre dans l'Espagnol, prendre dans l'Italien, et lire tous les vieux Bouquains" (52; sc. 8).

7. See Viala, *Naissance* 90–96. In "Qu'est-ce qu'un Auteur?," Foucault asserts that as of the seventeenth century, "les discours littéraires ne peuvent plus être reçus que dotés de la fonction-auteur: à tout texte de poésie ou de fiction on demandera d'où il vient, qui l'a écrit, à quelle date . . . le statut ou la valeur qu'on lui reconnaît dépendent de la manière dont on répond à ces questions" (85). Molière's critics can be said to manipulate this logic to discredit the playwright when they attribute his works to a promiscuous "basin" rather than a proper running spring.

8. For a fuller examination of the question of authorship and invention in relation to Molière, see Norman, "Molière, Rhapsode"; in relation to the classical age, see Chartier, *L'Ordre des Livres*, and Viala, *Naissance;* for a broad theoretical analysis of literary originality, see Meltzer, *Hot Properties*.

9. The "épître" to *Le Menteur* is particularly interesting, for the playwright boasts of his copying at the same moment he expounds on the genre of comedy. He first assures the reader that he is the play's true author: despite the great change in style, this new comedy is indeed "de la même main" that created his recent tragedy *Pompée*. Corneille then dramatizes his role as author, attributing to himself

that comic writers should be able to imitate others writers, just as tragic playwrights imitate the Ancients.[10] It thus seems quite natural that Molière should have shamelessly proclaimed, as is reported, "I take my goods where I get them" [je prends mon bien où je le trouve].[11]

Hence Molière's opponents needed to find a more daring strategy for

as creator the traits associated with his own heroes. The transition he has undertaken from tragedy to comedy ("du héroïque au naïf" [336]) is presented as a daring descent from on high (he has "osé descendre de si haut"), somewhat like the generous action contemplated by the wavering Auguste in *Cinna*. Having thus firmly established the engagement of his artistic will in the composition of the piece, he then presents the copying as an outright exploit of heroic dimensions. He directly proclaims that the play is pure imitation: "ce n'est ici qu'une copie d'un excellent original." The daring nature of the imitation lies in the fact that the original is Spanish and thus belongs to the cultural army of the current enemy of the French crown. Corneille asserts the artist's superiority to such national concerns, and following Horace, "qui donne liberté de tout oser aux poètes ainsi qu'aux peintres, j'ai cru que nonobstant la guerre des deux couronnes, il m'était permis de trafiquer en Espagne." In an ironic final display of literary heroics, Corneille presents an alternative interpretation of his copying: it isn't trading with the enemy, but instead a ruthless *pillage* which should be acceptable even to the most ardent supporters of the French crown ("Ceux qui ne voudront pas me pardonner cette intelligence avec nos ennemis approuveront du moins que je pille chez eux" [336]).

Playful though this passage be, it does show that one of the best remedies to the charge of plagiarism is a declaration by the author of willful, and thus conscious, larceny, as Corneille himself called it ("larcin"). It is as though the generosity with which the crime is committed can add to the glory of the author. Corneille assumes the kind of immoral grandeur which he later attributes to his heroine Rodogune: "tous ces crimes sont accompagnés d'une grandeur d'âme qui a quelque chose de si haut qu'en même temps qu'on déteste ses actions, on admire la source dont elles partent" ("Discours . . . du poème dramatique" 826)

There is nothing new in this kind of appropriation; Montaigne no doubt provides the most authoritative example of making literary loans his own: "Parmy tant d'emprunts je suis bien aise d'en pouvoir desrober quelqu'un, les déguisant et difformant à nouveau service" (III, 12, p. 267). Indeed, individual "judgment" itself is formed by accumulating one's wealth from other writings. Thus the young pupil must know how to "approprier": "Les pièces empruntées d'autruy, il les transformera et les confondera, pour en faire un ouvrage tout sien, à sçavoir son jugement" (I, 26, p. 199). Appropriation becomes simple possession: "La vérité et la raison sont communes à un chacun, et ne sont plus à qui les a dites premièrement, qu'à qui les dict après. Ce n'est non plus selon Platon que selon moy . . . " (ibid.). See Antoine Compagnon on Montaigne's perspective on appropriation and judgment (291–98).

10. Confronted with the accusation of plagiarism, a defender of Molière in *La Guerre comique* demands why the distinction between comedy and tragedy in matters of literary imitation should be maintained. "Je crois que la *Précaution Inutile* et les *Histoires de Straparolle* lui ont fourny quelque chose de son sujet, qu'il lit les Italiens et les Espagnols, qu'il en tire quelque idée dans l'occasion; mais le bon usage qu'il fait de ces choses le rend encor plus loüable. Je voudrois bien sçavoir par quelle raison un Autheur Comique n'a pas la liberté de se servir des lectures qu'il fait et pourquoy les Poëtes tragiques prennent des sujets entiers, traduisent des centaines de Vers dans une Pièce, et se parent des plus beaux endroits des Anciens. Il faut estre bien déraisonnable pour establir une pareille inégalité. (*Querelle* 452; "Dispute IV")." Molière's defender makes it clear that the playwright's imitations are consciously reworked, indeed improved, and put to use toward the design ("sujet") chosen by the artist. The author's role is safely preserved. It is in this sense that we can understand the following formula used by Chapelain to describe Molière in his *Mémoire des gens de lettres vivans en 1662:* "L'invention de ses meilleures pièces est imitée, mais judicieusement." (qtd. in Mélèse 129). The word "invention" is taken here in its rhetorical sense as the choice of the subject matter and the materials used to develop it. In this sense, the "invention" of the subject need not bring to the world anything new or unseen; it must simply reflect the conscious choice of the author. Molière *invents by copying.*

11. Unfortunately, Molière's forceful declaration has the distinct disadvantage of being unpublished in the author's time: it is first quoted posthumously in Grimarest's 1705 *Vie de M. de Molière*. During his lifetime, Molière remained in general suspiciously silent about the literary "originals" that

depreciating his literary currency. It is Jean Donneau de Visé who sharpens this new weapon against the playwright. The young critic does so in his 1663 *Nouvelles nouvelles,* a long passage of which constitutes the first biographical sketch and in-depth criticism of Molière. According to the critic, Molière did not simply steal from books, but, more importantly, from his own audience. However, Molière's copying here is not the result of theft, but of gifts freely given. According to Donneau de Visé, Parisian elites ("les gens de qualité") were so infatuated by the playwright's satire of themselves in *Les Précieuses* that they rushed to supply him with new material—from their own hands.

> [I]ls donnèrent eux-mêmes, avec beaucoup d'empressement, à l'auteur . . . des mémoires de tout ce qui se passait dans le monde, et des portraits de leurs propres défauts, et de ceux de leurs meilleurs amis, croyant qu'il y avait de la gloire pour eux que l'on reconnût leurs impertinences dans ses ouvrages. (*OC* 1: 1019)

> They [people of quality] eagerly gave to the author . . . accounts of all that was happening in society, and portraits of their own faults, and of those of their best friends, believing that they would be glorified by having their impertinences recognized in his works.

All that remains for Molière the "rhapsode" is to stitch together the morsels. And the material is abundant:

> [N]otre auteur . . . reçut des mémoires en telle confusion, que, de ceux qui lui restaient, et de ceux qu'il recevait tous les jours, il en aurait eu de quoi travailler toute sa vie" (1020).

> Our author . . . received these accounts in such a flood that, from what remained, as well as from those he was receiving everyday, he would be able to work all his life.

Molière's role as an editor of this material is variable. Sometimes the stitching is so reckless as to preclude any sign of the author's active presence: *Les Fâcheux,* for example, is nothing but "a mass of detached portraits, all pulled from these accounts" [un amas de portraits détachés, et tirés de ces mémoires] (1020). In the case of certain other plays, however, Donneau de Visé admits that the author has "stitched together well" [bien

---

he was accused of copying. Molière's lack of declaration regarding his imitations disturbed his critics as much as the actual imitations. See for example Somaize's *Les Véritables Prétieuses,* where the "baron" adds to his observation that everyone is aware of Molière's plagiarism, "mais Mascarille pourtant soûtient n'avoir imité en rien celle [la comédie] des Italiens" (52; sc. 7).

cousu] the public's portraits according to a conscious dramatic design (1022).

Whether well stitched or not, the play itself has become, through the intermediary of a more or less competent author, a kind of *self-portrait* of the public. Social peers write portraits one of the other and then hand them over to Molière for staging. The theater is both the mirror and the publisher of its own audience. According to Donneau de Visé, it is in particular what we might call the "publicizing" function of Molière's plays that attracts his audience members, for it is there that they will see the work of their own wits displayed before their peers:

> [T]ous ceux qui lui donnent des mémoires veulent voir s'il s'en sert bien; tel y va pour un vers, tel pour un demi-vers, tel pour un mot, et tel pour une pensée, dont il l'aura prié de se servir . . . ce qui fait croire justement que la quantité d'auditeurs intéressés qui vont voir ces pièces les font réussir. (1020)

> All those who give him *mémoires* want to see if he [Molière] uses them well; some go there [to his plays] for half a verse, others for a word, others for a thought, which they have asked him to use . . . all of which makes one believe that the great number of self-interested theatergoers who go to these plays is what makes them succeed.

The function of the author as intermediary seems to have all but disintegrated.

It is admittedly quite unlikely that Donneau de Visé's account is entirely accurate here. But what astonishes is that such an account is possible within the literary and social imagination of the time. Donneau de Visé is masterfully in tune with that collective imagination. His hold on popular opinion may lead to breathtaking inconsistencies, as we will see later when he switches camps to defend Molière and *Le Misanthrope*. But it is this shameless desire to catch the mood of the moment that will make him in years to come such a successful journalist and playwright of polemical and satirical comedies.[12]

Let us then take quite seriously—if with a good grain of salt—Donneau de Visé's version of the publicizing mirror. A public transfixed by its own image creates its simulacrum collectively and regards it with delight. Indeed, in a final turn of the polemicist's screw, the literary transaction of exchanging *mémoires* is rendered unnecessary, as we will see. Molière may simply take dictation from members of the public as they recount anec-

---

12. On Donneau de Visé, see Mongrédien, *Querelle* 3–10. For a keen analysis of his later journalism, see Dejean, *Ancients* 56–66, passim.

dotes, or he may wander the streets and infiltrate social transactions with his own notebook. But as Molière advances from transcribing writings to transcribing reality, we find ourselves confronted with a new set of problems, problems that concern less literary imitation than the imitation of life. The inventive role of the author has been seriously diminished: representation is considered a spontaneous and transparent screen to life. According to this vision, the fidelity of the portrait is what counts, not the artistry and originality of the portraitist. But this emphasis on fidelity, on the transcription of reality, raises its own problems concerning the classical notion of mimesis, problems that lie at the heart of Molière's mirror project.

Three

❖

THE PORTRAIT—
A SECOND PERSON

The same tensions that define the aesthetics of literary imitation are at play in the imitation of life. If one simply copies one's contemporaries, is one an artist? Is the resulting "copy" a work of art? These are the questions raised by Molière's critics when they attack his alleged use of amateur transcriptions of real persons and events. The debate around the *mémoires'* artless descriptions invokes the widest issues concerning poetic representation: what is the "Nature" to be reproduced? The Aristotelian ideal of imitating a universalized nature—"what should be"—as opposed to the historical singularities of "what is" (*Poetics* ch. 9) is largely adopted in the seventeenth century with the preference for the lifelike, the verisimilar *(le vraisemblable),* to life itself, truth *(le vrai).*[1] Pierre Pasquier has shown how French classical treatises on dramatic mimesis continually valorize "selection and correction" (25–37) above "duplication." The artist's genius is reassuringly at work when constructing a generalized portrait; copying singularities of nature, on the other hand, is at best the work of a historian rather than a poet. The radicalness of Molière vaunting his use of transcriptions of the real can perhaps best be understood today by analogy with the first appearances early in the twentieth century of "found objects" in art exhibitions. The transposition of the real into a framework supposedly assigned to artistic craftsmanship and transcendence breaks with all ex-

---

1. On the seventeenth-century adaptation of Aristotle's precepts on mimesis toward the notion of "vraisemblance," see Pasquier (13–68), Bray (*Doctrine* 191–214), and Tocanne (*L'Idée de nature* 309–10). On the related issue of the idealized "belle nature" as a preferred object of imitation, see Pasquier (69–80), Bray (*Doctrine* 150–52), Kibédi Varga (*Poétiques* 27–30), and Annie Becq's chapter, "L'Imitation de la Nature," in *Genèse de l'esthétique* (79–94).

isting rules concerning the selective and transformative role of the artist.[2] In both cases the eruption of the real provokes a storm of critical opposition.

However, it is important not to oversimplify the aesthetic canons of the French classical age, particularly in relation to comedy. Even though Molière's realism appears to many of his contemporaries to be a striking transgression of all poetic norms, the fact is that Molière's supposed violation of the code of "selection and correction" arises quite naturally from an ambiguity inherent in the classical conception of the comic genre. The requirement to transform nature can be applied easily to tragedy, but comedy is the site of a polar requirement, one that insists that it present an image of daily life, a mirror to manners. Such is, after all, the definition of the genre attributed to Cicero, a definition that held considerable sway in the seventeenth century: *imitatio vitae, speculum consuetudinis.*[3] Comedy was above all *naïve* in its depiction, frank and simple, aiming toward the transparent.[4] The genre was thus the site of a battle between those who followed this precept of mimetic fidelity to the letter and those who insisted that comedy transform nature. The latter group generally aligned themselves with Aristotle's definition of comedy as presenting humans not as they are but rather *worse* than they are, as portraying not exact replicas of individual faults but instead as portraying the *essence of the ridiculous.*[5] In short, comedy is a genre wavering between duplication and transformation, between ephemeral contemporary manners and the timelessly ridiculous, between the biting satire of Aristophanes and the transcendental elegance of Menander.

A passage in La Bruyère's *Les Caractères,* written a decade and a half after Molière's death, reveals the depth of this tension.

> Ce n'est point assez que les moeurs du théâtre ne soient point mauvaises, il faut encore qu'elles soit décentes et instructives. Il peut y avoir un ridicule

2. I work here with Thomas Pavel's analysis of the profound contradiction between the "found object" and classical aesthetics (368–93).

3. This formula attributed to Cicero is quoted by Donatus in his *Fragmentum de Comoedia et Tragoedia.* The implications for Molière's theater of this conventional formula are discussed by Defaux (62–69 and passim) and Dandrey (*Molière* 15–20).

4. Corneille, for example, famously credits the success of his first comedy, *Mélite,* to the "style naïf qui faisait une peinture de la conversation des honnêtes gens." Boileau qualifies the portraits of comedy as "les images naïves" of current life (*L'Art poétique* III.367).

5. After defining painters as either portraying their models as better, as the same, or as worse than their contemporaries, Aristotle then eliminates the most "faithful" of the three styles when he distinguishes comedy from tragedy: "one [comedy] aims to imitate men worse, the other better than their contemporaries" (ch. 2, 1448a). On the reception of this tradition in the aesthetic treatises of seventeenth-century France, see Bury, "Comédie et science des moeurs."

si bas et si grossier, ou même si fade et si indifférent, qu'il n'est ni permis au poète d'y faire attention, ni possible aux spectateurs de s'en divertir. Le paysan ou l'ivrogne fournit quelques scènes à un farceur; il n'entre qu'à peine dans le vrai comique: comment pourrait-il faire le fond ou l'action principale de la comédie? "Ces caractères, dit-on, sont naturels." ("Des Ouvrages de l'esprit" no. 52)

It is not enough that the characters and manners of the theater be not bad, they must moreover be decent and instructive. There can be ridiculous qualities so low and gross, or even so bland and indifferent, that it is not permitted to the poet to pay attention to them, nor possible for the spectator to be entertained by them. The peasant or the drunk furnish a few scenes to a *farceur;* but they hardly enter into the truly comic: how can they form the foundation or the principal action of a comedy? "But these characters," it is said, "are natural."

Once again the hierarchical distinction between comedy and farce is put in polemical play. But this time farce is not so much accused of excessive physicality and staginess as of excessive fidelity to reality. Comedy is associated with dramatic structure (a "principal action") and a coherent foundation; farce with loose depictions of social conditions unworthy of representation. A comic poet selects and constructs judiciously; a "farceur" copies arbitrarily. One can never underestimate the classical age's obsession not simply with design, but with *conscious* design. Indeed, the most important treatise on theater in the period, the abbé d'Aubignac's 1657 *La Pratique du théâtre,* devotes an exhaustive chapter to the formidable "Study of Theory" that a playwright must undertake before committing pen to paper. This is the discipline lacking in the mere observer, whose farces duplicate their model.

But the case is not quite so simple as it may seem. The last line of the above passage reminds us that there is a tension present in the very definition of comedy, a tension that even the stern La Bruyère cannot ignore. If indeed "'these characters . . . are natural,'" has not the comic poet in fact perfectly performed his function and created a credible mirror to life, an *imitatio vitae*? La Bruyère's responds:

Ainsi par cette règle, on occupera bientôt tout l'amphithéâtre d'un laquais qui siffle, d'un malade qui dort ou qui vomit: y a-t-il rien de plus naturel? C'est le propre d'un efféminé de se lever tard, de passer une partie du jour à sa toilette, de se voir au miroir, de se parfumer, de se mettre des mouches, de recevoir des billets et d'y faire réponse. Mettez ce rôle sur la scène. Plus longtemps vous le ferez durer, un acte, deux actes, plus il sera naturel et conforme à son original; mais plus aussi il sera froid et insipide.

According to this rule, the audience would soon be diverted with lackeys whistling, invalids sleeping or vomiting: Is there anything more natural? It is the nature of an effeminate man to rise late, to spend part of his day at his *toilette,* to look in the mirror, to perfume himself, to put on beauty spots, to receive notes and respond to them. Put this role on stage. The longer you make it last, one act, two acts, the more it will be natural and resemble its model; but also the more it will be uninteresting [cold, *froid*] and insipid.

La Bruyère appeals directly to the spectator here and shifts his critique from the moral ground to the realm of the delectable. The commentator is no longer concerned with the decency of an effeminate man, but instead with the pleasure that his representation may give an audience. The problem is this: the unmediated "natural" will by nature leave the audience "cold" and bored. For the purely pragmatic reasons of exciting and warming his audience, the playwright must select and construct, rather than transcribe. By referring specifically to the "act" structure of comedy, La Bruyère posits a basic distinction between dramatic structure and portraiture, between *action* and *depiction,* in which the former is valorized at the expense of the latter. It must not be forgotten that the basic governing principles of classical form, the famous three unities, are designed largely to assure an essential density to the representation of time, space, and action, to create a compactness that precludes any fidelity to the meandering contingencies of chronological and spatial specificity—to insure, in short, that an ideal formal structure repress the eruption of realistic detail.

And yet the dogmatic La Bruyère, at the very moment he embraces idealized form and rejects haphazard realism, cannot help seducing his audience, warming them up, with the kind of depictive acumen for which he himself is famous as a "moralist," as a painter of contemporary character types. The very phrasing swells with the effeminate details whose depiction it denounces: "It is the nature of an effeminate man to rise late, to spend part of his day at his *toilette,* to look in the mirror, to perfume himself, to put on beauty spots." This is just the kind of acute observation that La Bruyère knows his public loves, and that fills his own book. After all, he himself describes his book as a "portrait" of the public painted "after nature" [d'après nature] (preface 61).

Indeed, La Bruyère's *Caractères* was criticized for precisely the same kind of unstructured realism for which he denounces the "farceur." Hence this critique from the journal *Mercure Galant* dating from 1693, three years after the edition in which La Bruyère published the passage above:

Ce n'est qu'un amas de pièces détachées. . . . Rien n'est plus aisé que de faire trois ou quatre pages d'un portrait, qui ne demande point d'ordre, et il n'y a point de génie si borné qui ne soit capable de coudre ensemble quelques médisances de son prochain, et d'ajouter ce qui lui paraît capable de faire rire.[6]

It is nothing but a mass of detached morsels. . . . Nothing is easier than making a portrait of three or four pages, which requires no order, and there is no mind so dull that it could not stitch together some nasty descriptions [médisance] of his peers and add something that he thinks might make one laugh.

The vocabulary is astonishingly close to that used against Molière. Like the playwright, La Bruyère does nothing but "stitch together" portraits without conscious design ("ordre"), and furthermore he does so in the style of social gossip, of *médisance*—a term frequently applied to Molière and one to which I will return later. There is no doubt that the classical moralist like La Bruyère—that specialist in "the science of describing *mores*" ("Discours sur Théophraste" 3)—cannot escape the tensions between lifelike imitation and literary construction, between duplication and transcendence, which haunts all those writers who claim to hold a mirror to their public.

And yet the comparison between the moralist and the playwright may simply not occur to La Bruyère. There is no doubt that in the period's aesthetic framework the comedy's representation *as visual spectacle* seems to differentiate it radically from a literary representation. La Bruyère carefully specifies generic particularities here: he speaks of a stage to be filled, not a page; of acts to be constructed, not chapters; of spectators to be diverted, not readers. What differentiates the two forms? The response lies in the classical imagination of representation, where the stage projects a more immediate image of the original, one more dangerously natural because it passes directly through the eyes. This is what Pascal suggested when he warned:

Tous les grands divertissements sont dangereux pour la vie chrétienne; mais entre tous ceux que le monde a inventés, il n'y en a point qui soit plus à craindre que la comédie. C'est une représentation si naturelle et si délicate des passions, qu'elle les émeut et les fait naître dans notre coeur." (Br. no. 11).

All grand entertainments are dangerous for Christian life; but among all those the world has invented, nothing is to be more feared than theater. It is such a natural and subtle representation of passions that it engenders and agitates them in our heart.

This presumption of the superlative immediacy of theatrical representation is no doubt what causes La Bruyère to situate comedy at the heart of the

---

6. *Mercure Galant* June 1693, qtd. in Jaouën 121. Jaouën analyzes this passage in an excellent study of the problem of the fragmentary form (119–24).

quarrel over depiction. Though his own portrait of the *efféminé* shows the extent to which moralist writing is rife with the same tensions between transformation and duplication, there is nevertheless no doubt that for the classical age comedy—linked as it is with visual portraiture—is the privileged battleground for competing norms of mimesis.

Although La Bruyère is generally thought to target here Molière's protégé Baron, the commentary seems to invite application to Molière himself. On an anecdotal level, one can compare La Bruyère's *efféminé* with Molière's own fatuous creature, the *petit marquis*. Of course it can be argued that no character sketch of a *petit marquis* ever formed the principal action of a Molière comedy. Nevertheless, we have already seen *Les Fâcheux* described by Donneau de Visé as nothing but a similar collection of such little portraits of characters who, if they conform to the eponymous title of play (best translated as "The Bores"), hardly merit our attention. The *précieuse,* a seeming counterpart in affectation to La Bruyère's *efféminé,* also holds the principal role of a comedy, in which, we might add, the action of looking in a mirror (the famous "conseiller des grâces") forms a highlight.

The fact is that years before La Bruyère's commentary, critics rehearsed the same argument against Molière. I return again to Donneau de Visé, who comments here on Molière's characters, called "the fools that one paints from nature" [fous que l'on peint d'après nature]:

> [C]es peintures ne sont pas difficiles, l'on remarque aisement leurs postures; on entend leurs discours; l'on voit leurs habits; et l'on peut sans beaucoup de peine venir à bout de leur portrait. ("Lettre sur les affaires" 306)

> These portraits are not difficult, one remarks quite easily their [the models'] posture; one listens to their speech; one sees their clothes; and without any effort one can finish their portrait.

The playwright as realistic portraitist is reduced to the status of a banal observer, the equivalent of any reasonably perceptive social being who contemplates his peers, and who possesses no particular art. The prestige of the playwright is effaced by the facility of copying.

Donneau de Visé's commentary is a response to Molière's own justification of comic portraiture in *La Critique,* part of which we have already seen; I now return to the passage in its entirety to examine the relationship between playwright and portraitist:

> Lorsque vous peignez des héros, vous faites ce que vous voulez. Ce sont des portraits à plaisir, où l'on ne cherche point de ressemblance; et vous n'avez qu'à suivre les traits d'une imagination qui se donne l'essor, et qui souvent

laisse le vrai pour attraper le merveilleux. Mais lorsque vous peignez les hommes, il faut peindre d'après nature. On veut que ces portraits ressemblent; et vous n'avez rien fait, si vous n'y faites reconnaître les gens de votre siècle. (1: 661; sc. 6)

When you paint heroes, you can do what you want. They are portraits of fancy [à plaisir], where one does not look for likeness; and you have only to follow the lines of a soaring imagination, which often departs from the true toward the incredible [merveilleux]. But when you paint men, you must paint from life. People want these portraits to be lifelike; and you haven't done anything if you don't make the audience recognize the people of your times.

The distinction between painting "heroes" and "men" is that between tragedy and comedy. In Aristotelian terms it is the difference between painting humans as they are and painting them better than they are. Molière pushes this distinction by taking the radical step of aligning comedy with verity *(vrai)* rather than verisimilitude *(vraisemblance),* that is, with reality over essence. Tragic verisimilitude, generally considered the highest form of imitation, is here belittled by Molière as a purely imaginary essence, and thus, paradoxically an arbitrary essence. The tragic portrayal is arbitrary because it is not submitted to the only test that counts for the spectator: the test of a comparison with life. Comic portraiture is the difficult art because it must pass the *proof of recognition.*

By the end of the seventeenth century, this proof had become a comic topos for classical poetics. So it is that the philologist Anne Dacier echoes Molière nearly perfectly three decades later in her commentary on Terence, though she seeks in Aristotelian poetics a justification for the proof of recognition.

Il y a des manieres differentes de peindre le moeurs; car comme Aristote l'a fort bien remarqué, ou vous faites les hommes comme ils sont, ou vous les faites pires, ou vous les faites meilleurs. Des trois manieres, les deux dernieres sont, à mon avis, les plus faciles & les plus imparfaites; *car comme vous ne suivez alors que votre idée,* moy qui n'ay pas la même idée que vous, je ne puis juger de la perfection de vostre ouvrage, parce que *je n'ay point de modele sur quoy je puisse juger de la ressemblance de vos portraits.* Il n'en est pas de mesme de celuy qui fait les hommes comme ils sont, *tout le monde a en soy ou devant les yeux l'original qu'il a voulu copier, chacun en peut juger par soy-mesme, & c'est ce qui en fait la difficulté.* (*Comédies de Térence* 6; emphasis added)

There are different ways to paint characters and manners, for as Aristotle so well remarked, either you make men as they are, or you make them worse, or you make them better. Of the three ways, the two last are, in my mind, the easiest and the most imperfect; for as you then follow only your own idea, I—who have not the same idea as you—cannot judge the perfection of your work, because I have no *model by which to judge the likeness of your portraits*. It is not the same with those who paint men as they are; *everyone has in their mind or before their eyes the original that you want to copy, and one can judge by oneself and that is what makes it difficult.*

In a revealing omission, Dacier overlooks Aristotle's definition of comedy as a portrayal of men worse than average and seeks Aristotelian authority for a rather un-Aristotelian realism.

This shift in comic aesthetics, away from idealization (of the ridiculous) and toward fidelity to real models, is in line with an increasingly vocal justification of portrait painting in the seventeenth century. We have seen the persistence of the portrait metaphor in discourses on comedy; this analogy, though rooted in poetic treatises since antiquity, assumes a new power during this period as portrait painting seeks to assure its place in the hierarchy of genres.[7] Just as tragedy reigned as the grand genre above middling comedy, so too did historical painting reign over portraiture. Like tragedy, historical painting is defined as *action;* it is a narrative art. Portraiture and comedy, on the other hand, take the radical step of promoting the decorative and rhetorical function of description as the *raison d'être* of art. Critical discourse on portraiture also dares to embrace the true above the grand or marvelous, as Molière urges. While Dutch painters were dethroning historical painting in favor of what Svetlana Alpers has labeled the "art of describing," in France the portraitists were still insurgents, strenuously defending their art as noble, while maintaining its distinctive realism.[8] I do not use the word lightly here: indeed, the probable first use of the term "realism" in an aesthetic context (in 1835) occurred in a commentary pitting Rembrandt's portraits against idealized historical painting.[9]

Under Louis XIV, the debate around portraiture did not simply divide critics into opposing camps, it divided individual critics in their own writings, sowing their discourse with contradictory proposals.[10] If important seventeenth-century theorists of painting like Félibien and Roger de Piles

7. On the relation between literary and painterly portraits in the second half of the seventeenth century see Harth 96–128, Plantié 115–44, and Bonfait.

8. See Coquery, "Le Portrait Français" 17, and Bonfait 41–44.

9. See Watt 10.

10. Jacques Thuillier places this tension at the center of French classical art theory: "L'art au XVIIe siècle, est toujours prisonnier de sa double définition: d'une part comme *mimèsis,* soit l'imitation de la nature qui conduit à ce *vrai simple,* et de l'autre comme *expression de belles idées,* au sens platonicien du terme, laquelle aboutit à la notion de *vrai idéal*" (xxiv–xxv).

criticized certain portraitists for being "copyists" and for aiming toward simple "faithful imitation of nature" instead of the more essential "living expressions of the passions of the soul,"[11] these same theorists were also tempted to justify portraiture and even to admit that a certain kind of copying was harder than imagining. While this lifelike resemblance gained a very hesitant foothold among erudite critics, it was above all prized by the nonprofessional public, who sought a transparent image of the model they already knew in life.[12] This popular desire for the proof of recognition was hardly in accord with the aesthetic norms of representational transformation. For a critic like Roger de Piles, this vulgar obsession is so dangerous that he advises the portraitist not to allow an audience to compare his painting with the model:

> Il ne faut non plus en présence du modèle demander le sentiment des gens qui ne s'y connaissent pas: parce que regardant le modèle d'une vue et le voyant d'une autre dans le tableau, ils seront d'avis que l'on raccommode les parties que leur imagination leur représente défectueses. (146)

> It also important not to request the opinion of nonconnoisseurs while in the presence of the model: because looking at the model with one view and seeing the painting with the other, they will suggest that one change those parts that their imagination represents to them as defective.

According to the critic, the accomplished artist understands the selection and correction necessary in imitation; the "nonconnoisseurs," on the other hand, seek a perfect transparency of the image. For the amateur, the "view" of the portrait must be perfectly congruous with the view of the model. We will return to the shifting gaze of the spectator from the real-life model to the theatrical portrayal later, but for the moment I want to suggest that this effacement of art, this victory of social presentation (the model in life) over artistic representation, is above all the desire of the nonprofessional public, as Roger de Piles remarks. Of course, in the realm of representation, visual depiction has been since Plato the figure for transparency, for the natural, rather than artificial or written, sign.[13] We have seen the danger this transparency poses for certain thinkers in Pascal's warning against the theatrical transmission of unruly passions. But a contradictory idealization of this illusion of *immaterial representation* also took hold in the

---

11. Roger de Piles on Titien, cited in Bonfait 40. Bonfait situates this remark among similar critiques by Félibien (40).

12. Coquery presents some reception texts from the period on "likeness" in "Le Portrait vu du Grand Siècle" (25–26).

13. *Cratylus* 434.

French classical age, and the desire for immediacy was channeled through the genre of the portrait, due precisely to the potential effacement of the portrait's artifice, overpowered by the perceived presence of its living model. The theorist Félibien describes portraits as "true images where nature seemed to have formed a second person" [les images véritables où la nature semblait avoir formé une seconde personne](qtd. in Marin, *Champaigne* 89–90). As Louis Marin has remarked, this self-effacement pushes the very definition of the genre to the state of aporia, and we have already seen the contradictions it engenders in the writings of classical critics. The paradox of the truly successful portrait is that it is no longer a portrait: it is, in fact, the *person*. And it is, as Félibien writes, no longer a work formed by a portraitist, but instead one formed by *nature* itself. This is true for the comic stage as well the canvas. Thus when Boileau turns to his defense of comedy in *L'Art poétique,* he offers this immediacy as the very triumph of comic depiction, exemplified by Terence's stage.

> Ce n'est pas un portrait, une image semblable;
> C'est un amant, un fils, un père véritable. (III.419–20)

> It is not a portrait, a like image;
> It is a lover, a son, a real father.

Boileau's remark is clearly meant as praise for Terence's great art, in this case that art which hides art *(ars est celare artem).* However, a simple reading of the literal level suggests that art seems less to hide itself than to destroy itself: it is, after all, "not a portrait." And while this kind of radical mimeticism seemed indeed a final destruction of art for some, as Poussin's famous dismissal of Caravaggio's realism illustrates, it is nevertheless the surest way to please a public eager to see itself.[14] To see itself, or to believe that it sees itself, in person, rather than in portraiture.

To return to the question of the *mémoires,* we can now understand how Molière turned to his advantage the accusation of copying those portrait sketches written by the nonprofessional public about itself. By abandoning his role of poet to an untrained public, he guarantees the fidelity of his depiction. If the goal of the comedy is to replace the screen of artistic representation ("a portrait") with the immediacy of social presentation ("a real father"), what better way to succeed than to replace poetic mediation ("imagination," "construction") with direct social observation? The transparency of the depiction is thus incarnated in the transparency of its

---

14. Poussin's remark is of course the inspiration of Marin's *To Destroy Painting (Détruire la peinture).*

creation: the public crafts its own self-portrait, undiluted by the hand of the artist. It is *nature*—here, the unmediated social commerce of self-presentation—that generates not a portrait of itself but a second reality on stage.

Molière can thus embrace the social practice of observation as the best means toward delectable recognition, that is, a recognition whose pleasure results from the identicalness of copy and original. I will explore later the problems that arise from this recognition, but first I return to the scene of public self-attribution in *La Critique* to see how this union of social practice and poetic creation is played out in the period's collective imagination, both in its fictions of public authorship and in its tales of Molière the man.

Four

◈

The Social Commerce
of Representation

In rereading the conclusion of *La Critique,* it becomes clear just how perfectly the scene serves as a creation myth for transparent comic depiction. Here the characters reflect on their own conversation and discover that it is in itself a comedy that needs only to be staged—or perhaps one should say restaged:

> Uranie: Il se passe des choses assez plaisantes dans notre dispute. Je trouve qu'on en pourrait bien faire une petite comédie, et que cela ne serait pas trop mal à la queue de *l'Ecole des femmes.*
>
> Dorante: Vous avez raison.
>
> Le Marquis: Parbleu! Chevalier, tu jouerais là-dedans un rôle qui ne te serait pas avantageux.
>
> Dorante: Il est vrai, Marquis.
>
> Climène: Pour moi, je souhaiterais que cela se fît, pourvu qu'on traitât l'affaire comme elle s'est passée.
>
> Elise: Et moi, je fournirais de bon coeur mon personnage.
>
> Lysidas: Je ne refuserais pas le mien, que je pense.
>
> Uranie: Puisque chacun en serait content, Chevalier, faites un mémoire de tout, et le donnez à Molière, que vous connaissez, pour le mettre en comédie.

> Uranie: Our conversation has had some rather amusing moments. I think that it could make a little comedy and that it would not be too bad at the end of *L'Ecole des femmes.*
>
> Dorante: You're right.
>
> Le Marquis: Egad, knight, you'd play a part in it that would not be at all to your advantage.
>
> Dorante: It's true, Marquis.

CLIMÈNE: As for myself, I am happy that it be done, provided that the whole affair be treated just as it happened.

ELISE: And I'd furnish my character with all my heart.

LYSIDAS: I don't think I would refuse my own.

URANIE: Since everyone would be satisfied, knight, write an account [mémoire] of it and give it to Molière, whom you know, to make it a comedy.

The fluidity of terms operating between portraits and models, between social personalities and *dramatis personae,* is breathtaking here. Elise's expression "my character" [mon personnage] is intriguingly ambiguous: it is the future role of "Elise," to be performed when the transcription is staged, but it is also Elise herself, that is to say, the social persona she—as a participant in the conversation—presents to the world. The comedy becomes the self-presentation of the "originals," rather than the representation of copies. When the marquis says to Dorante in regard to the comedy, "*you'd play a part* in it that would not be at all to your advantage," it is apparently Dorante, his social interlocutor, who "plays" himself, effortlessly crossing the border separating salon and stage. The portrayal becomes a loan of one's personage granted temporarily to the theater; the transaction is so traceless that the change of hands is forgotten. Is it Dorante playing Dorante, or one of Molière's actors playing Dorante? So too when Elise asserts "*I'd furnish* my character" she speaks as though the donation was an autonomous act of personal will. No playwright need intervene. The model realizes her portrait alone and simply *appears* in the representation.

It is now clear just how radical this mythification of comic creation is. The transparency of transcription creates a conflation of portrait and model so thorough that the terms are confounded. But the question remains: why will this simple recording of a conversation be delectable to an audience and not insipid and "cold" as La Bruyère warns? Surely this risk must exist despite the popular desire we have seen for transparency. Is the theater audience truly so fascinated with itself that it would endlessly watch its social interactions projected on the stage? Would the audience of *La Critique's* depiction of an audience in turn wish to see itself projected on stage? Is the cycle of mirroring endlessly captivating? The answer is quite arguably "yes" for this mid-seventeenth-century public. The fact is that Molière's critics responded with plays depicting audiences that had seen the audience of *La Critique:* indeed, Molière himself depicts members of his public discussing *La Critique* in his next polemical play, *L'Impromptu de Versailles.* I will look at some of these scenes later, but for the moment the simple existence of this spiral of audience portrayals on the Paris stage (and in printed form in the Paris bookshops, for not all were performed) shows the extent to which the audience was fascinated to see itself as it is, that is, as an audience, discussing plays about other audiences.

Of course this new craze was not without its precedents. This kind of conversational criticism follows a larger tradition of the philosophical dialogue, which in the Italian Renaissance assumed the form of polite conversation; the form was thoroughly embraced in mid-seventeenth-century France.[1] But it is precisely the transparency of this kind of representation that is pushed to its limit during the polemics over Molière's comedy. That limit is the edge on which the last play of the Quarrel, *La Guerre comique,* balances so delicately. This text (never staged, for reasons that will be apparent) presents a play much like *La Critique,* in which audience members discuss on stage the merits of Molière's theater. However, in a stunning disruption of dramatic space, the conversation is interrupted by a member of the theater audience—that is, a member of the audience watching the play *La Guerre comique*—who joins the conversationalists on stage. The scene brilliantly captures the excitement created by seeing a perfect simulacrum of oneself as audience member: it is an excitement that propels the spectator to slide—or simply to slip, so soft is the slope—from audience to stage and thus effortlessly to become a second person in portrait form.

It is clear now that the triumph of transparency in *La Guerre comique* is much more than a polemical peculiarity: it is instead a necessary consequence of a certain public's desire to see itself, and to believe that it is really seeing itself, on stage. And yet it must be admitted that this myth of immediate representation, as profoundly rooted as it may be in the classical imagination, is not entirely satisfying as a paradigm for the production for Molière's comedy. It remains just that—a myth, a construction of the collective imagination that leaves us searching for its foundations, for those historical conditions that render it plausible. We have seen how a certain aesthetic discourse can facilitate the illusion of transparency; I now explore how a certain conception of social exchange further promotes the myth of spontaneous public self-portraiture. Social commerce in itself is viewed in the classical period as a perpetual site of artistic creation; it achieves this status in two different ways, both made possible by the contemporary evolution of what has been called the civilization of manners. The first concerns the subject of representation, the slice of society that is depicted or "transcribed" on the stage: social intercourse is conceived of as an art in

---

1. See Fumaroli, "Rhétorique, dramaturgie."

itself, an art that, when fully realized, meets the most rigorous standards of order, decorum, wit, and (to reply to La Bruyère) liveliness demanded of a comic subject. The public is the art. The second concerns the means of representation, the feasibility of a nonprofessional public creating its own portrait: social commerce is conceived of as a site of depiction, even as a highly sophisticated arena of satire. The public is the effective agent of depiction. The public is the artist, even the playwright.

Social Commerce as Art

Why should a transcribed conversation satisfy the demands of art? The beginning of the response is found in Uranie's remark, "Our conversation has had some rather amusing moments. I think that it could make a little comedy." Uranie suggests that the justification for future staging is found in the quality of the conversation, amusing in itself and without any need of modification. By creating an entertaining discussion, the participants believe they have authored a solid comic dialogue. Such will be the "action" of the play. And indeed any difference between representation and reality is not to be countenanced. This is the demand made by Climène, that the "whole affair be treated just as it happened." In her insistence on fidelity, Climène speaks as a coauthor insisting that the "art" of the comedy be her art—that which she displayed in authoring her part of the conversation and not the art of an outside author who might exercise some invention, who might employ an Aristotelian poetics of transformative imitation. She also speaks as a future spectator of the play, who insists on fidelity because she is content with her own person and does not wish to see her copy deformed on stage. Climène believes exact transcription will assure her "role will be to her advantage," as the marquis might say. What she fails to understand is that no modification could possibly make her more risible than she is. This mistake on her part is perfectly emblematic of what we will see to be the blindness of models before their own portraits.

Yet despite her particular foibles, Climène is quite typical of her society when she esteems herself an artwork. As a contemporary observer remarks, "One knows certain people who are the most *beautiful works* in the world" [On connaît de certaines gens qui sont les plus *beaux ouvrages* du monde].[2] The seventeenth-century will toward "the self as art" has been brilliantly analyzed by Domna Stanton; but the title of her work, *The Aristocrat as Art,* unjustly narrows the sociological scope of this tendency. It is the aim

2. Morvan de Bellegarde, *Réflexions sur le ridicule* 176..

of a broad social elite that extends well beyond the aristocracy. The perfection of self-presentation as art finds its mythic expression in the famous concept of *honnêteté,* that almost mystical blend of cultivation and self-effacement, elegance and transparency, distinction and decorum.[3] It is above all a quality vaunted for its power to transform social commerce into art: the *honnête homme* serves up just enough wit and brilliance to embellish a conversation without crushing it with affectation or bravura. *Honnêteté,* therefore, is an emblem for a perfect aestheticization of social commerce, one in which the highest sign of distinction becomes an art that hides itself; the art of self-representation emulates the same ideal of *ars est celare artem* that governs poetic representation. This aestheticization of social exchange has of course other marks of distinction, those that are on the contrary mocked in Molière's theater: affected *préciosité,* self-conscious wit *(bel esprit),* ostentatious propriety.

Now the link between aestheticized social practices and the art of comedy is not simply fortuitous. For the seventeenth century, the relationship between social practice and comic performance is generative: the first produces the second. At the end of the century, the critic Saint-Evremond narrates such a genesis tale for comedy in his commentary on Roman theater.

> La Tragédie fut le premier plaisir de l'ancienne République & les vieux Romains, possédés seulement d'une âpre vertu, n'allaient chercher aux Théâtres que des exemples qui pouvaient fortifier leur naturel & entretenir leurs dures & austères habitudes. *Quand on joignit la douceur de l'esprit pour la conversation à la force de l'âme pour les grandes choses, on se plût aussi à la Comédie.* ("De la comédie italienne" 3:52; emphasis added)

> Tragedy was the first pleasure of the ancient republic, and the old Romans, possessed by sober virtue, sought in the theaters only examples that could fortify their natural disposition and support their hard and austere customs. *Once they had joined the mildness of spirit necessary for conversation to the strength of their souls for great actions, they also took pleasure in comedy.*

Saint-Evremond suggests that the social evolution of a brutal warring society into a "civilization of manners" provokes yet another evolution, a theatrical evolution from heroic tragedy to manners comedy. Of course Saint-Evremond transposes here to ancient Rome a vision of his own century's evolution. It is after all precisely in the seventeenth century that the "civiliz-

---

3. The founding research on the literary traits of this new public (defined by *honnêteté*) is found in Maurice Magendie's *La Politesse mondaine.* Emmanuel Bury's recent book provides an excellent overview of the topic. On the social practice of conversation, see Fumaroli, "Conversation"; Goldsmith; and the recent collection of essays, *Art de la lettre, art de la conversation* (Bray and Strosetzky).

ing process," as Elias has termed it, comes to its culmination with the domestication of feudal warriors as the courtiers of Versailles. Though this domestication of former warring heroes as elegant conversationalists certainly met with some powerful resistance, the dominant discourse of the latter half of the century is that of a tranquil self-satisfaction with the supposed progress of manners.[4] And writers did not hesitate to consider the rise of "respectable" comedy to be a powerful tribute to their culture's exceptional refinement. Already a generation before Molière's Paris success, Corneille claimed to construct a new type of comedy whose simplicity of depiction was made possible by the cultivated elegance of his public. In short, according to the playwright, the stage only reflected the audience's luminous *honnêteté*. Such is Corneille's explanation for the success of his first comedy, the 1629 *Mélite,* which he credits to its "artless style that portrayed the conversation of *honnêtes gens*" [style naïf qui faisait une peinture de la conversation des honnêtes gens]. The pleasure of comic dialogue is attributed to the conversational skill of the elite public, to the "lively spirit of people of quality" [humeur enjouée des gens [de] condition] ("Examen," *Mélite* 28). Boileau as well equates the comic mirror, its artless fidelity in portraiture, with the conversational practices of a certain public. "The faithful images" [les images naïves] of comedy succeed only when they reflect a certain condition of social exchange—one characterized by sociological outlines: "The actors must bandy their wit *nobly*" [Il faut que [les] acteurs badinent *noblement*] using a cultivated language ("l'agréable et le fin") (III.405, 397). These precepts remind Boileau's reader that comedy, like all poetry, must never imitate a language associated with unrefined exchange ("le langage des halles") (I.84), that is to say, a language associated with market commerce rather than leisured commerce.

I will return to this point in the final section in order to gauge how Molière's theater exploits artful conversation as the very foundation of its

4. The view that aristocratic opposition to its own domestication dies out in literature after the mid-century failure of the Fronde—a perspective that was literary history doxa for decades after Paul Bénichou's 1948 *Morales du grand siècle*—has been nuanced in recent years, perhaps most importantly by DeJean's *Tender Geographies.* DeJean sees in the post-Fronde movement of *préciosité* and its ideal of "writing nobly" a political project that continues the aristocratic critique of monarchy in earlier heroic novels. DeJean has recently carried her argument further, contending in *Ancients against Moderns* that the Modern party, led by "liberal aristocrats" (38) and women's salons, advances a radical critique of the reigning political and social order. This argument unfortunately must disregard the Modern party's full complicity with absolutism, clearly inscribed in the first manifesto of the movement, Perrault's 1687 "Le Siècle de Louis le Grand." I would argue on the contrary that the Ancient party formulates perhaps the strongest critique admissible not only of absolutism, but also of the codes of domesticated politeness that attend its power. A text such as Dacier's introduction to her *Iliade* denounces court etiquette and its "soft manners" in terms that foreshadow the language of Saint-Simon's *Mémoires* and its analysis of the "gilded cage" of Versailles (see Norman, "Subversive Ancients?").

dramaturgy, whether it be among the affectations of provincial bourgeoisie *(Les Précieuses)* or the elegance of a Paris salon *(Le Misanthrope)*. For the moment, however, we have begun to see the underlying principles that allow the classical age to conceive of social exchange as a form of spontaneous comic creation. Nevertheless, the question of mediation cannot be entirely dismissed. Despite the apparent transparency of the conversation on stage, even the somewhat fantastic texts we have seen do not totally efface the act of representation. The public must, after all, write up accounts of itself to give Molière, whether it be Donneau de Visé's character sketches or *La Critique*'s transcription of a conversation.

Social Commerce as Representation

In short, the public must be an active *agent of depiction*. But what guarantees the quality of these amateur descriptions? Again, the answer is in the evolution of social exchange. For if the social being is a work of art, he or she is also a critic of other works of art, that is, of other social beings. When Bellegarde remarks, "One knows certain people who are the most beautiful works in the world," he posits not only the artistry of "certain people," but also the active appreciation of their beholders, of their peers in society, the "ones" who observe and judge them. The necessary corollary of *social exchange as art* is *social exchange as criticism.* If the self-as-art seeks distinction, it needs a circle of spectators to judge it. If each individual is defined by his social relationships to others, then the individual exists through his *representation* in the eyes of others. As Elias shows, the closed society of the court provides the model framework for this "art of human observation" (478). The art of knowing men, as Cureau de la Chambre's 1659 *L'Art de connaître les hommes* calls it, is the subject of numerous treatises in the seventeenth century, all designed, as Cureau phrases it, to help the reader "discover the inclinations, the manners and the designs of others[,] . . . [which] is the surest guide that one has for one's conduct in civil life, and . . . he who wishes to use it may avoid a thousand errors and a thousand dangers" [découvrir les inclinations, les moeurs et les dessins d'autrui ⁙ . . . c'est le guide le plus asseuré que l'on puisse prendre pour se conduire dans la vie civile, et . . . celuy qui s'en voudra servir, pourra éviter mille fautes et mille dangers] (5). The "mascarade" of social commerce, as Molière's contemporaries frequently noted, necessitates a continual penetration of others' masks.[5] All of this leaves no escape from the gaze of the "world": it is no

5. For Marmet this "mascarade" (150) makes it necessary to examine one's peers' masks (46) and to dissimulate in turn: "Tasche donc de couvrir tes defauts; if faut du moins paroistre vertueux, et feindre de l'estre, pour estre estimé tel" (150–51). See also Mme de Schomberg's 1663 letter on La Roche-

surprise that Gracián transforms the old adage, "the walls have eyes," into a founding principle of his "arte de prudencia," the art of acting well one's role before the spectators of one's peers: in a word, "always behave as though others were watching"(*Oraculo* n. 297). The paranoia of *prudencia* is the lucidity of the classical age. Everyone *is* watching.

Social intercourse becomes theatrical performance, and conversation, theater. Indeed the very word "theater" applies at the time to any space subjected to the public's conscious gaze. The theater is simply a place where one is seen, whether one is an actor on stage or simply a participant in the parade of Paris's leisurely life. And for the city's bourgeois elites and aristocracy it is being part of the spectacle that matters, and not the actual pleasure of conversing with one's peers. La Bruyère pushes the ambiguity of the word "theater" to its limit, describing Paris's fashionable parks and shopping spots in terms of stage, audience, and critics:

> Dans ces lieux d'un concours général . . . on ne se promène pas avec une compagne par la nécessité de la conversation; on se joint ensemble pour se rassurer sur le théâtre, s'apprivoiser avec le public, et se raffermir contre la critique: c'est là précisément qu'on se parle sans se rien dire, ou plutôt qu'on parle pour les passants. ("De la ville" no. 3)

> In these public places . . . one does not stroll with company for the sake of conversation; people come together in order to assert themselves on the theater, to familiarize and ingratiate themselves with the public, and to strengthen their position against criticism; it is precisely there that one speaks without saying anything, or rather that one speaks for those passing by.

As La Bruyère suggests, this social practice of observation produces a certain dynamism, not just in the exchange of glances, but more importantly in the commerce of representation, in reciprocal efforts at describing, criticizing, and judging those performing on the social stage. "People go out in Paris . . . so as to look each other in the face and to disapprove of each other" [L'on se donne à Paris . . . pour se regarder au visage et se désapprouver les uns les autres] (no. 1).[6] Observation, conjugated with a

---

foucauld's *Maximes:* "Il y a longtemps je l'ai pensé, et j'ai dit que tout le monde était en mascarade et mieux déguisé que l'on ne l'est à celle du Louvre, car l'on n'y reconnaît personne" (qtd. in La Rochefoucauld 566).

6. Jürgen Habermas attributes precisely to such bourgeois attempts at aristocratic distinction the origin of "the equation of theatrical performance with public representation" (14). Habermas posits the birth of the public sphere in the aristocratic culture of representation that flowered in the salons and that, with the infusion of cultivated bourgeoisie in the late seventeenth century, shifted its critical eye to literature and the arts. This "literary precursor of the public sphere . . . provided the training ground for a critical public reflection still preoccupied with itself"; and though it was in good part bourgeois, it preserved, Habermas notes, "a certain continuity with the publicity involved in the representation enacted at the prince's court" (29). It is no doubt in the realm of theater that this movement from social representation to literary criticism first takes place; I would argue that the very ambiguity of the

certain literary cultivation, permits the evolution from mere contemplation to critical depiction: "The observation of people that life in the courtly circle demands finds it literary expression in an art of human portraiture . . . in court memoirs, letters, or aphorisms." (Elias 479). Though Elias writes here of "court people," he himself suggested that the basic paradigm can be extended to a considerably broader group, including the "honnêtes gens" of the town and all others who identify themselves (credibly or not) with cultivated manners (464–67). Furthermore the art of description is hardly limited to such specifically literary forms as the memoirs. The seventeenth century conceived of social commerce itself as a commerce of representation. Three centuries before the sociologist Erving Goffman dissected the mechanics of self-presentation in the theater of everyday life, the Jansenist moral philosopher Nicole devoted in 1675 an important essay to his own analysis of this dynamic:

> Le commerce de la civilité du monde . . . est tout rempli de témoignages d'estime, d'égards, d'application, il donne lieu de se représenter à soi-même comme aimé et estimé et par conséquent comme aimable et estimable.[7]

> The commerce of polite civility is full of signs of esteem, favorable regard, and consideration; it provides a place to represent oneself to oneself as being loved and esteemed, and thus lovable and estimable.

Nicole imagines this traffic in representation as a kind of exchange of portraitists: each individual is both a portraitist of others and a model for other portraitists.

> [L'homme] ne forme pas seulement son portrait sur ce qu'il connaît de soi par lui-même, mais aussi sur la vue des portraits qu'il en découvre dans l'esprit des autres. Car nous sommes tous à l'égard les uns des autres comme cet homme qui sert de modèle dans les Académies des peintres. Chacun de ceux qui nous environnent se forme un portrait de nous. . . . Mais ce qu'il y a de plus considérable en ceci, c'est que les hommes ne font pas seulement les portraits des autres, mais qu'ils peuvent voir aussi ceux que l'on fait d'eux.[8]

> [Man] does not form his own portrait on what he knows about himself through himself, but also by seeing the portraits that he discovers in the

---

term "theater" provides the kind of open border that allows the public to move from criticizing itself to criticizing its literary (and theatrical) representation. On this subject, Hélène Merlin offers a general critique of Habermas on seventeenth-century France and, more specifically, on tragic drama and the *querelle du Cid* (*Public* 24–32, 153–93), and Hartmut Stenzel provides a sobering analysis of Habermas's applicability to Molière's theater, particularly as concerns its political and institutional implications.

7. Nicole, "Traité de la connaissance de soi-même," *Essais de morale* 3: 11.

8. This passage (3: 16) has been commented on by Marin (*Champaigne* 105–6) and Louis van Delft (*Le Moraliste classique* 323).

minds of others. Because we are to one another like the man who serves as a model in the Academy of Painting. Each of those who surround us creates a portrait of us. . . . But what is most significant in this is that men do not simply make the portraits of others, but that they can also see the portraits that one makes of them.

What are the tools at the disposition of this social academy of painting? I return here to La Bruyère. When the moralist addressed his public in order to explain the success of *Les Caractères*, he explicitly credited the existence of such a collection of character portraits to the custom of observation and description so prevalent in polite society:

> Les femmes . . . , les gens de la cour, et tous ceux qui n'ont que beaucoup d'esprit sans érudition, indifférents pour toutes les choses qui les ont précédés, sont avides de celles qui se passent à leurs yeux. . . . Ils les examinent, ils les discernent, ils ne perdent pas de vue les personnes qui les entourent, si charmés des descriptions et des peintures que l'on fait de leurs contemporains, de leurs concitoyens, de ceux enfin qui leur ressemblent et à qui ils ne croient pas ressembler. . . . ("Discours sur Théophraste," *Les Caractères* 4).

> Women . . . , courtiers, and all those who have lively minds but without erudition, indifferent for all things that have preceded them, are avid for all those that happen before their eyes. . . . They examine them, they discern them, they do not let out of their view the persons who surround them, so charmed by the description and the portraits that one makes of their contemporaries, of their peers, of those finally who resemble them and whom they believe they do not resemble. . . .

La Bruyère attributes to a certain group (women, courtiers, the cultivated but unscholarly *honnêtes gens*) a penchant for the examination of their social world, a penchant that is both supported and advanced by literary depictions. The art of conversation is thus harnessed to a system of peer interobservation and representation, one that is exploited in various "genres mondains" and in particular in the "portrait," a form practiced orally and collectively in salons, but also printed anonymously in collections.[9]

It is important to remark that satire also exists at this confluence of

9. The social appropriation of the literary tradition of the character sketch has been examined by Louis van Delft (in his chapter on "mondanité" in *Le Moraliste classique*) and by Marc Fumaroli (in his chapter on *Les Peintures morales* in *L'Age de l'éloquence* [379–91]), who describes the adaptation of Theophrastan "characters" and Ciceronian "notatio" for the tastes of "le Grand Monde" [388]. The inscription of mimetic genres such as satire and encomium in a conversational framework is analyzed from different perspectives in Alain Génetiot's *Les Genres lyriques mondains* and Alain Viala's introduction to *L'Esthétique galante*. For a study of both the social history and the form of the literary portrait at the time, see Jacqueline Plantié's *La Mode du portrait littéraire*.

literary and social practices: indeed the very definition of the word evokes both domains. The three major dictionaries of the late seventeenth century agree that satire applies to both literature and worldly conversation. Thus in the 1694 *Dictionnaire de l'Académie,* next to the definition "a work in prose or verse, made to reprove, to censure vices" [ouvrage en prose ou en vers, fait pour reprendre, pour censurer les vices], we find this application to conversation: "*Satire* signifies also any piquant, disobliging speech. *He made a long satire against you*" [*Satyre,* signifie aussi, tout discours piquant, médisant. *Il a fait une longue satyre contre vous*].[10] Indeed, a veritable mania for satiric exchange seems to be in the air, as is noted in the definition of *satyriser:* "to mock someone in a piquant and satiric fashion: *He's a man who satirizes his best friends: all he does is satirize*" [railler quelqu'un d'une manière piquante et satyrique. *C'est un homme qui satyrise ses meilleurs amis: il ne fait autre chose que satyriser*].

The above passages demonstrate the powerful hold that the social exchange of depiction and satire exerts on the classical imagination; it remains to be seen just what are the underlying foundations of this intercourse. With what aim does one depict others? For whom does one "satirize one's best friends"? Is there a final arbiter of character, a privileged beholder of the portraits in the social "academy of painting," a privileged laugher in the arena of satiric exchange? It is, I believe, precisely the absence of a definitive judge that creates the necessary condition for the spiraling practice of observation and depiction. This absence is first of all a metaphysical one: God as an active spectator and judge increasingly disappears from the social landscape. Thomas Pavel is right to attribute to the absence of divine surveillance—as illustrated by the rise of the Jansenist vision of a hidden God—the rising importance of worldly surveillance. The retreating glance of God leaves in its place "a society severely controlled by the gaze of its participants" [une société sévèrement controllée par les regards de ses participants] (330–31). This certainly describes the world depicted in Molière's comedy, where those who appeal to heaven's gaze are inevitably a subject of ridicule, whether they be jealous lovers like Arnolphe, paternal despots like Orgon, or inept valets like Scagnarelle.

But if God is no longer an active observer of the social comedy, is there not a temporal gaze that may fill this lofty place? Does not the king, and

---

10. The adjectival form summons as well two types of examples: first "Ouvrage satyrique . . . Poëte satyrique," then *"Homme satyrique, esprit satyrique, langue satyrique."* Likewise Richelet's 1679 *Dictionnaire françois* offers for *satirique* this all-encompassing entry: "ce mot se dit des choses et des personnes. Il signifie mordant, piquant." Finally, under *satyre* Furetière places next to the entry "une espèce de poëme inventé pour . . . reprendre les moeurs" this other acceptation: *"satyre,* se dit aussi de toute médisance et raillerie piquante."

the state administration of absolute monarchy, take the place of the hidden God as ultimate judge? If indeed the "society of manners" is linked to the end of feudalism and the rise of absolutism, is not the king the maker and breaker of reputation? It is certainly a commonplace of the epoch that reputation is a currency whose fluctuating value is determined by royal decree. But the descriptions of the social commerce of representation that we have just seen are noticeably lacking in reference to royal surveillance; and Molière's portrayal of this commerce likewise neglects almost entirely the king's arbitration. With the notable exception of *Tartuffe*'s *deus ex machina,* the king is elsewhere when it comes to gauging reputation; and those few characters who claim personally to possess the king's or court's esteem prove as ridiculous as those who seek recourse to divine arbitration. Certain aristocrats in *Le Misanthrope* vaunt their distinction in the king's eyes, but whether it be Arsinoé the prude or Acaste the fop, their declarations are but signs of ludicrous vanity; the audience is well aware that Louis XIV has other concerns than judging the amiability of a *petit marquis* or the sonority of Oronte's sonnet. In any case, it is in general "le monde" and in particular Célimène, a peer among peers, who judge manners in *Le Misanthrope*'s closed world. The approval one seeks, the gaze one desires, is that of one's interlocutors. This is all the more true in the bourgeois realm of *Les Précieuses, L'Ecole des femmes,* or *Tartuffe,* where each character is sharply aware of the collective gaze of *la ville, les gens,* and *le monde.* After all, the king is surely indifferent to whether Arnolphe is a cuckold, or whether Cathos and Magdelon overindulge in euphemisms. The monarchy does not need to enter the business of administering ridicule; the petty spoils of polite prestige can be divided up without royal intervention.

The social commerce of civility, whether practiced in aristocratic salons or in the homes of the cultivated bourgeoisie, may thus indeed present an ideal space protected from the etiquette of court, a world apart where each speaker is treated according to his or her wit and judgment regardless of questions of rank and ceremony.[11] Yet it must be admitted that this apparent utopia may in itself be viewed as instrumental to absolutism. If absolutist power structures have little concern with the correction of individual manners, they do in contrast have an important stake in the energetic functioning of the social commerce of observation: it is an essential dynamic of the "gilded cage" in which the emasculated aristocracy competes for flattery and enjoys the spectacle of each other's follies; it furthermore drives a rich bourgeoisie, to which the monarchy is allied, to busy

---

11. This vision, contested by historians such as Roger Chartier, is elaborated by Fumaroli ("Conversation") and Daniel Gordon.

itself in a search for distinction in manners. The social commerce of representation in short provides a perfect distraction from the more brutal machinery of politics. The king may withdraw from this realm of social control and allow the elites and near-elites to control themselves by mutual observation. So satire famously flourishes under absolute monarchy. As La Bruyère observed, in a world where it was impossible to contest the monarchy and the Church, the only recourse left was the critical depiction of social *mores:* "A man born French and Christian finds himself constrained in satire; the grand subjects are prohibited to him" [Un homme né chrétien et Français se trouve contraint dans la satire: les grands sujets lui sont défendus] ("Des ouvrages" 65). The concentration of power in absolutism leaves a certain range of freedom to the satirist who may now depict those elites who seem powerful but are in fact ultimately disarmed. A half century later Montesquieu clearly credits such satirical liberty to the monarchical system, in contrast to the aristocratic one; in an aristocracy the diffusion of power allows too many individuals the right to suppress satire deemed injurious to them.[12] The king, on the other hand, has little concern for the individual outcomes of the game of shifting reputations; indeed he profits from the diversion. This game of reciprocal surveillance ultimately acts then as a kind of superior panopticon, one in which the central tower has been withdrawn from the plans, and the detainees observe each other, each from their cell in the perfect circumference of the prison.[13]

But what is important for us is that the prisoners actually *enjoy the show.* Satire, that controlling eye of social admonishment, is an instrument

12. Montesquieu compares monarchy's self-serving tolerance of satire to its total suppression in aristocratic regimes: "Dans la monarchie . . . on [fait des satires] plutôt un sujet de police, que de crime. Ils peuvent amuser la malignité générale, consoler les mécontents, diminuer l'envie contre les places, donner au peuple la patience de souffrir, et le faire rire de ses souffrances. L'aristocratie est le gouvernement qui proscrit le plus les ouvrages satiriques. Les magistrats y sont des petits souverains qui ne sont pas assez grands pour mépriser les injures." (*Esprit des lois* 12: 13, 267).

13. Even a critic like Jean-Marie Apostolidès, who fetishizes the surveilling role of the king in representational exchanges—whether they be theatrical or social—admits that the central viewing power of "l'entourage monarchique" is effaced as the century progresses, replaced by a more or less autonomous functioning (*Le Prince* 32). Apostolidès furthermore recognizes that, in Molière's comedy, the dominant model for exchange is not the fixed authority of political power but instead the flux of economic exchange (134). Yet here again, Apostolidès, citing only the last act of *Tartuffe,* insists that "le regard du roi" governs even in the realm of daily social life depicted in comedy (135). This leads him to insist that in the case of *Le Misanthrope,* the characters' merit is determined by the king's gaze (152). Apostolidès however offers no evidence from the text, where the justification for such an argument would be, as I have shown, very weak. Larry Riggs offers an interesting challenge to this reading: he agrees with Apostolidès on the hegemony of the king's role as central spectator to the social field, but argues that Molière's comedies contest any attempt to control the world through visual representation (*"Dom Juan"* 12).

at the disposal of each participant in the game. And what is more, the act of satiric depiction actually intensifies the pleasure of the social spectacle. It provokes a reaction, it livens up the scene of conversation. If we return now to another scene in *La Critique,* we will see precisely how this exchange of observation and judgment is manipulated by the participants in order to heighten the thrill of salon banter. From the beginning of the play the two hostesses, Elise and Uranie, speak of their arriving guests as so many characters in a comedy, the spectacle of which will either entertain or annoy them. Commenting on their invitees, Uranie says: "I appreciate those that are reasonable, and *I entertain* myself with the foolish ones" [je goûte ceux qui sont raisonnables, et *me divertis* des extravagants]. Uranie's attitude remains somewhat passive here, but Elise goes further in a key moment in the play; she actually directs the conversation by encouraging the "ridiculous" aspects of her peers. And she does this by offering a satiric portrait, couched in terms of ironic praise, of Climène. Elise presents a verbal mirror—more private than public, it must be admitted—to her interlocutor in order to delight in the spectacle of vanity and misrecognition.

> ELISE: On . . . voit bien, Madame, . . . que tout est naturel en vous. Vos paroles, le ton de votre voix, vos regards, vos pas, votre action et votre ajustement, ont je ne sais quel air de qualité qui enchante les gens. Je vous étudie des yeux et des oreilles; et je suis si remplie de vous, que je tâche d'être votre singe et de vous contrefaire en tout. (1: 650; sc. 3)

> ELISE: One . . . sees quite well, madam, . . . that all is natural in you. Your words, the tone of your voice, your glances, your step, your action and your grooming all have an air of quality that enchants people. I study you with my eyes and ears; and I am so taken by you that I want to try to ape you and imitate [counterfeit] you in everything.

This passage rehearses all the elements we have analyzed in the social commerce of representation. First the "self as art": when Elise describes Climène as model to imitate, much like a canonical painting or poem, she views her interlocutor more as a finished "work," to follow Morvan de Bellegarde's words, than an organism. Second, the mechanics of social observation: Elise devotes her sensory apparatus to the meticulous "study" of her peer. Finally, the conversational act of representation: the social gaze is translated into a verbal evaluation, which in this case is apparently laudatory. But of course, the depiction is double edged: the excess of praise is an open invitation to read the remark ironically. This irony is all the more apparent no doubt in the face of Climène's affected social performance, which is anything but "natural."

The ball has been tossed. The exchange of representation and recognition may begin. How will Climène react? She cannot ignore the extravagance of the flattery in Elise's portrait; her response therefore wavers between vanity (she believes the praise is sincere) and indignation (she fears the praise is laced with irony). Elise nurses Climène's response for all the spectacle it can provide:

> CLIMÈNE: Vous vous moquez de moi, Madame.
>
> ELISE: Pardonnez-moi, Madame. Qui voudrait se moquer de vous?
>
> CLIMÈNE: Je ne suis pas un bon modèle, Madame.
>
> ELISE: Oh! que si, Madame!
>
> CLIMÈNE: Vous me flattez, Madame.
>
> ELISE: Point du tout, Madame.
>
> CLIMÈNE: Epargnez-moi, s'il vous plaît, Madame.
>
> ELISE: Je vous épargne aussi, Madame, et je ne dis pas la moitié de ce que je pense, Madame.
>
> CLIMÈNE: Ah! mon Dieu! brisons-là, de grâce. Vous me jetteriez dans une confusion épouvantable.

> CLIMÈNE: You mock me, madam.
>
> ELISE: Pardon me, madam, but who could mock you?
>
> CLIMÈNE: I am not a good model, madam.
>
> ELISE: Oh! But you are, madam!
>
> CLIMÈNE: You flatter me, madam.
>
> ELISE: Not at all, madam.
>
> CLIMÈNE: Spare me, please, madam.
>
> ELISE: And so I am sparing you now by not saying half of what I think of you, madam.
>
> CLIMÈNE: Ah! Good God! Let us stop here. You are throwing me into a frightful embarrassment.

Climène, after some initial suspicion ("You mock me"), abandons herself to the charm of flattery, and, in a spectacular display of blindness, ignores Elise's irony. Elise pushes the comedy further by dancing on the edge of overt sarcasm, testing the depth of Climène's vanity with the treacherous wordplay on "sparing" her interlocutor (by saying only "half of" what she thinks). The final words show that Elise has pulled off her act quite adroitly: Climène is disturbed, yes, but not due to a justified sense of indignation. It is instead Climène's embarrassed modesty, overwhelmed as she is by praise whose sarcasm she fails to decode, which causes her to put Elise's volley to a stop. Irony and blindness allow the satiric exchange to follow its own dramatic arc in the theater of the salon.

Five

⟐

PLAYWRIGHTING AND POLITENESS

Elise's performance in *La Critique* demonstrates just how exquisite the so-cial art of representation may be, and just how dynamic the play with rec-ognition is. But if the scene perfectly illustrates the potential for social commerce to transform itself into comedy, there yet remains one question to be answered before we can accept the model of public authorship. I return to La Bruyère's critique here. Can a comedy be crafted purely by depiction, even if that depiction is guaranteed by the public's uncontested talent at satire? Is there not need for action, for dramatic structure? And can a public of amateur portraitists create that structure?

These are the questions that the characters of *La Critique* pose for themselves. For, even if they feel that the amusing quality of their conver-sation qualifies them as a more diverting subject than La Bruyère's banal *efféminé,* a doubt persists. Thus immediately after deciding to record their discussion, they turn to the notion of theatrical aesthetics:

> DORANTE: Mais quel dénouement pourrait-il trouver à ceci? car il ne saur-ait y avoir ni mariage, ni reconnaissance; et je ne sais point par où l'on pourrait faire finir la dispute.
> URANIE: Il faudrait rêver quelque incident pour cela.

> DORANTE: But what dénouement can we give it? For it seems to me that there is neither a marriage, nor a recognition scene; and I don't know how we can bring to an end the dispute.
> URANIE: We'll have to dream up some incident for that.

Once they conceive of their conversation as a comedy to be staged, the characters momentarily abandon the ideal of naïve transcription. The in-tervention of artifice, of a fictional ending, proves necessary in order to give the representation shape. A dénouement apparently must be *invented,* rather than simply recorded from life: the expression *rêver,* dream up, recalls the soaring imagination of the tragic poet rather than the faithful observation of the comic one. Furthermore, to properly design such a dénouement demands, as we have seen, a sufficient knowledge of the art, "une estude de Theorie," as d'Aubignac suggests. Can these polite conversationalists summon the poetic imagination and the theoretical knowledge necessary to craft comic action?

La Critique does not fail to answer the question. First of all, the nonprofessional public's mastery of the art is assured by its mastery of another role they adroitly assume throughout the play: that of critic. In the classical framework, the authority of a poet, as constituted by possession of a theoretical background, is *a fortiori* that of the critic.[1] To prove *La Critique's* characters' competence as critics, and as poets, there is no need to look beyond Dorante's own utterance recognizing the need for a dénouement. He not only understands the formal element that is needed, but furthermore knows its canonical incarnations in practice (marriage, recognition). As for the other aspects of poetic theory, Dorante claims elsewhere that he knows perfectly the famous classical "rules" of art: "he has read them, thank God, as well as anyone else" [il les a lues, Dieu merci, autant qu'un autre] (1: 664; sc. 6).

This theoretical mastery is no minor point. After all, *La Critique*'s polemical power depends entirely on the perceived capacity of the public to judge a play: otherwise Molière would not dare place his self-defense in the mouths of his audience. Indeed, the entire Quarrel is grounded on the audience's appropriation of the power of critical arbitration. From the opening text, Donneau de Visé's *Nouvelles nouvelles* (February 1663), through its last ember, La Croix's *La Guerre comique* (March 1664), the polemical texts place in discussion audience members, some perspicacious and some not, but in the whole forming a competent court of last appeal in critical matters. This perceived competence results from a much remarked popular craze for poetic theory at the time. When d'Aubignac, for example, introduces the subject of the "unity of time" in *La Pratique,* he comments on the fascination the heretofore arcane subject holds for contemporary polite society:

Souvent les Poëtes en parlent, de leur costé les Comédiens s'en entretiennent en toute rencontre, aussi bien que ceux qui fréquentent le Theatre; il n'y a

---

1. So it is that Boileau, when commenting on structure, commands the poet to be in spirit a critic: "Soyez-vous à vous-même un sévère critique" (*L'Art poétique* I.184). *La Critique* can be said to be an ironic application of this rule, for by criticizing himself, Molière justifies himself.

point de Ruelles de lict où les femmes n'entreprennent d'en faire des leçons. (bk. 2, ch. 7, p. 113)

Often Poets talk about them [the rules]; as for actors, they discuss them at each encounter, as well as those who frequent the theater; there is not a single salon [Ruelle] where women do not undertake to give lessons about them.

Molière exploits this convergence of playwrights and nonprofessional public (theatergoers, women in salons). However, he also exploits a certain difference between the professionals, whether scholars (*doctes*) or poets, and the lay audience, in order to valorize the amateur public. He does so in *La Critique* by presenting the satiric portrayal of a Parisian playwright, Lysidas, whose very name reveals his exclusive identity as a poet, an identity that necessarily precludes any claim to cultivated politeness. His ostentatious specialization robs him of the universal adaptability that Pascal ascribes to easy cultivation: Lysidas would appear to be Molière's illustration of the *pensée* denouncing the social impairments of literary professionalism: "Poète et non honnête homme" (Br. no. 38).[2] Thus when Lysidas's jargon-laden theoretical discourse punctures the elegant conversation of the salon, the *honnête homme* Dorante capitalizes on the impolite obscurity of the terms ("la protase, l'épitase, et la péripétie") to dash his opponent:

Ah! Monsieur Lysidas, vous nous assommez avec vos grands mots. Ne paraissez point si savant, de grâce. Humanisez votre discours, et parlez pour être entendu. Pensez-vous qu'un nom grec donne plus de poids à vos raisons? Et ne trouveriez-vous pas qu'il fût aussi beau de dire l'exposition du sujet, que la protase, le noeud, que l'épitase, et le dénouement, que la péripétie? (1: 664; sc. 6)

Ah! Monsieur Lysidas, don't overwhelm us with your big words. Please try to appear less scholarly. Humanize your speech and talk in order to be understood. Do you think that a Greek term gives more weight to your argument? And don't you find that it is as good to say exposition of the subject instead of protasis, plot complications [noeud] instead of epitasis, and dénouement instead of peripeteia?

Interestingly enough, Dorante associates effective dramatic theory with effective social commerce: critical terms are valid when they can be absorbed by polite conversation, when they are understood by everyone—in short when they are, according to Dorante's sense of the word, human. And it is of course precisely the common French expression "dénouement"

---

2. Of course, Pascal in no way suggests here that an *honnête homme* cannot write or criticize poetry: on the contrary, poetry might be one of his chief talents, but not one that impinges upon social adaptability. "Les gens universels ne sont appelés ni poètes, ni géomètres, etc.; mais ils sont tout cela et juges de tous ceux-là. On ne les devine point" (Br. no. 34).

that these nonprofessionals use when they think of "dreaming up" the conclusion to *La Critique*.

On a broader level, Molière stresses throughout his career this practical approach, one that pits the learned against the lay. He seizes on this strategy from his first printed preface, that of *Les Précieuses,* where he ironically imagines the commentary he might have written had he more leisure:

> [J]'aurais tâché de faire une belle et docte préface; et je ne manque point de livres qui m'auraient fourni tout ce qu'on peut dire de savant sur la tragédie et la comédie, l'étymologie de toutes deux, leur origine, leur définition et le reste. (1: 264)

> I would have worked up a beautiful and scholarly preface; and I do not lack the books that would have furnished everything erudite that can be said about tragedy and comedy, the etymology of both terms, their definition and all the rest.

Molière refers here to the flood of such learned prefaces beginning in the 1630s and culminating with Corneille's *examens* and *discours* in his 1660 *Oeuvres*. It is certain that Molière's attitude is part of a large movement away from the mid-century theoretical approach (which was unavoidable even for the practical Corneille) and toward a greater emphasis on amateur taste and audience pleasure. However, Molière goes considerably further in crafting an alliance with his audience. A comparison with Racine is instructive here. Dorante's remarks on the rules in *La Critique* have often been compared to Racine's preface of *Bérénice* (written seven years later in 1670) and its so-called attack on the *doctes*. Indeed the two texts bear a remarkable similarity in phrasing:

MOLIÈRE

Je voudrais bien savoir si la grande règle de toutes les règles n'est pas de plaire, et si une pièce de théâtre qui a attrapé son but n'a pas suivi un bon chemin. (1: 663; sc. 6)

RACINE

La principale règle est de plaire et de toucher. Toutes les autres ne sont faites que pour parvenir à cette première. (1:467)

MOLIÈRE

I would like to know if the most important rule of all the rules is not simply to please, and if a play that has attained its goal has not followed a good route.

RACINE

The principal rule is to please and to move: all the other rules are created only to attain this first one.

Racine apparently joins Molière here in rejecting the need for esoteric rules. Furthermore, in a later passage the tragedian echoes Dorante's tirade against Greek terminology, attacking a critic who employs the term "protasis," "as if he knew what the word meant" [protase comme s'il entendait ce mot](467). Yet despite the similar tactics embraced here by the two playwrights, there is in fact an important difference in their approach to the artist's relation to the public. Racine, unlike Molière, in no way intends to bring the poet closer to the public and its level of literary capabilities. In fact, he makes an important distinction between the theoretical knowledge of the poet and that of the amateurs, as the passage that immediately follows Racine's above remark shows. Here Racine places the "them" of the audience, interested only in its pleasure, in opposition to the "us" of the poets, those who are cursed with the burden of special knowledge and skills. The audience is told to leave the poet's science to the poets:

> Mais toutes ces règles sont d'un long détail, dont je ne leur conseille pas de s'embarrasser. [. . .] Qu'ils se reposent sur nous de la fatigue d'éclaircir les difficultés de la poétique d'Aristote; qu'ils se réservent le plaisir de pleurer et d'être attendris; et qu'ils me permettent de leur dire ce qu'un musicien disait à Philippe, roi de Macédoine, qui prétendait qu'une chanson n'était pas selon les règles: "A Dieu ne plaise, Seigneur, que vous soyez jamais si malheureux que de savoir ces choses-là mieux que moi!" (1:467)[3]

> But all these rules are full of details, which I advise them [the audience] not to bother themselves with. . . . Let them rest on us the burden of explaining the difficulties of Aristotle's poetics; let them keep the pleasure of weeping and being moved; and let them allow me to say to them what a musician said to Philip, king of Macedonia, who claimed that a song did not follow the rules of art: "God forbid, sire, that you ever be so unhappy as to know all those things better than I do."

The fable of the musician and the king accentuates the distinction between artist and audience on two levels. First, by placing the musician before his patron, addressed here as "sire," the artist is designated as *servant* to his audience, socially isolated from it. Second, this isolated space is the result of a kind of sanctified solitude that accompanies his superior knowledge. This is the artist's curse. The classical precursor to the romantic "poète maudit" is this figure of a suffering repository of poetic theory: the poet's "unhappiness" is in his technical knowledge. Racine certainly envisions no

---

3. The preface to *Bérénice* is often cited as an attack against pedantic critics, the bothersome "doctes." (See, for example, Picard [*Racine polémiste* 86] and Tocanne, "L'Efflorescence classique" 224). However, the presence of a king—who is hardly a professional critic or scholar—in this targeted group seems to suggest that the audience members criticized here represent a much larger and more diverse group, one that comprises any member of the public who feels competent in theoretical issues.

possibility here for the king (little less the courtier and the bourgeoisie) to take up the instrument and start playing; nor, in consequence, for the audience to pen a well-constructed play.

The difference in attitudes toward the audience results no doubt from an established distinction in genres. Racine is of course writing as a tragic poet, and as such, his subject matter is drawn from extraordinary actions and passions. His heroes must be distanced from the public, either by history or by geography. In a curiously phrased passage, Racine explicitly prohibits the tragic portrayal of a peer to the spectators. It is, according to the playwright, forbidden to

> mettre des héros sur le théâtre qui auraient été connus de la plupart des spectateurs. Les personnages tragiques doivent être regardés d'un autre oeil que nous ne regardons d'ordinaire les personnages que nous avons vus de si près. (*Bajazet* 1:530; "Seconde Préface")

> put on stage heroes who might be known by most of the spectators. Tragic characters must be viewed with another eye than that with which we ordinarily view the people whom we have seen so closely.

I would argue that for Racine, the need for an "other eye" to envision the tragic hero necessitates in turn an "other hand" to depict him. To portray such an extraordinary human, one who so escapes the public's common gaze, is an act that requires an extraordinary art, one that in turn escapes the public's powers of portraiture. In contrast, it is precisely the goal of the comic stage to engage the same eye that the public uses to perceive its social peers, or at least to trick the audience into believing it is using the same eye when the comic portrait replaces the social original. It is, as Boileau suggested, the same gaze that regards indifferently the "true father" and Terence's portrait. Given that this proximity between the portraitist and the model so eases the task of comic representation, the amateur's theoretical capacities prove perfectly sufficient, constrained though they are by the rules of politeness.

We now see that Molière's salon critics have been granted the competence to take on the creation of a conclusion for their conversational comedy. What do they do? Immediately following Uranie's suggestion that the characters think up an appropriate ending, the servant Galopin enters. The following is the last scene of the play in its entirety.

GALOPIN: Madame, on a servi sur table.
DORANTE: Ah! voilà justement ce qu'il faut pour le dénouement que nous cherchions, et l'on ne peut rien trouver de plus naturel. On disputera fort

et ferme de part et d'autre, comme nous avons fait, sans que personne se rende; un petit laquais viendra dire qu'on a servi; on se lèvera, et chacun ira souper.

URANIE: La comédie ne peut pas mieux finir, et nous ferons bien d'en demeurer là.

GALOPIN: Madam, the table has been served.

DORANTE: Ah! That's just what we need for the dénouement we are looking for, and one could find nothing more natural. Everyone disputes with each other strongly and firmly, as we have done, without anyone giving in; a little lackey comes in to say the meal is served, we get up, and everyone goes to supper.

URANIE: The comedy couldn't end better, and we'd best stop right there.

Reality proves the best invention. After a short attempt at fictional creation, the characters return to the principle of the artless copy. Certainly nothing could be "more natural" than this ending, as Dorante suggests. Indeed, given that under Louis XIV most plays ended at around eight o'clock, the players on stage seem to be joining in a "communal ritual" with the audience, as Ronald Tobin has remarked.[4] The characters' evening ends in perfect harmony with Paris daily life.

But then, La Bruyère might ask caustically: "Is there anything more natural?" His objection to arbitrary and artless naturalism could never be more relevant. The conclusion of the comedy is nothing but a haphazard event, totally unprepared by the previous action; indeed, the "authors" proudly proclaim their refusal to resolve the conflict: "no one gives up." In short it is no dénouement at all according to dramatic conventions. Has Uranie's salon here abandoned what theoretical understanding it possessed? Or has the principle of naturalism actually overturned all rules of art? I would argue the latter.

As is so often the case, we can read the characters' discourse here as lightly ironic or quite serious. As ironic, the suggestion that dinner is an effective dénouement is less an affirmation than a simple refusal: a refusal to adhere to the conventions of dramatic resolution. According to this reading, when Uranie says that the comedy couldn't finish better, she simply means *no one really cares how a comedy ends.* These audience members suggest that they are quite above the artificial contrivances of a typical

---

4. Tobin makes the remark in his general introduction to gastronomy in Molière's plays (17). More specifically, he sees in the conclusion to *La Critique* an appeal to the audience's tastes: Molière envisions his plays as a *ragoût*, or a stew of many flavors, in which there is something to meet the tastes of each spectator and thus to end discord (39–41). I think such a reading can perfectly coexist with Molière's adoption of the audience's taste for the natural and distaste for the hackneyed.

dénouement, such as the unlikely recognition scene that terminates *L'Ecole des femmes*. This ironic nonchalance has obvious implications for Molière's own dramaturgy. Molière was much attacked for his dénouements during the polemic over *L'Ecole* (Mongrédien, *Querelle* xlii–xliii), but his critics fail to see how Molière's use of the *deus ex machina* is brillantly playful; they are part of a more general tendency toward self-consciously ironic resolutions.[5] In their lighthearted invention of the dénouement, the characters of *La Critique* certainly echo here something of the parodic endings of Molière's plays.

It is quite clear that this sophisticated indifference to dramatic action results directly from an overriding concern with depiction. And the depth of this indifference suggests a reading that is less ironic than affirmative. In choosing to end the play with neither a marriage nor a scene of recognition, the characters do not simply mock conventional happy endings; they go much further and take a conscious step toward liberating comedy from such structural constraints. By allowing the contingencies of everyday experience to determine the very shape of the comedy, they reject all the mechanisms of poetic unity designed to concentrate the story to its essence, to its Aristotelian universality rather than its historic exactitude. In its place, they actively embrace an aesthetic associated with the novel, a genre that, well before the "modern" realism of a Defoe or Prévost, was already associated with the representation of the contingent and the particular rather than the probable and the general.[6] Indeed, the modern novel of manners, as pioneered only a few years later by Furetière, explicitly balks at all formal rules in its pursuit of the "chance events" [le hasard] of real daily life.[7] *La Critique*'s rejection of the generic constraints of comedy also

5. Eustis devotes a considerable amount of analysis to Molière's dénouements, which are, according to the scholar, "presented in such a way as to poke fun, precisely, at the conventions of traditional romantic comedy" (102).

6. Corneille, for example, defines the novel as the form that is free to follow verisimilar action without concerns for aesthetic unity: after commenting on the the the "incommodités" of the unities of place and time, Corneille observes: "Le roman n'a aucune de ces contraintes: il donne aux actions qu'il décrit tout le loisir qu'il leur faut pour arriver." The novel, in short, may faithfully follow the contingencies of each "action particulière" (*Discours de la tragédie* 837). According to classical poetics, any theatrical attempt to capture the novel's meandering exactitude is by nature ridiculous; thus the comic scene in Desmaret's 1637 *Les Visionnaires* where a madwoman recounts a play she is writing, in which the action follows the character faithfully through his life, regardless of the essentializing constraints of dramatic form. I am tempted to ask what the audience of *Les Visionnaires* would make of a plot summary of the ambling *La Critique*, or of *Le Misanthrope* for that matter.

7. In his preface ("Au lecteur") to the second book of *Le Roman Bourgeois*, Furetière rejects both the three unities and the traditions of comic dénouement in order to faithfully pursue his "très véritable et très sincère récit" (1024). A. Adam, in his introduction to the novel, comments on Molière's important influence on the birth of the novel of manners and goes so far as to trace a lineage from Molière to the naturalism of the late nineteenth century (45–50).

foreshadows the birth of the *drame* in the next century, a theatrical form that refuses hierachical poetic distinctions in its proclaimed attempt to faithfully depict the bourgeois life.

Molière of course is neither Richardson nor Diderot, and I hardly want to reduce his work to a prehistoric episode in the rise of the realistic novel or of middling drama. Nevertheless, Molière is using the polemical one-act form here to conduct bold experiments on the outskirts of the comic genre, experiments with important repercussions. I have already suggested the importance of the play in the evolution of Molière's satiric program: its self-proclaimed realistic depiction of an aristocratic salon opens the ground for the great first French comedy of manners, *Le Misanthrope*. We can now see how the rejection of comic conventions by Uranie's salon furthermore creates the conditions necessary in order to allow *Le Misanthrope* to become the first *grande comédie* to conclude with neither a traditional recognition scene nor the marriage of the principal young lovers. As such it served as an aesthetic model for the next century in its drive to find new forms for the representation of manners; the play was a model for realistic drama (even among those who contested its moral perspective), and it became the canonical example of the exact portrayal of conversation. I will return later to these questions of dramatic form, but for the moment, I want to emphasize the formative role of the myth of spontaneous comic creation in revolutionizing literary representation.

Nevertheless, it must be admitted that despite the importance of public self-portraiture in this myth, the collaboration between Molière and his audience held less sway for posterity than another parallel myth, one built on the same foundation of the social commerce of observation and representation. In this myth, it is not the amateur public that creates the play, but the playwright Molière himself. However, the Molière in question is less an exclusively professional playwright, in the mode of a Lysidas, than *honnête homme;* Molière becomes a polite interloper in the closed world of social life, a newcomer who integrates himself into the salons in order to better transcribe his observations. The biographical construction of a "Molière, observer" transforms the professional playwright into a member of his own audience, rather than transforming members of the audience into playwrights. However, the same rules govern both forms of comic creation.

Six

MOLIÈRE THE SPY AND ZÉLINDE

The myth of spontaneous comic creation naturally has its limits. *La Critique* is after all the only play that Molière explicitly credits in its entirety to his public. But the model does not falter at these boundaries: instead it absorbs the very figure of Molière the author. It does so by dissolving the playwright into the audience and its social intercourse. Molière himself suggests such an assimilation at the end of *La Critique*. Let us return to Uranie's project for staging the conversation:

> URANIE: Since everyone would be satisfied, knight, write an account [mémoire] of it and give it to Molière, whom you know, to make it a comedy.

Molière may only be necessary as the man who stages the transcription; nevertheless the play's existence depends on its transmission from Dorante to the man of theater. And the mode of the transmission is most important. The exchange is based on an amicable association. It is in Molière's quality as *honnête homme,* that is, as a friend of the *honnête homme* Dorante, that he has access to the *mémoire;* it is as a man of the world that Molière appropriates the public's self-portraits. And the playwright's integration into the social world he depicts has further implications: it allows him not only access to these *mémoires,* but also a close vantage point from which to observe his models in their natural social habitat. Just as Dorante has acted as Molière's spy in the salon of Elise and Uranie, so too Molière can act as his own spy in society.

Molière's skill as an inside observer was much celebrated during his life and was canonized in literary history with the first edition of his collected works (1682), where the introduction explicitly links Molière's status as a man of society with the creation of his comedies[1]:

> [I]l se fit remarquer à la Cour comme un homme civil et honnête . . . possédant et exerçant toutes les qualités d'un parfaitement honnête homme. . . . Quoi qu'il fût très agréable en conversation lorsque les gens lui plaisaient, il ne parlait guère en compagnie. . . . Mais s'il parlait peu, il parlait juste; et d'ailleurs il observait les manières et les moeurs de tout le monde; il trouvait moyen ensuite d'en faire des applications dans les comédies, où l'on peut dire qu'il a joué tout le monde. (*OC* 1: 999)

> He was remarked at the court as a civil and politely cultivated (*honnête*) man . . . possessing and exercising all the qualities of a perfect *honnête homme*. . . . Though he was most pleasant in conversation when he liked people, he hardly spoke when in company. . . . But if he spoke little, he spoke well; and moreover he observed the manners and the characteristics of everyone; he then found the means to apply this in his comedies, where one could say that he mockingly depicted [played, *joué*] everyone.

"Molière, honnête homme," then, serves as a cover for "Molière, observer," who assumes certain social graces to better spy on his peers, as well as a cover for "Molière, rhapsode," who amasses anecdotes for future use. Again, it is Donneau de Visé's 1662 *Nouvelles nouvelles* that presents the first account of Molière slyly placing his affability in the service of theater. Donneau de Visé is obsessed with Molière's social climbing, with his sly assimilation into the elite classes he satirizes. According Donneau de Visé, the playwright's first step upon his arrival in Paris is to ingratiate himself with "people of quality" in order to guarantee the favor of those whose opinions count.

> Comme il avait de l'esprit, et qu'il savait ce qu'il fallait faire pour réussir, il n'ouvrit son théâtre qu'après avoir fait plusieurs visites, et brigué quantité d'approbateurs. (1: 1018)

> As he was smart and knew what it took to succeed, he did not open his theater until he had first made several social calls and worked up a number of supporters.

At this point his socializing is aimed only at courting potential audience members and not at observing potential models for satire. According to Donneau de Visé, the playwright's effort at winning the favor of the Paris elite works so well that soon people of rank are calling on him, rather than

1. This anonymous preface was probably written by the actor Marcel (see *OC* 1: 1373).

he on them. After the success of his first two plays, *L'Etourdi* and *Le Dépit amoureux,*

> son théâtre commença à se trouver continuellement rempli de gens de qua-
> lité, non pas tant pour le divertissement . . . que parce que le monde ayant
> pris habitude d'y aller. Ceux qui aimaient la compagnie, et qui aimaient à
> se faire voir, y trouvaient amplement de quoi se contenter. (1: 1018)

> his theater began to be constantly filled with people of quality, not only for
> the pleasure of the entertainment . . . but also because good society had
> taken up the habit of going there. Those that loved company, and loved
> being seen, found there everything that could satisfy them.

The spectators come to the theater in order to see each other in the seats—
to admire the social spectacle they offer each other—rather than to view
the stage. The audience space becomes the site of social commerce. Its
members are less passive spectators than active participants, engaged in
their own spectacle of exchanging glances and performances. As such, they
become a subject for comic depiction, and Molière does not fail to turn
his attention to the audience. Donneau de Visé continues his narrative:

> Pendant cela notre auteur fit réflexion sur ce qui se passait dans le monde,
> et surtout parmi les gens de qualité, pour en reconnaître les défauts; mais
> comme il n'était encore ni assez hardi pour entreprendre une satire, ni assez
> capable pour en venir à bout, il eut recours aux Italiens, ses bons amis, et
> accommoda *Les Précieuses* au théâtre français, qui avaient été jouées sur le
> leur, et qui leur avaient été données par un abbé des plus galants. (1: 1018)

> During this time our author reflected on what was going on in the world of
> society, and particularly among people of quality, in order to recognize their
> foibles; but as he was not yet daring enough to undertake a satire, nor ca-
> pable enough to succeed in the task, he had recourse to the Italian troupe,
> his good friends, and adapted for the French stage *Les Précieuses,* a play that
> had been performed on theirs, and that had been given to them by a most
> gallant abbot.

Molière is not yet either audacious or competent enough to imitate his
public, so he settles for a simple literary imitation. His choice of material is,
however, most interesting; to copy this particular play hardly fits the nor-
mal definition of literary plagiarism. First of all, the Italians did not work
from a written play, but from a loose scenario; there is thus no text to copy.
More importantly, the author of this particular scenario is designated not
so much as a man of letters as a man of the world, a "most gallant abbot"
of the type that circulated in the period's salons. The tale of Molière's imi-

tation of the Italians' *Les Précieuses* has a number of twists that interest us, and I will return to it. For the moment let us note that in copying the work of an "abbé galant," Molière copies less the work of a professional playwright than that of an inside observer of polite society. The advantage for Molière is that the portrait of society coming from such a hand will certainly be well informed. Thus, though the playwright dare not yet create his own satire, according to Donneau de Visé, the success of *Les Précieuses* is due—thanks to the abbot—to its satiric keenness. The audience delights in its own image, produced by one of its own. Molière profits from the experience:

> [L]a réussite qu'elles [*Les Précieuses*] eurent lui fit connaître que l'on aimait la satire. . . . Il apprit que les gens de qualité ne voulaient rire qu'à leurs dépens, et qu'ils voulaient que l'on fît voir leurs défauts en public. (1: 1019)

> The play's success showed him that the audience loved satire. . . . He learned that people of quality only liked to laugh at their own expense, and that they wanted everyone to see their faults in public.

An important new element enters the narrative here. The public is no longer content to display itself ("se faire voir") in its allotted place the audience; it now wants the stage "to display" its own faults ("que l'on fît voir leurs défauts"). It is here that the *mémoires* enter as an initiative undertaken by the "gens de qualité" in order to see themselves on stage. We can now understand the mode of transmission for these accounts, as it is envisioned by Donneau de Visé.

> Notre auteur . . . reçut des gens de qualité plus de mémoires que jamais, dont l'on le pria de se servir dans [les pièces] qu'il devait faire ensuite, et je le vis bien embarrassé un soir après la comédie, qui cherchait partout des tablettes, pour écrire ce que lui disaient plusieurs personnes de condition, dont il était environné. (1: 1019)

> Our author . . . received from people of quality more *mémoires* than ever, which they begged him to put in they plays he was to create thereafter, and I saw him quite overwhelmed one evening after the comedy, looking everywhere for tablets in order to write what several people of condition, who surrounded him, were telling him.

Where this somewhat fantastic scene takes place we do not know. But the image of Molière surrounded by people whose elite social status is so insistently affirmed by Donneau de Visé ("gens de qualité" / "gens de condition") is, I think, of interest in itself. In this intimacy the transmission of portraits from public to author can dispense with written accounts; the communication becomes oral. With the *mémoires* no longer necessary, social commerce replaces textual transmission as the site of creation. This allows Molière to take the dictation of the Parisian elite and to become, a century and a half before Balzac, quite literally the secretary of French society.

But Molière does not simply await the oral accounts of his informers; he also infiltrates that society in order to copy its words and manners. His domain extends beyond the theater; his dictation sessions with the public become leisurely exercises in the town's social life. Indeed, fashionable dinners become the site of the transfer of gossipy reports and portraits:

> Ces messieurs lui donnent souvent à dîner, pour avoir le temps de l'instruire en dînant de tout ce qu'ils veulent lui faire mettre dans ses pièces; mais comme ceux qui croient avoir du mérite ne manquent jamais de vanité, il rend tous les repas qu'il reçoit, son esprit le faisant aller de pair avec beaucoup de gens, qui sont beaucoup au-dessus de lui. (1: 1020)

> These gentlemen invited him [Molière] often to dinner in order to have time while dining to instruct him of everything that they wanted him to put in his plays; but as those that believe they have merit never lack vanity, he returned all the dinners that he received, his wit making him act the equal of many people who are above him.

The professional playwright is replaced here by the absorbent interlocutor of leisurely conversation. The poetic isolation of the genius-servant *à la* Racine is supplanted by the perfect gregariousness of a dinner companion. And Molière, claims Donneau de Visé, does not fail to profit from these dinners in his effort to assert himself as a social equal. To return to *La Critique,* the playwright thus arrives at a social position in which he may well be the "friend" of an aristocrat such as the "Chevalier" Dorante. We can even imagine that Dorante might render his transcript to Molière at one of these dinners portrayed by Donneau de Visé.

Molière's social evolution as painted by Donneau de Visé, though, allows the playwright not only to receive Dorante and others' oral accounts or *mémoires,* but also to become himself a peer-observer like Dorante and the other "gens de qualité." Molière can now write his own *mémoires* from his personal engagement in—and surveillance of—social commerce. We can trace the following movement in Molière's career as a public depository: first, the transmission of written *mémoires;* second, oral dictation of prepared accounts; third, informal recounting at dinner parties; and finally, active observation by the playwright. Importantly, this movement places progressively more and more of the effort of representation in Molière's hands. Once fully integrated into the social world in question, Molière may transcribe on his tablets not just the public's dictations, but his own observations.

In his polemical play *Zélinde* (1663), Donneau de Visé best develops this model for Molière's inspiration. The character Argimont here describes observing Molière:

> ARGIMONT: Il avait les yeux colez sur trois ou quatre personnes de qualité, [. . .] il paroissoit attentif à leurs discours, et il sembloit, par le mouvement de ses yeux, qu'il regardoit jusques au fond de leurs ames pour y voir ce qu'elles ne disoient pas. Je crois même qu'il avoit des tablettes, et qu'à la faveur de son manteau, il a escrit, sans être apperceu, ce qu'elles ont dit de plus remarquable.
>
> ORIANE: Peut-estre que c'estoit un crayon, et qu'il dessignoit leurs grimaces, pour les faire representer au naturel sur son theatre.
>
> ARGIMONT: S'il ne les a dessignées sur ses tablettes, je ne doute point qu'il ne les ait imprimées dans son imagination. C'est un dangereux personnage: . . . il ne va point sans ses yeux, ny sans ses oreilles. (Mongrédien 1: 37–38; sc. 6)

> ARGIMONT: He [Molière] had his eyes stuck on three or four people of quality. . . . He appeared attentive to all their words and it seemed that, by a movement of his eyes, he looked right into the depths of their soul to see what they were not saying. I even believe that he had tablets, and that, with the help of his coat, he wrote, without being seen, all the most remarkable things they said.
>
> ORIANE: Maybe it was a crayon, and he drew their expressions in order to represent them as perfectly lifelike [au natural] on stage.
>
> ARGIMONT: If he did not draw them on the tablets, I don't doubt that he printed them in his imagination. He is a dangerous person: . . . he doesn't do anything without his eyes or without his ears.

The only sign distinguishing Molière from his peers is the tablets he may be using to copy down his observations. Yet even his possession of these professional instruments is uncertain. The tablets remain almost invisible—certainly invisible enough to call their existence into question. Furthermore, the tablets themselves are profoundly ambiguous in their function: as *literary tools,* they can serve to record the speakers' conversation as well as Molière's observation of their character; as *graphic tools* they copy their facial expressions. Of course, the tablets' ambiguity plays on the double role of Molière himself, both author and actor, one who imitates both speech in writing and gestures in play. However, this double function, rather than increasing the technical signification of the tablets, that is, their role as specialized instruments of the professional artist, tends instead to create a kind a vagueness around their necessity. Thus they can be replaced by the simple memory of the observer, which imprints in the mind what has been seen. This process of observation, memory, and mimicry is one open to all; the author really has no more need of the tools of his trade.

Yet there is still a doubt as to Molière's perfect assumption of the role of nondistinct *honnête homme,* as one observer in a social sea of observers. Molière's talents as observer—and author and actor—make him, as Argimont says, "un dangereux personage." The public's apprehension regarding Molière is further supported by Argimont's interlocutor, Oriane: "Some are beginning to mistrust him, and I know people who do not want him to come to their homes any longer" [On commence à se defier par tout de luy, et je sçay des personnes qui ne veulent plus qu'il vienne chez elles] (38; sc. 6). And yet the play itself demonstrates that this danger to Molière's social success is hardly fatal. For, Argimont reports that he has seen Molière whisked away by a person of quality, "un homme de Robbe," who says to Molière:

> Il faut que vous veniez aujourd'hui disner avec moy; il y a bien à profiter; je traite trois ou quatre Turlupins, et je suis asseuré que vous ne vous en retournerez pas sans emporter des sujets pour deux ou trois Comedies. (38; sc. 6)

> You must come to dine with me today; there's stuff to profit from; I am inviting three or four buffoons [Turlupins], and I am assured that you won't leave without taking with you the subjects for two or three comedies.

Here Molière's friends present the "originals" directly to the playwright. Rather than giving Molière a portrait of the Marquis Turlupin, they introduce him to the Marquis Turlupin in person. They appreciate the spectacle and want to see it reproduced on stage, just as Elise and Uranie no doubt look forward to the spectacle of Climène on stage.

The construction of Molière as a kind of private eye publicizing the personal foibles of Parisian elites is apparently so well established that by his death in 1673 his public is mourning the loss of this inside observer. Such is certainly the impression given by Mme de Sévigné's letter regretting the loss of the playwright two years earlier: she speaks of Molière's death as one might of a trustworthy gossip's: "It is too bad Molière is dead: he would make a very good farce out of what is happening at the Bellièvre's townhouse" [C'est dommage que Molière soit mort. Il ferait une très-bonne farce de ce qui se passe à l'hôtel de Bellièvre] (10 July 1675).

Mme de Sévigné does not say how Molière would gather his material, and it must be admitted that it is unlikely that the *grande dame* would invite the playwright to the Bellièvre's home, as did the gentlemen in the scene above. This of course reminds us that Molière's role as actor hardly permits a full integration into society, one that a nonacting poet of the bourgeoisie might attain. After all, Molière, head of his own troupe, is the "man of the theater" *par excellence.* As such he is marginalized in a number of ways, not the least of which is living excommunicated in a Catholic state. But if the *honnête homme* may not easily take to the stage, the fact is that respectable elites, while insisting on class distinctions, managed a certain social exchange with actors. The social status of the actor in the second half of the seventeenth century is of course problematic. On the one hand, the admittance of Molière as a social peer of the "gens de qualité"—though based primarily, as we have seen, on his role as nonpedantic poet—was apparently not disturbed by his parallel profession as actor. On the other hand, there is no doubt that Molière's decision to become an actor represented a serious fall in status, "une véritable déchéance sociale" in his bourgeois milieu, as Bray notes (*Molière* 47). The ambiguous status of actors is the subject of much commentary at the time (Mélèse 167–70) and is perfectly summarized by La Bruyère: "The condition of actors was infamous among the Romans and honorable among the Greeks: what is it among us? We think like the Romans, we live with them like the Greeks" [La condition des comédiens était infame chez les Romains et honorable chez les Grecs: qu'est-elle chez nous? On pense comme les Romains, on vit avec eux comme les Grecs] ("Des Jugements" no. 15). Whether or not most of the town or court made a serious effort, as La Bruyère asserts, to "live with" an actor like Molière, it is evident even to Molière's critics that *he* found a way to live with *them.* I would argue that it is not really necessary to establish whether Molière ever really created comedies while supping with gentlemen; what matters is that it was considered possible, and more importantly, that it fit a model of comic genesis that was in favor at the time.

This model held sway even in Donneau de Visé's conception of his own comedy, *Zélinde,* in which he attacks Molière's "transcription." Donneau de Visé's vision of Molière, though driven perhaps by envy or rivalry, is nevertheless much more than a result of polemical desperation. It is often suggested that Donneau de Visé's narratives of Molière can be dismissed simply as an irrational fit of critical choler—a fit that leads him to embrace contradictory strategies.[2] And yet we have already seen how difficult it is

2. It is precisely these scenes from Donneau de Visé that Dandrey has used to assail the image of Molière the satirist, claiming that the accusation of direct and malicious depiction is simply a trumped-up charge expediently employed by Molière's muddled critics (*Molière* 55–68). Interestingly enough,

to reject offhand these narratives, given how profoundly Molière embraces the alliance with the social art of observation and reproduction. In fact, his critics must embrace it also.

Donneau de Visé finds himself in a bind. He wishes to discredit Molière by showing that he copies his material from his public, whether through *mémoires,* dictation, or simple observation. If, however, Donneau de Visé wishes to denigrate Molière by portraying him as a simple observer and transcriber with no more art than his amateur public, then he must belittle the public's social art of portraiture. Otherwise Molière is not as *little* talented as his audience, but as *highly* talented as they in the art of comic portraiture. Hence the problem: Donneau de Visé can hardly denigrate the competency of this public in a polemical treatise aimed at winning its approval and flattering its role as final arbiter in questions of theatrical depiction.

Zélinde thus ultimately adopts the premise of a public that is an effective comic author. The case of the character Argimont is exemplary. Ironically enough, the very scene in which he describes Molière's tactics of observation and copying acts as a perfect demonstration of comic creation by the amateur public. In the scene we are presented with a portrait of Molière drawn by Argimont, who proves to be a particularly intriguing representative of the theater public. Although Argimont is only a lace merchant on the very bourgeois rue Saint Denis, and therefore not a "personne de qualité," he is nevertheless a perfectly cultivated critic and conversationalist, and one who can integrate himself into the ideal audience of *honnêtes gens.* To prove so Argimont recounts the adventure of another merchant who successfully entered into a conversation about the theater when making a delivery at the home of an aristocrat. The merchant

> entra chez une Dame de qualité, où il avoit affaire, comme plusieurs personnes s'entretenoient d'une Piece nouvelle que l'on joüoit alors. L'on luy fit l'honneur de luy en demander son sentiment, qu'il dit d'une maniere qui surprit toute l'assemblée, et qui fit advoüer que l'on sçait bien juger d'une Piece de Theâtre, à la ruë Saint Denis. (19; sc. 3)

---

in response to Donneau de Visé, Dandrey cites the passage on public mirrors, the tricky ambiguity of which should, I have shown, disqualify it as an earnest apology. It must be noted though that in rejecting the use of satire in Molière, Dandrey defines the genre in a limited fashion, concentrating on its *ad hominem* aspects (65). I am arguing in response simply that direct satire is an operating element of Molière's comedy, part of its creative impulse, but consistently challenged and counterbalanced by a competing tendency toward the generic and universal.

entered the home of a lady of quality, where he had some business, just as several people were discussing a new play that was then being performed. He had the honor of being asked his opinion, which he delivered in such a way as surprised the entire company, and which made them admit that one knows how to judge a play on the rue Saint Denis.

Like Molière, Argimont is a bourgeois admitted into aristocratic company because of the distinction he has attained in matters of dramatic aesthetics.[3] And again like Molière, Argimont practices his own brand of careful social observation and description to please his public. It is thus that he reports back to his clients what he has seen of "Elomire" (i.e., Molière) and his tablets. Let us now reconstruct the action that leads to Argimont's description of the playwright. After criticizing *L'Ecole* in the third scene, he hears from his shop assistant that Elomire himself is in the neighborhood. Argimont exclaims:

> Elomire! ah! Madame, permettez que je descende, je meurs d'envie de l'entretenir, et de sçavoir si sa conversation répond à son esprit. (34; sc. 4)

3. In fact, according to Argimont, the merchants of the rue Saint Denis are important tastemakers: "Il y a quinze ou seize Marchands de cette ruë, qui [. . .] ont veu toutes les Comedies que l'on a joüées; [. . .] tout ce qu'il y a d'illustres Bourgeois à Paris se rapporte au sentiment de ces Messieurs" (19; sc. 3). Auerbach, in his article "La Cour et la ville," uses the figure of Argimont to argue that the literary public of the time, despite the great differences in its members' social stations, was united in a "self-contained, homogenous society" (179). Under the sign of *les honnêtes gens* is placed a spectrum that runs from these theater-going merchants to the *noblesse d'épée,* passing through the upper bourgeoisie and the *noblesse de robe.* The merchant class "was of one mind with court society, and this is what made possible the remarkable unity of style and taste that characterized the great century" (155). Auerbach denies the existence of a "Marxian class struggle" between the merchant class, who largely formed the parterre, and the nobility (154). Auerbach's conception of an unified theater public has been recently disputed by Jeffrey Ravel ("Définir le parterre au XVIIe siècle"), Merlin (*Public et littérature* 24–25), and Viala (*Naissance* 123–51). In contrast, scholars such as Kibédi Varga continue today to embrace Auerbach's depiction of a coherent literary public in the classical age ("Réflexions"). I also tend to believe that different classes found themselves homogenized as a theater public, but with the distinguo that it is precisely *as a theater audience* that they found a momentary collective identity. While Auerbach posits that the two classes share *a priori* a certain common outlook as a result of shared interests and that this shared ideology then produces a shared aesthetic taste, I would argue that the scene from *Zélinde* shows, quite to the contrary, that the integration of classes operates in reverse order: it is the commonality of taste that permits the integration of the merchant in the salon. It is clear that a certain preexisting gulf divides the merchant and the aristocrats who offer him the rare "honor" of demanding his opinion. It is the merchant's demonstration of a certain level of cultivation or "taste" that then permits a certain homogenization of classes. The "surprise" registered by the aristocrats at the merchant's capable judgment certainly demonstrates the existence of prejudices regarding his social position. The merchant breaks these prejudices by displaying the kind of critical acumen upon which these people pride themselves. It is precisely his quality as a theater critic that makes him *honnête.* I believe that Argimont's integration into the social commerce of "les gens de qualité" then is quite similar to Molière's: as in the case of the playwright, it is his competency in matters of theater that opens the doors of the Paris elite.

Elomire! Ah! Madam, permit me to go downstairs, I am dying to talk to
him and to know if his conversation is as keen as his talent.

Argimont desires to observe the spectacle of Molière *honnête homme,*
as conversationalist in the social world, rather than Molière the actor or
author. Upon his return from his adventure in observation, Argimont delivers the portrait of Molière that we have seen. Appropriately enough, the
scene he observes and describes for his clients is that of Molière observing
and transcribing for his public. One might even ask if Argimont had his
own tablets to record Elomire's movements, or perhaps, like the playwright, Argimont has simply "engraved them in his imagination." In either
case, Argimont's portrait of Molière not only entertains his clients within
the play's fictional world, but it is also presumably effective enough to entertain the audience (or readers) of the play *Zélinde,* where the portrait
constitutes one of the few direct satires of Molière as a personage.

As in Molière's *La Critique,* then, Donneau de Visé uses the wit and
conversation of the public as the creative source of the satire. It must be
admitted, though, that Donneau de Visé does not stage a self-attribution
scene like that in *La Critique.* The characters never promise to transcribe
their dialogue for future performance. Nevertheless, on several occasions
Zélinde favorably compares the wit of its spectator-characters to that of the
playwright Molière. The first example concerns the keen observation for
which these Parisians pride themselves. The remark is made by Zélinde,
the eponymous heroine of the play, in reply to a verbal portrait drawn by
her interlocutor, the *honnête homme* Mélante, who has just satirized the
frondeurs, that is, the critical cabals that manipulated audience reaction to
plays in Paris at the time. Zélinde lauds the portrait:

> Jamais Elomire n'a fait de Portraits si ressemblans que celuy des frondeurs
> de Pieces, que vous venez de faire. (79; sc. 10)

> Never has Elomire made portraits more lifelike than that of the theater ca-
> bals that you have just made.

The quote admirably summarizes the position of Mélante as *honnête
homme:* he is a *spectator* of comedies, as his firsthand knowledge of critical
cabals demonstrates; he is furthermore the *subject of comic portraits,* as one
of the *personnes de qualité* who are the privileged models for Molière's (and
Donneau de Visé's) plays; and finally he is a *creator* of lifelike portraits,
such as those of the *frondeurs* he sketches here. Indeed in this case, his
portraits are deemed even more "lifelike" than those of Molière. Given that
likeness is the key criterion for comic portraits, as is stated in *La Critique,*

this comparison between Mélante's skill and Molière's is particularly strik-ing. Donneau de Visé thus places satiric creation in the hands of the pub-lic—just what he has accused Molière of doing.

Even more remarkably, the play contains its own scene depicting the transmission of portraits from amateur public to professional author. When Zélinde encounters the poet and playwright Aristide, she states:

> Il faut que vous me veniez voir un de ces jours; j'ai les choses du monde les plus plaisantes à vous donner, et qui produiront de merveilleux effets au Theatre: ce sont de ces choses du temps qui sont presentement à la mode et qui de plus sont veritables. (50; sc. 8)

> You must come to see me one of these days; I have the most entertaining things in the world to show you, and which will produce marvelous effects on stage: they are timely matters that are now all the fashion and that are moreover true [véritables].

This scene presents precisely the kind of donation of *mémoires* for which Donneau de Visé denigrates Molière. Furthermore, the portraits that Zélinde offers the playwright are qualified as "true" [véritable] rather than simply verisimilar. Donneau de Visé embraces here the very aesthetic of transcription he seemed to attack. Indeed the character Aristide—a mouthpiece for Donneau de Visé's position and, as a playwright, no doubt a double for the author—shows himself to be most interested in staging Zélinde's portraits: he offers no resistance to this kind of rhapsodism. But the irony is in fact even more delicious: Donneau de Visé uses the *mémoire* in question for his own play, *Zélinde.* How? The character Zélinde fortu-nately remembers the subject of the portrait sketch she has just offered playwright Aristide, that of a malicious wit about town, a *médisante,* which she then recites to the other characters. As such, it constitutes one of the verbal satires that embellish the play, much like Argimont's sketch of Mo-lière. After Zélinde delivers her satire, the playwright Aristide comments on its appropriateness for comic representation:

> Ah! Je tourneray cela à merveille, et je ne doute point du succez, puis que les Satires sont à la mode. (52; sc. 8)

> Ah! I will treat it marvelously, and I do not doubt its success, as satires are in fashion.

Zélinde and Aristide then proceed beyond this act of creation of a comic role toward collaboration on an entire play. Zélinde again inspires the playwright Aristide, this time suggesting a play that will be a burlesque inversion of Molière's *La Critique:*

Il faudroit que vous fissiez la Critique, sous le nom d'Apologie. Ah! que ce seroit une bonne Pièce! [. . .] L'on pourroit, de son sujet, faire une Satire inimitable, en faisant seulement que ceux qui deffendent l'Escolle des Femmes, la combattent, et que ceux qui la combattent la deffendent. (55–56; sc.8)

You should make a Critique, under the name of an Apology. Ah! That would be a good play! One could make a inimitable satire from this subject, just by making those that defend the play attack it, and those that attack the play defend it.

Here, as in *La Critique,* the creative act, the very genesis of the comedy, transpires in social commerce. Aristide follows with his own contribution, and even the noble lady Oriane interjects with advice on the projected play. Though this scene is not, like the end of *La Critique,* properly speaking a spontaneous creation by the characters of their own play (it is not a description of the play they are in, *Zélinde*), the little group's project of an inverted *Critique* will in fact be realized during the course of the Quarrel of *L'Ecole des femmes.* The play outlined in this moment of conversational intoxication will be authored not by Donneau de Visé, but instead by another of Molière's critics, Boursault, in *Le Portrait du peintre, ou la contre-critique de l'Ecole des femmes.* Once again the public (as represented on stage) creates a comedy for its own future viewing.

To sum up: Donneau de Visé cannot escape accrediting the act of comic depiction to its own future audience because the link between the portrayed and the portrayer implacably displaces the act of representation away from poetic invention and toward the social practice of observation. Satires are, as Donneau de Visé himself admits, "in fashion," and their delectable transparency require audience collaboration. But if the audience seeks to recognize easily the model, that recognition poses its own problems. The satirist is "a dangerous personage." Satire tends less to correct than to provoke angry retaliation, as we see have seen in these polemical counterattacks, and as the title "Portrait of the Painter" suggests. But here we need to move beyond the creation myths of the plays to the tale of their reception, and their audience's often violent reaction.

*Part
Two*

RECOGNITION
RECOGNITION

We have seen that the "fidelity imperative" commands the comedy to absorb its own audience, as observers and portraitists, into the act of comic creation. But the very existence of this imperative results, in turn, from another function of the public: not that of creator, but of spectator. For it is first and foremost the desire of the audience members to see their world represented as they picture it that creates the conditions for their mythic collaboration with Molière. I have until now considered only implicitly the public's role as spectators, glancing, for example, at Climène's uneasy desire to see herself portrayed on stage in the projected *La Critique*. Now I situate more fully the public before its portrayal and examine the self-recognitions and misrecognitions that result. The audience's confrontation with its own portrait is not simply the terminal point in the process of comic depiction; it is instead at the center of its creative dynamics: it provides a second spectacle that not only complements the comedy on stage, but that also provides material for future comic representations.

Molière's theater capitalizes here on one of the defining ambitions of French classical literature: the desire to stimulate a sense of self-recognition in the audience. Indeed, the persistent emphasis on verisimilitude is arguably simply the symptom of a kind of collective narcissism; verisimilitude is, as one scholar has remarked, the necessary result of a culture that "needs to eliminate from the representation everything that does not resemble its own world, everything in which it cannot recognize itself" [besoin d'écarter de la représentation tout ce qui ne ressemble pas à son propre monde, tout ce en quoi elle ne peut pas se reconnaître] (Tocanne, *L'Idée* 310). But if the audience desires to recognize its world in the work of art, it can also be repulsed by the view of its faults. The aesthetic elixir that would allow recognition without repulsion is the much sought after philosophers' stone; and the formula for that elixir is an attainable goal. Such is the moral of La Fontaine's *L'Homme et son image,* an homage to the cynically debunking *Maximes* of La Rochefoucauld. The fable's hero, a modern Narcissus, cannot bear the disappointment of seeing himself exactly reflected; he quits society to avoid all sight of mirrors, no longer able to bear their fidelity to reality. However, in his exile he encounters a beautiful canal, the waters of which are irresistible, despite the unflattering mirror they form to his imperfections. He is forced to confront his reflection. La Fontaine draws the moral:

> Notre âme, c'est cet homme amoureux de lui-même;
> Tant de miroirs, ce sont les sottises d'autrui,
> Miroirs, de nos défauts les peintres légitimes;
> Et quant au canal, c'est celui
> Que chacun sait, le livre des *Maximes.* (24–28)

> Our soul is this man in love with himself;
> All these mirrors are the foibles of others,
> Mirrors that are the legitimate portraitists of our faults;
> And as for the canal, it is,
> As everyone knows, the book of the *Maximes.*

If the art of representation makes self-recognition temporarily attractive to the audience, La Fontaine does not underestimate the continuing resistance to it: even in the beautiful frame of the canal, the hero wishes, albeit futilely, to flee the mirror:

> Il fait tout ce qu'il peut pour éviter cette eau;
> Mais quoi? le canal est si beau
> Qu'il ne le quitte qu'avec peine. (19–21)

> He does everything he can to avoid this water;
> But how? The canal is so beautiful
> That he cannot easily leave it.

The author's task, then, is to negotiate the audience's contentious self-love, or *l'amour-propre,* in order to perform the miracle of presenting the audience with a desirable mirror of its repulsive vices.

La Fontaine's parable is built on a crucial comparison: that between the self-recognition of "our faults" which occurs in confronting social reality (the "foolishness of others") and that which takes place in confronting its representation (the "book of the *Maximes*"). However, despite the equivalence of the two forms of self-recognition, La Fontaine notes that there is an essential modification that sweetens the confrontation with literary representation, as opposed to harsh reality. This modification varies according to the genre, and we might catalogue the possible attenuations as follows: in tragedy, it is the transforming process of universalizing verisimilitude that allows the mirror to be a softened one, displaced as it is in the setting of a distant epoch and country, a heroic realm far from the audience's world; in the form of moral maxims or essays, it is the generalizing taxonomy to which particular faults are subjected and thus depersonalized; in the case of La Fontaine's own fabulous mirror, it is the disguise of allegory that renders the reflection bearable.

The self-recognition produced by the comedy-mirror is of another, and much more direct, order. We have seen comedy's adoption of the true *(vrai)* as opposed to the *seemingly* true *(vraisemblable)*; we have seen that the comedy's spectator does not employ an "other eye" for the representation, as does that of tragedy. The sense of recognition produced by the comic portrait and that produced by its social model are thus confounded. Indeed the conflation of the two is so complete that an eye untrained in the social world cannot even begin to appreciate its depiction on stage. Simply put, to recognize the fidelity of the portrait, one must personally know the model. Such is the sense of Donneau de Visé's apology for *Le Misanthrope*, written three years after the Quarrel of *L'Ecole des femmes*—and after the polemist spectacularly switched camps to become a tireless defender of Molière.

> [L]'on ne peut ne la pas trouver bonne sans faire voir que l'on n'est pas de ce monde, et que l'on ignore la manière de vivre de la cour et celle des plus illustres personnes de la ville. (*OC* 2: 140; "Lettre [sur] *Le Misanthrope*")

> One cannot refuse to find it [*Le Misanthrope*] good without showing that one is not of this world, and that one ignores the manners of the court and those of the most illustrious persons of the town.

The sense of recognition produced by the comic portrait depends on the viewer's placement in the closed social world depicted. As another of Molière's apologists (again in a Donneau de Visé text) says of a young provincial woman who criticizes Molière's portrayal of *petits marquis:*

> Comme elle ne sçait pas encore ce que c'est que le monde, elle ne peut pas connoistre encore le fin d'un Ouvrage (*Response* 271; sc. 3)

> As she knows nothing yet of the polite world, she cannot understand the subtlety of the work.

One views comic depiction as one views the world. The perspective is from the inside. Recognition operates here in what Roland Barthes has called the *"inland* de la mondanité" that defines classical society: it is the closure that results from "a phenomena of which our societies of mass lose more and more any idea: everybody in it knows each other" [un phénomène dont nos sociétés de masse perdent de plus en plus l'idée: *tout le monde s'y connaît*] ("La Bruyère" 227, 228–29). It is only from within this world that one can understand its representations, be they social or theatrical. Such is the sense of Alceste's description in *Le Misanthrope* of his opponent's hypocritical self-representation:

> *Au travers de son masque on voit à plein le traître;*
> Partout il est connu pour tout ce qu'il peut être;
> Et ses roulements d'yeux et son ton radouci
> N'imposent qu'a *des gens qui ne sont point d'ici.* (I.i.125–28; emphasis
>   added)

> *One fully sees the villain through his mask;*
> Everywhere he is known for what he is;
> And his rolling eyes and sweetened voice
> Fool only those *people who are not from here.*

Social representation follows the same insiders' rules as comic depiction. The hypocrite's mask, like the portraits of the comedy, can be deciphered only by those who have observed the world in which they are situated, and who are adept at the art of comparing the representation and the represented, the portrait and the true model.

Part 2 closely follows the spectator's gaze as it shifts from portrait to model, from stage to audience. In order to gain a preliminary purchase on the problem of viewer recognition as it operates in the closed social world of *mondanité*, I first compare two examples of the portrayal of *préciosité*, one from Molière and the other from his immediate forerunner, the abbé de Pure. Both cases pose larger theoretical questions regarding the relationship between portrayal and beholder—questions I will examine in chapter 8, before undertaking in chapters 9 and 10 a larger look at the dynamic exchange between Molière and the targets of his satires.

Seven

◈

PRECIOUS RECOGNITIONS

La Prétieuse

The abbé de Pure's inextant play *La Prétieuse* is often cited as a precursor of Molière's *Les Précieuses ridicules*. Indeed, at the time of *Les Précieuses*'s performance, Molière was accused of plagiarizing de Pure's play, which was apparently staged at the *comédie des italiens* in Paris three years earlier, in 1656, though never printed.[1] There is, though, a troubling irony in the accusation. The charge of plagiarism against Molière naturally assumes that the abbé de Pure is the authoritative creator of the comedy in question: literary theft assumes original literary property. However, if we look at de Pure's own account of the play, we see that the author attributes the composition of *La Prétieuse* not to himself, but instead to members of the play's future public, to friends of the social personages to be represented on stage. As Couton has remarked of the play, "it is created from a little coterie conspiracy" [elle est née d'une petite conspiration mondaine] (*OC* 1: 253). A close look at this social comedy opens some important questions about the utility of such representational "conspiracies," questions that Molière's version of the play a few years later answers in some surprising ways.

Though little information about the comedy *La Prétieuse* exists, the abbé de Pure describes the creation, staging, and reception of the play in

---

1. In his 1660 preface to his own *Véritables Prétieuses,* the writer Somaize labels Molière nothing more than "the so-called author" [l'autheur prétendu] of the comedy, because the playwright "copied" the "Pretieuses de Monsieur l'abbé de Pure" (Mongrédien, *Comédies et Pamphlets* 36). Donneau de Visé follows up with the same accusation in his *Nouvelles nouvelles* (*OC* 1: 1019). For information on the circumstances surrounding the play see *OC* 1: 250–51 and Michaut 65.

the third part (1657) of his lengthy novel of literary manners, *La Prétieuse ou le Mystère des ruelles*. The heroine of the story, Aurélie, is in love with a poet, Scaratide. Her friends and relations do not approve of the match, which they find most disadvantageous for her, and they plot to change her affections. They first scheme to introduce her to a rival for her affections, one who is an *honnête homme* rather than a disreputable poet. They then plot to create a play that will represent her situation on stage. The idea is to publicly embarrass Aurélie by exposing her unsuitable preference for the poet (2: 170–71). The heroine describes the story line of this little comedy plotted by her friends: "a girl finds herself preferring a fake poet to a real and respectable gallant" [une fille se trouvoit préférer un faux Poëte à un galant effectif et de condition] (2: 173).

Aurélie's social peers take on the role of playwright with the sole objective of provoking a scene of self-recognition from the model and viewer of the portrait, Aurélie. They take her to the theater where she will see herself and her beloved poet represented on stage. Aurélie's account of the painful episode constitutes the core of the novel's passage concerning the play. The first-person narration begins when one of the plotters (who is referred to as both friend and family relation ["une parente"]) comes to take Aurélie to the theater to see what will be *La Prétieuse*.

> [C]ette mesme amie me vint prendre en carosse et m'invita à la Comedie des Italiens. [. . .] [J]e n'eus pas veu plustot paroitre un Poëte contrefaict, que sans avoir besoin de ces frequents regards que celle qui me donnoit la Comedie m'addressoit de temps en temps, je connus bien que l'on m'avoit joüée sur le Theatre, et que ma passion avoit esté exposée au peuple pour m'en faire concevoir, par un conseil public, une honte particuliere. J'advouë que le dépit et la colere s'éleverent dans mon ame avec quelque sorte d'impetuosité et je n'eus pas assez de force sur moy-mesme pour retenir cette indignation que j'avois de l'affront que je recevois de Gelasire tout ensemble et de ma parente. (2: 172)

> This same friend picked me up in a carriage and took me to the Italian theater. . . . I no sooner saw a poet imitated [on stage] than, even without needing the frequent glances I received from the woman who gave me the comedy, I knew that they were playing me on stage, and that my passion had been exposed to the public in order to provoke a private sense of shame through a public admonishment [conseil public]. I admit that spite and anger impetuously arose in me, and I did not have the self-control to hold back the indignation I felt from the affront that I received from Gelasire and my cousin.

The first development related here is Aurélie's discovery of the authors of the comedy, that is, Gelasire and her cousin. The key to her attribution lies in the moment of her self-recognition. This process of self-recognition remains somewhat implicit. As soon as she sees the staged poet, she realizes that she is being portrayed on stage. What is to be assumed here is that the poet on stage is an exact reproduction of the one courting Aurélie. When she recognizes the poet, she recognizes her own situation. Aurélie assumes that such an *identical* copy of her situation can only be the work of someone who knows the original, and who is thus close to her and her poet. She therefore refines her attribution; the indefinite "they" [on] of "they were playing me on stage" is replaced by the names of specific members of her entourage, Gelasire and her cousin. This model of representation as exact copy—as a mirror created in the interior of a social group—creates a confusion between reality and representation. When Aurélie remarks, "they were playing *me* on stage," she elides the word "role"; this elision is significant, for she recognizes at that moment no distinction between her person and the "role" that it had inspired. This is the same blurring of person and portrayal that characterizes the marquis's and Elise's remarks at the end of *La Critique*.

In addition to Aurélie's own self-recognition, there is another sign that the play is a portrayal of her created by her friends: the scrutiny under which she is placed during the performance. Aurélie claims that she determined she was being played on stage even without taking into account the glances cast her way by "the woman who gave me the comedy"— that is, by her scheming friend. The evidence provided by these glances may be, as Aurélie asserts, secondary and nonessential; nevertheless it is important enough to be repeated in her account. The scrutiny directed to her person in the audience is a necessary consequence of her being the model of the character portrayed on stage. Aurélie understands that the spectators are regarding a dual spectacle: her dramatic *representation* on stage is doubled by her physical *presence* in the theater audience. The public is comparing the original and the copy.

In addition to the simple interest of comparing the portrait to its model, the "real" Aurélie in the audience provides an additional fascination: Aurélie's reaction to seeing herself is in itself a performance. Her friend watches Aurélie watching herself in order to gauge the effect of this self-recognition: an effect that is qualified as "shame" by Aurélie. From the friend's perspective, the spectacle is provided by Aurélie herself, just as for the others it is provided by her portrayal on stage. The ambiguity of Aurélie's expression "they were playing me" exploits the double nature of the spectacle. By having the actors *play the role* of Aurélie on stage, the authors *play a trick* upon Aurélie in the audience. The double sense in classical French of "jouer quelqu'un" is deployed here; it can either mean to theatrically portray someone or simply to fool them, that is, to make a fool of them.[2] In this case, the two senses are integrally linked. Aurélie's friends make a spectacle of her (as spectator) by presenting her with the spectacle of her role on stage. They then watch the spectator for the pleasure of the reactions that the stage performance engenders. In this sense, they are doubly authors: first by creating the comedy, then by placing Aurélie in the audience of the comedy and thereby provoking a new comedy as Aurélie watches herself. In short, portrayal provokes the reaction of the portrait's model and thereby creates a second spectacle.

We have already seen this strategy in play in *La Critique,* when Elise provokes the ridiculous vanity of Climène by drawing the portrait of her manners and presenting it to her. Whether it be a verbal portrait, as in the case of Elise, or a staged portrait, as in the case of Aurélie's friends, the portraiture is conceived as a pragmatic exercise by these "authors." They seek to incite reaction by presenting a "mirror" to the model. In Aurélie's account, the desired moral effect of the portrait defines its very nature: rather than a simple public mirror, Aurélie calls her depiction on stage a "public admonishment." Its corrective value is placed above its specular function. But of course Molière's own *miroirs publics* have also been defined as serving as a "lesson" and a "censure," as Uranie states. In fact, the utility of the comic portrait as a counselor depends on its efficacy as a mirror: to correct oneself, one must see oneself.

But above all what Aurélie's account tells us is that this moment of the spectator's self-recognition is in itself a spectacle, and one carefully designed by the authors for *their own pleasure.* Aurélie's expression of indignation may very well provide an occasion for the authors to verify the moral utility of their spectacle, and we can assume that the "shame" reflected on Aurélie's face satisfies the creators that the comedy is a success on this front. But there is also the suggestion that the spectacle of Aurélie's self-recognition is in itself delectable to her beholders as a comedy, regardless of any corrective effect it may hold.

The spectacle of self-recognition gives rise thus to both the future promise of moral improvement and the immediate (and cruel) pleasure of visible humiliation in the expressions of the one targeted for ridicule. The tensions between these two apparently opposing outcomes will be fully exploited in Molière's reworking of the play's themes a few years later. But before proceeding to *Les Précieuses ridicules,* let me summarize: in his novel

---

2. For an example of this usage, see Th. Corneille's *Amour à la mode* (1651): "Cet Oronte me fourbe, il me joue, il me brave" (V.ii).

La Prétieuse, the abbé de Pure accounts for the creation of his comedy by attributing it to an act of social observation and representation, to a closed system of scrutiny and identification enacted within the world to be portrayed. Furthermore, the authors are credited not only with creating a mirror of reality, but also of submitting the viewer to the recognition of moral faults in this mirror. There is no way to know if the abbé de Pure's account in the novel reflects the true circumstances of the creation of the play (in which case, Gelasire should be read as the abbé de Pure himself), or if it is a purely imaginative framework. In this second case, we can define Aurélie's narrative as a fictional supplement to the comedy designed as a kind of creation myth reinforcing the play's realism, much like the self-attribution scene that concludes *La Critique.* Whether such scenes are fact or fiction, what concerns us here is the model it provides for the creation and reception of the comedy, a model of observation, representation, and viewer recognition. I now compare the abbé de Pure's deployment of this system in the paratextual framework for *La Prétieuse* with the framework contained in the very text of Molière's *Les Précieuses ridicules.*

Les Précieuses ridicules

In order to gauge the parallel between the two plays, let us return briefly to the polemic over Molière's debt to *La Prétieuse.* I have already noted that the accusation of plagiarism against Molière is ironic, since the abbé de Pure laid no personal claim to the stolen property in question, a play that he attributes to a social intrigue and not to himself. Naturally, this paradox hardly impedes Molière's critics from publicizing the accusation, even though the abbé de Pure himself apparently never complained of being its victim.[3] The charge against Molière was most aggressively pursued by Somaize, who wrote his own version of a *précieuses* satire, *Les Véritables Précieuses,* one year after Molière's play. Somaize's comedy presents a description of de Pure's *La Prétieuse* designed to maximize the similarity with Molière's play and thus reinforce the evidence against Molière. Here is his comparison of the two plays:

> [C]'est la mesme chose, ce sont deux valets tout de mesme qui se deguisent pour plaire à deux femmes, et que leurs Maistres battent à la fin: Il y a seulement cette petite difference, que dans la premiere les valets le font à

3. Gustave Michaut makes clear that de Pure could easily have joined the polemic against Molière, but consciously chose not to accuse the playwright (66).

l'inceu de leurs Maistres, et que dans la derniere, ce sont eux qui leur font faire. (52–53; sc. 7)

It is the same thing: there are two valets who disguise themselves to please two women, and their masters beat them at the end: there is only this little difference, that in the first [de Pure's play] the valets do it without their master's knowing it, and in the second [Molière's], it is the masters who make them do it.

This description of de Pure's play has left Molière apologists searching for means by which to defend the playwright from the charge of plagiarism. The strongest tactic has been to assert that Somaize's description of de Pure's play, written after Molière's play was performed, is skewed in order to exaggerate the resemblance between the two. In order to justify Molière, de Pure's own report of the play, which as we have seen makes no mention of disguised valets, is presented by scholars as a more reliable version, written as it is two years before Molière's play was staged and thus free from any contamination from the latter.[4]

It is surprising that, despite the close attention paid to de Pure's description of the play, the comparison between what Couton calls the "conspiration mondaine" that creates *La Prétieuse* and the social conspiracy that provokes the action of *Les Précieuses ridicules* has been overlooked. This second conspiracy is, of course, enacted in the play rather than recounted in a subsequent text. It is the conspiracy devised in the first scene by the two rejected suitors of the *précieuses,* La Grange and Du Croisy, who have observed the two women's conduct and resolved to ridicule them. As in *La Prétieuse,* the conspiracy also involves the performance of a "poëte contrefaict," Mascarille (assisted here by fellow valet Jodelet), who will court the two young women with a burlesque imitation of fashionable Parisian affectations. The performance of the mock-poet Mascarille will create in the last scene the same shameful self-recognition on the part of the *précieuses* (who understand they are the subject of public mockery) that de Pure's counterfeit poet produces in Aurélie. In short, the three principal steps operating in the creation and reception of *La Prétieuse* are reenacted here: *observation* of the model made possible by social contiguity; *representation* of the faults associated with the model through play-acting; and

---

4. The abbé de Pure's account was first used to exculpate Molière in 1880, and Michaut exploits this resurrection of de Pure's text to thoroughly vindicate Molière's inventiveness, arriving at the following conclusion: "Ainsi il n'est pas prouvé que *La Précieuse* de l'abbé de Pure et *Les Précieuses ridicules* de Molière soient semblables dans leur conduite générale." More recently, this argument has received important support in Couton's "Notice" to *Les Précieuses* (1: 251–53).

finally, the model's *recognition* of personal faults as represented in the spectacle.

We can therefore isolate the principal body of the play—the valet Mascarille's ridiculous aping of fashionable manners before the admiring Cathos and Magdelon—as a kind of comedy in the comedy, which is conceived by the two plotting suitors. This internal comedy is framed by the opening and closing scenes of *Les Précieuses.* The opening scene presents the creation of the internal comedy: here, the two suitors devise the plot involving Mascarille's disguise. The final three scenes present the reception of the internal comedy: the suitors return to expose the truth about their "play" and force the *précieuses* to recognize their folly. Indeed, both of the scenes contain strong allusions to the theatrical nature of the trick played upon the women. The word *pièce,* suggesting both a theatrical "play" and a "trick" or practical joke, is used first by the plotters themselves to describe their enterprise: La Grange says, "we will play them a trick that will make them see their foolishness" [nous leur jouerons tous deux une pièce qui leur fera voir leur sottise] (1: 266; sc. 1). The word *pièce* reappears at the end of the play, this time employed by one of those who has been "played upon," Magdelon: "Oh! Father, what a dirty trick [or play] they have concocted for us!" [Ah! mon père, c'est une pièce sanglante qu'ils nous ont faite!] (1: 286, sc.16).

Of course, these allusions to theatrical representation remain just that: allusions. The two suitors do not create an actual theatrical performance or comic text. They instead devise a feint to be enacted in the house of their victim, for an immediate audience of two. In this sense, there is a real difference between the characters of *Les Précieuses ridicules,* on the one hand, and on the other, Aurélie's scheming friends or the transcribers of *La Critique,* who are all explicitly credited with the function of comic authors. My analysis thus shifts realms: from the character as an *explicit* figure of the author to the character as a figure *analogous* to the author. I have already suggested the power of this analogy by comparing characters and authors as portraitists. This analogy clearly opens large questions pertaining to the implicitly reflexive nature of characters' action and discourse—even when not clearly labeled as "literary" in its enactment—and I will turn to the structure of such allusive reflexivity in part 3.

Les Précieuses opens *in medias res,* with the two suitors discussing the shabby welcome they have just received from the two women. What is interesting here is that the two speak of the previous encounter as though it were a spectacle viewed by an outside observer. La Grange begins the play with the following speech:

A-t-on jamais vu, dites-moi, deux pecques provinciales faire plus les renché-
ries que celles-là, et deux hommes traités avec plus de mépris que nous?
[. . .] Je n'ai jamais vu tant parler à l'oreille qu'elles ont fait entre elles, tant
bâiller, tant se frotter les yeux et demander tant de fois: "Quelle heure est-
il?" (1: 265–66; sc. 1)

Has one ever seen, tell me, two provincial fools be more pretentious than
these two, and two men treated with more scorn than us? . . . I have never
seen so much whispering in the ears, so much yawning, so much rubbing
of the eyes and so many demands of "What time is it?"

La Grange's assumption of the role of detached observer is radical. He first
assumes the perspective of a third party: the indefinite "one" that surveys
the scene. This "one" represents at the same time La Grange *and* society in
general, or at least an amalgam of men such as La Grange that circulate
in that society and normally observe the visits paid by suitors to young
women. By situating his observation point outside the scene, La Grange
describes not only what he has seen, that is, the women's conduct, but also,
and more strikingly, what he cannot see: himself. This indefinite observer
sees how the two suitors have been treated. It is revealing that La Grange
uses the generic term "men" [des hommes] to refer to himself and his
friend. La Grange has radically abstracted himself and his friend. The scene
of their welcome is rendered here as just another theoretical case in an
endless series of possible scenes of suitors' visits. Just as La Grange sees
himself in the general role of a "man," so too he places the two women
into a general category: that of "pecques provinciales." This is important,
for even if he later describes in detail the specific actions of the women, we
see here that he has not only observed their particular mannerism, but that
he has also placed them in a social category based on larger observations.

It is indeed this categorization of the *précieuses,* based upon various
social observations drawn together to define a general character trait, that
provides the foundation for the comedy they intend to play on the *précieuses.* Thus La Grange:

[J]e veux me venger de cette impertinence. Je connais ce qui nous a fait
mépriser. L'air précieux n'a pas seulement infecté Paris, il s'est aussi répandu
dans les provinces, et nos donzelles ridicules en ont humé leur bonne part.
En un mot, c'est un ambigu de précieuse et de coquette que leur personne.
Je vois ce qu'il faut être pour en être bien reçu; et, si vous m'en croyez, nous
leur jouerons tous deux une pièce qui leur fera voir leur sottise, et pourra
leur apprendre à connaître un peu mieux leur monde. (1: 266; sc.1)

I want my revenge for this impertinence. I know what made them scorn us.
That air of *préciosité* has not only infected Paris, but it has also spread to the

provinces where our ridiculous damsels have inhaled their share of it. In a word, they are a hybrid of a *précieuse* and a coquette. I see what it takes to be well received here, and if you follow me, we will make a little show [jouer une pièce] that will make them see their foolishness and teach them to know a bit better their place in the world.

La Grange advances his analysis here. He claims first to have located the problem, to "know" the source of the women's disdain. This source is found not in their specific condition, but in a general social manner, in an "air" that has infected the women.[5] La Grange asserts that he knows the world and its ways. His observations have permitted typification. As a moralist he has created a taxonomy of the social creature. La Grange concludes sagely that the women are a hybrid ("ambigu") of two species: the *précieuse* and the coquette.

Observation followed by analytic description provides the necessary materials for the next step: representation. Having located the network of manners that define the women, he knows how to reproduce them: he knows "what one must be" [ce qu'il faut être] to be welcomed into the women's society. As one Molière scholar pointed out, the use here of "be" [être] rather than "appear" [paraître] is important: in the society depicted "there can be no demarcation between appearance and essence, affectation and profound personality, public and private image" (Hubert 17). Indeed, in this world where beings are profoundly "infected" by fashion and where the taxonomy of character is so absolute, manner absolutely defines the person.

To "be" the same as the *précieuses* is to play the role perfectly, to represent their manners in such a way that the representation becomes indistinguishable from reality. Such is the nature of the "play" enacted by the two valets. They will provide an image of the *précieuses* as incarnated in masculine form—in the persons of Mascarille and Jodelet. To what purpose? The intended goal of this representation is made clear. The play is intended to *make seen* the faults of the women ("une pièce qui leur fera voir leur sottise," says La Grange), to render their manners visible to themselves, so that they too can know themselves and their situation, that is, "know their world" [connaître leur monde] the way La Grange and Du Croisy know theirs.

But this lesson of lucidity will not be taken lightly. After the fun and games of the two valets' visit is over, and their real status as servants is revealed to the two women, the intended "lesson" is in fact taken very

---

5. As Roger Duchêne has remarked on La Grange's description, in classical French the term "air" is primarily social in its application: "L'air se rapporte à la conduite en société" (357).

much as an "affront" (1: 286; sc. 16)—the same word Aurélie applied to her lesson. Furthermore, the affront is as public as Aurelie's "conseil." There is no doubt that the audience of this *pièce* will extend well beyond the house of old Gorgibus, father and uncle to Magdelon and Cathos: the spectacle of the valet's wooing of the women will be recounted throughout the town. So it is that the reactionary Gorgibus laments in the last scene:

> Nous allons servir de fable et de risée à tout le monde, et voilà ce que vous vous êtes attiré par vos extravagances. Allez vous cacher, vilaines; allez vous cacher pour jamais. (1: 287; sc. 17)

> We will be the talk and the laughingstock of the town, and now you see what your foolishness has brought you. Go and hide yourselves, wretches; go hide yourselves forever.

Exile from the world appears to be the only recourse left to the humiliated *précieuses.*

We cannot know with certainty if the two women will, like Aurélie, "learn a lesson" from this cruel affront, but I think we must assume they will not. Indeed I believe that Molière's version of the story presents a radically more skeptical vision of the moral utility of representation and recognition. First of all, it must be admitted that enraged malice rather than generous pedagogy motivates the two authors of Cathos and Magdelon's humiliation. The two suitors force the women to recognize their fault, but the two do so, as La Grange suggests, only in order to seek "revenge" for their humiliation before the eyes of the world. This lack of moral elevation clearly distinguishes them from Aurélie's companions, who seek to better her condition. But even more importantly, whatever the impulse may be behind the valet's little comedy, its outcome is undeniably ugly. After learning that they have been the dupe of a "nasty play" performed by two valets, the women in turn promise to avenge their own humiliation: Magdelon declares, "I swear that we will get revenge" [Je jure que nous en serons vengées], repeating the language used by La Grange in the first scene (1: 286; sc. 16). Will the women's revenge also feature its own little comedy to be played out? In any case, such a cycle of malevolent comedies seems to offer little hope for the correction of vices. There is no hint of a corrective shame here, the kind of helpful introspection that Aurélie undertook after seeing herself represented. Instead, Magdelon's final lines are characterized by unreflective anger: "I'm dying with spite" [Je crève de dépit], she exclaims (1: 286; sc. 15).

But of course in a world where such representations are part of a closed social game, played out between the twin acts of observation and identifi-

cation, rancor and malice are powerful motives—and perhaps the only real
ones. The bile of the satirist—whether professional playwright or simple
participant in social intercourse—inspires many bitingly faithful portraits.
And there is, unfortunately, nowhere to hide. The eyes of the world are
upon each member of this society. The attempt to flee the common gaze
animates many a comic character, as the attempt to flee the gods' gaze
propels a tragic heroine like Phèdre. Cathos and Magdelon may, as their
father urges, rush off stage to hide from the affront they have suffered. In
doing so they join Arnolphe at the end of *L'Ecole* and Alceste at the end of
Le Misanthrope. However, the spectator is offered no information about
where they might go to escape the laughter of the world and its continual
drive to describe and ridicule the other. This desire to escape the world's
system of representation—and to recognize oneself in it no longer—is of
course none other than the desire Alceste nurses for his distant desert, or
the desire that La Fontaine's Narcissus feels for his mirrorless utopia. A
place, unfortunately, that has no real existence for those locked into the
stage of the theater, or into the stage of social commerce.

Eight

⟡

ILLUSION AND REFLEXIVITY

The case of *La Prétieuse* illustrates how spectators view comic copies with the "same eye" used for their social originals, their models in the public. By provoking Aurélie's powerful sense of self-recognition, the comic mirror proves its efficacy and directness. This mirror, though, also proves to be somewhat less alluring than that allegorized by La Fontaine: Aurélie hardly finds the situation of her depiction "irresistible." Nevertheless, the moral medicine seems to take, and Aurélie is reformed. The same cannot be said of Cathos and Magdelon, who flee from the laughter of the world, promising only to retaliate in kind against those who have rendered them a public spectacle and have held up a mirror to their faults.

These specific reactions to the comic mirror indicate both the power of its image and the forcefulness of the spectator's resistance to it. I now situate these tensions within the larger framework of French classical theater, both in terms of its practical operations and its aesthetic conventions. Though the period produces, even valorizes, a dynamic exchange between the stage portrait and its public, there remains a certain theoretical opposition to the blurring of the boundaries separating the two. In the 1630s, Corneille made the first move toward the comedy of current manners, pioneering the use of contemporary Parisian settings for his comedies; thereafter throughout the century the aesthetic barrier between the world of comic characters and that of the theater audience was progressively effaced. Indeed, by the time Rapin wrote his *Réflexions sur la Poétique d'Aristote* in 1674, the ideal relationship between the stage and the audience of comedy was one of a transparent conversation. Rapin here cites Terence as the model for this perfect convergence of spectator and actor:

Les Romains *pensoient estre en conversation quand ils assistoient aux Comédies* de Terence, car ils n'y trouvoient rien, que ce qu'ils avoient coutume de trouver dans les compagnies ordinaires: c'est le grand art de la Comédie de s'attacher à la nature et de n'en sortir jamais d'avoir des sentiments communs. (139; emphasis added)

The Romans *thought they were in conversation when they went to the comedies* of Terence, for they found nothing but what they were accustomed to finding in daily society: it is the great art of comedy to attach itself to nature and never to depart from common feelings.

This ideal transparency also encounters serious opposition in the period. Resistance to it arose from certain aesthetic conventions of comic creation, as I have shown, but conventions governing spectatorship were no more indulgent: blurring the border between audience and stage was generally viewed as a threat to dramatic illusion, which depends upon the inviolability of the performance, upon a distance that preserves its integrity. There is a signal case of theoretical opposition to dissolving the barrier between stage and audience that demands our close attention: d'Aubignac's 1657 *La Pratique.* But before looking more closely at d'Aubignac's arguments, it is necessary to quickly sketch the seventeenth-century performance practices to which they respond.

The theater space of the French classical age has little to do with our own. The audience-stage relationship of the second half of the seventeenth century is defined by theatrical conventions that present striking contrasts to twentieth-century notions concerning the inviolable border between the stage and its audience. A summary of the modern conception of this impenetrable divide opens what is perhaps the most cited work on the sociology of theater:

Tout commande en effet cet aspect cérémoniel du théâtre: la solennité du lieu, la distinction d'un public, profane, et d'un groupe d'acteurs isolés dans un monde étroit, lumineux, le costume des comédiens, la rigueur des gestes, la particularité d'une langue poétique qui distingue radicalement la langue du théâtre, du bavardage quotidien. (Duvignaud 7)

Everything leads to this ceremonial aspect of theater: the solemnity of the place, the distinction between a lay audience and a group of actors isolated in a brightly lit and narrow world, the costume of the actors, the controlled gestures, and the specialness of the a poetic language that radically distinguishes the language of theater from daily chat.

Perhaps nothing seems more natural and self-evident to us than this evocation of the distant stage: Jean Duvignaud presents a thorough catalogue of what we generally assume to be the distinct boundary between daily social life and theatrical performance. Yet these strict demarcations hardly apply in the seventeenth century. The raucous theaters of the time were far from "solemn." The presence of seated spectators on the stage itself allowed the performance space very little "isolation" from the lay audience. Furthermore, though the actors were "illuminated," so was the audience, on whom the lights blazed brightly; spectator and actor were equally visible.[1] These theatrical conditions created an atmosphere in which, as one observer of the time noted, the audience provided a performance of equal interest to that on the stage:

> Dans la salle des spectacles, les Comédiens et les spectateurs se donnent réciproquement la comédie. Quand je suis dans une loge, ce qui se passe au Parterre m'excite autant à rire que ce qui se fait sur le Théâtre.[2]

> In the theater, the actors and the spectators mutually act out a play for each other. When I am in the balcony, what happens on the parterre makes me laugh as much as what happens on the stage.

Despite the increasingly policed nature of theaters after 1630, and during the 1640s and 1650s when d'Aubignac wrote *La Pratique*,[3] the theater space remained noisy and chaotic through the 1670s.[4] This much can be said for the general physical space for almost any theatrical representation at the time in Paris, whether it be a tragedy or a comedy. A look at the specific nature of the comic stage shows any stark barrier between audience and stage disintegrating even further. The costumes of the actors were generally the same as those of the portion of the public the play depicts. Indeed, this imitation was so close that, according to an anecdote from the abbé de Pure, the spectators seated on stage were often assumed to be actors:

> Combien de fois sur ces morceaux de vers: mais le voici . . . mais je le vois . . . , a-t-on pris pour un comédien et pour le personnage qu'on attendait, des hommes bien faits et bien mis qui entraient alors sur le théâtre et qui cherchaient des places, après même plusieurs scènes exécutées?[5]

1. The Italian practice of dimming the lights of the auditorium was not followed in France. See Banham 918.

2. Abbé Bourdelon in *Diversitez curieuses pour servir de récréation à l'esprit*, 1699 (1: 58), qtd. in Mélèse 214.

3. For the genesis of *La Pratique*, begun in 1640 and written through the 1650s, see P. Martino's preface to the 1927 edition (xii–xv).

4. "Bruyante, agitée, papotante" are the terms used by Mélèse (209–15).

5. From *Idée des spectacles anciens et modernes* (Paris, 1668 [174]), qtd. in Scherer, *Dramaturgie* 271. Scherer remarks of actors' costumes: "C'est trop peu de dire qu'ils reproduisent la réalité quotidienne du XVIIe siècle: ils sont cette réalité même" (150). For a full-length study of fashion in Molière, see Stephen Dock's *Costume and Fashion*. The question of the realism of costumes is addressed in the

How many times after these bits of dialogue: "but here he is . . ." "but I see him . . ." has the audience mistaken for an actor and for the character awaited the handsome, well-dressed men who entered just then on stage looking for their seats, even after several scenes had been played?

As for the gestures of the actors, they tended to duplicate the manners of the audience as closely as the costumes did current fashion. At least so much can be said of Molière's troupe, which, as we know from the first scene of *L'Impromptu,* aimed to imitate "le plus naturellement . . . possible" the behavior of their models in the public. The actor's style seeks a union of stage and society, qualified by Dandrey as "la transparence du jeu comique," where acting follows the code of naturalness and flexibility established by the social ideals of conversation.[6] And, finally, in the realm of literary expression the barrier between the stage and the audience collapses as well; Duvignaud's basic distinction between the language of the theater and everyday conversation is largely effaced in the comedy of manners, due to the growth of a cultivated literary public, whose self-proclaimed wit and elegance serves as the model for comic dialogue. Given the nature of the period's comic theater, Rapin's comparison with a salon, where characters and public converse, is more apt than Duvignaud's paradigm of a ceremony, where the anointed are distanced from the profane.

Ironically enough, though, the very lack of a practical, physical barrier between stage and spectators led some to seek an immaterial, aesthetic divide that could act as a kind of fourth wall to the dramatic space and prevent the kind of confusions between dramatic fiction and audience reality typical of the period. Preserving this barrier becomes a kind of driving mission for the abbé d'Aubignac, who devotes a good deal of his summa of dramatic theory, *La Pratique,* to presenting a paradigm of spectatorship that is at odds with what we have seen to be the period's general tendencies. Chapters 6 and 7 of the first book delineate what d'Aubignac considers the ideal perspective of the audience member, and, in so doing, distinguish two levels present in theatrical performance. One is the level of "representation" or "spectacle." This domain includes all that is linked to the physical situation of the theater: the actors and their costumes and props, as well

---

chapter on "The Emergence of Fashion in the First Parisian Comedies," which explores how current fashion on stage is essential in "revealing aspirations and defining character" (52).

6. In his chapter entitled "La transparence du jeu comique" (*Molière* 137–83), Dandrey thoroughly examines Molière's project of renovating the acting of the time, cutting through emphatic rhetorical and theatrical gestures and moving toward a flexible adaptation to the character at hand. Dandrey compares the actor's adaptability with social *bienséance;* he proposes "de définir l'art dramatique sur le modèle de la conversation, caractérisée par l'aisance et l'esprit d'à-propos" (143).

as the audience watching and their social situation. The other level is "The real story or the supposedly real story"[Histoire veritable ou que l'on suppose veritable]: this is the subject matter and the author's treatment of it, the characters and dramatic action (34–35). In short, d'Aubignac's two levels are (1) the story to be represented on stage ("l'Histoire") and (2) the means of that representation, the theater space and its activities ("le Spectacle" or "la Representation").[7] In the interest of dramatic illusion, d'Aubignac insists that these two levels never be confused, that considerations concerning the actors and the spectators never interfere with the story being staged: "one must never mix together what concerns the representation of a poem with the real action of the represented story" [il ne faut jamais méler ensemble ce qui concerne la representation d'un Poëme avec l'action véritable de l'histoire representée] (45). To illustrate the problem, d'Aubignac cites the example of the great French actor Floridor performing the role of Cinna. Floridor must efface himself as actor and ignore the audience in front of him: he must become truly Roman. He is never to make reference to contemporary seventeenth-century life—to "la Douceur de nos Dames" or to "les baricades de Paris" (45). D'Aubignac explains this precept as follows:

> [O]n ne souffriroit pas qu'il confondist la Ville de Rome avec celle de Paris, des actions si éloignées avec nos advantures presentes, et le jour de cette conjuration avec celui d'un divertissement public arrivé seize cents ans apres: car c'est pecher, non seulement contre des regles introduites par quelque consideration de bien-seance, mais encore contre le sens-commun. (45)

> One would not stand for [the actor] to confuse the city of Rome with that of Paris, or such distant actions with our own current events, or the day of this conspiracy [of Cinna] with the day of a public entertainment taking place sixteen hundred years later: for it is to sin, against not only the rules introduced by considerations of decorum, but also common sense.

In the case of such a tragedy, the distinction made between the situation of the theater and that of the dramatic action does indeed seem to be one dictated by common sense; Racine's "other eye" must after all be employed for the tragic stage. It would only confound the viewer to force her to use the same eye—that is, the same set of viewing assumptions—for Cinna that is used in everyday experience, the eye that sees Floridor in Paris instead of Cinna in Rome. But what of comedy, where the image is to be one of common daily life and thus does not demand such a leap of imagination on the part of the spectator? Here d'Aubignac proves himself re-

---

7. For further discussion of this distinction, see Pasquier (153–68) and Morrissey.

markably intransigent. He refuses to alter his paradigm for the specific nature of comedy. Having taken the position that the viewer's attention must be fully engaged in the represented action—and never distracted by the situation of its representation—he concludes that the action in question must be totally removed from the audience. Only by radically distancing the "real story" from the means of "representation" (that is, from the concerns of the actors and the audience) can the comic playwright avoid any risk that the two levels will be confused and the dramatic illusion broken.

There exists in the classical imagination a demon that excites all the fears associated with the elision of reality and depiction: it is the Old Comedy of Aristophanes. It is against this hobgoblin that D'Aubignac takes aim, commenting on *The Clouds:*

> En ce temps, la Representation étoit fort meslée avec la verité de l'action, elles estoient presque une mesme chose: car ce qu'on disoit contre le Socrate representé, s'addressoit au Socrate veritable, qui estoit présent. . . . [Aristophane] confond les interests des Acteurs avec ceux des Spectateurs, mesme l'histoire representée avec les affaires publiques. (46)

> During this time, the representation was completely mixed up with the true action [depicted in the play], they were almost the same thing: for what one said against the represented Socrates was addressed to the real Socrates, who was present. . . . [Aristophanes] confused the concerns of the actors with those of the spectators, even the represented story with public affairs of the time.

The common perception of a Socrates unjustly persecuted by Aristophanes played an important role in discrediting direct satire in classical aesthetics. But, as the passage suggests, the question was not simply a matter of preserving aesthetic boundaries; it was also a question of moral and legal propriety. Not only was direct satire viewed as indecorous, indeed perfidious, but it was illegal. Indeed, according to a judgment rendered against Boursault's 1668 comedy *La Critique des Satyres de Monsieur Boileau*—a play judged "defamatory of the honor" of the suppliant, Boileau—the use of proper names in comedies is "directly opposed to the laws and ordonnances of the kingdom."[8] The term used for this kind of direct satire is *médisance,* a difficult word to translate, as it denotes a kind of disparage-

---

8. From "Ordonnance du Parlement sur la Requête de Boileau contre Boursault." The judgement finds Boursault's play to be "une pièce diffamatoire contre l'honneur, la personne et les ouvrages du Suppliant; ce qui est directement contraire aux Lois et Ordonnances du Royaume, et qui serait d'une dangereuse conséquence, n'estant permis à des Farceurs et Comédiens de nommer les personnes connues et inconnues sur les Théâtres." From *Extraits des Registres du Parlement,* 22 October 1668, qtd. in full in Mélèse 423–24.

ment whose claims are not necessarily false: the literal translation of "bad-mouthing" would be more appropriate than "slander," for example. It is precisely the malicious wit of *médisance* that d'Aubignac denounces in the Old Comedy, which he qualifies as "a truly satiric poetry . . . that under the pretext of denouncing the people's vices in order to instruct them, instead indulges with impunity in lowly *médisance*" [une Poësie vrayement Satyrique . . . qui peu a peu sous pretexte de reprendre les vices du peuple pour l'instruire, s'emporta impunément dans une indigne medisance] (46). The term is echoed in the same context by Boileau, who while commenting on *les traits médisants* of Greek comedy, pities Socrates as the laughing-stock of Athens's "vile masses."[9]

I want to make it clear, though, that *médisance* is a highly problematic term of disapprobation in the classical age: it cannot be denied that this kind of malicious and direct criticism is, as we have seen, indissolubly bound up with satiric representation. To attack a vice is inevitably to attack those associated with it, even if unfairly so. Indeed, even those satirists who denounce *médisance* in one instance admit they practice it in another. Thus the very same Boileau who attacked Aristophanes' direct satire actually dared to proudly proclaim his very own poems to be pure *médisance*, rhyming (with impunity, I might add) his own brand of "satire" with "médire."[10] We will later see just how complex the relationship between *médisance* and moral truth proves to be in *Le Misanthrope*, where it is dramatized in the roles of Célimène and Arsinoé.

The problem of *médisance*—central as it may be for satiric representation—nevertheless does not constitute the principal failing of Old Comedy in d'Aubignac's view. Indeed, d'Aubignac only incidentally brings up the issue of injurious representation. His restriction on "mixing" the affairs of the audience with those of the comic characters extends well beyond a simple condemnation of defamation. His position concerns an absolute distinction in dramatic theory rather than incidental moral and legal issues. It is not simply a matter of avoiding slander, it is a matter of irrevocably divorcing comic depiction ("l'Histoire") from its audience ("le Spectacle"). Thus, after denouncing Old Comedy, he proceeds to set severe limits for New Comedy, where the stage action is invented on general prin-

9. We might suppose that Boileau, in attacking the laughter of the "vil amas du peuple"(*L'Art poétique* III.337, 344) is identifying here his own treatment by Boursault (six years earlier) with that of Socrates by Aristophanes.

10. He begins his "Satire VII" as follows: "Muse, changeons de style, et quittons la satire, / C'est un méchant métier que celui de médire." Of course, his renunciation is purely playful, and he concludes the poem by embracing the poetic "médisance" that he pretended to regret: "Je ne puis bien parler, et je ne saurois me taire," he boasts.

ciples rather than copied from specific events and personalities. D'Aubignac argues that not only must the comedy avoid portraying particular individuals, but that furthermore the comic fiction must avoid any contiguity whatsoever with the world of the theater and its audience. His dictum: the setting of the comedy must be completely separated from the situation of the public, just like tragedy.

> [La Nouvelle Comédie] receut des regles sur le modelle de la Tragedie, et devint la peinture et l'imitation des actions de la vie commune. Alors la representation en fut entierement separée, et tout ce qui se faisoit sur le Theatre, estoit considéré comme une histoire veritable, à laquelle ny la Republique, ny les Spectateurs n'avoient aucune part. On choisissoit des avantures que l'on supposoit estre arrivées dans des pays fort éloignés, avec lesquels la ville, où se faisoit la representation, n'avoit rien en commun. (47)

> [The New Comedy] took its rules from the model of Tragedy and became a portrait and imitation of the actions of common life. The representation was then entirely separated from it [the life of the audience] and all that was performed on the stage was considered as a real story, with which neither the republic nor the spectators had any part. Playwrights chose adventures that were supposed to take place in a distant land that had nothing in common with the city where the theatrical representation took place.

In addition to a marked geographic distance, the action of the comedy should also be historically distanced from the audience: the poet sets the play at "a time when the spectators could not have lived" (48), meaning, one imagines, that the play must take place no later than the date of birth of the oldest living citizen capable of transporting himself to the theater. D'Aubignac in fact demands for comedy the same geographic and historical divorce between hero and audience that Racine applies to tragedy. D'Aubignac's barrier between comic action and theater public is absolute:

> Ainsi l'Action Theatrale et la representation n'estoient plus confondues, parce qu'elles n'avoient plus rien en commun. (48)

> Thus the dramatic action and the representation were no longer confused, because they had nothing in common.

There appears to be a somewhat troubling paradox in d'Aubignac's claim: in order to insure that spectators can fully immerse themselves in the action of the comedy, that action must be placed as far as possible from the spectators' own world. In other words, in order to guarantee dramatic illusion, the viewer must not recognize his own surroundings in the image depicted. Such a recognition would distract the viewers from the story represented and move their attention toward current reality. Their gaze would shift from Socrates on stage toward the real Socrates in the audience. For d'Aubignac, the absorption of the viewers into the story depends upon an entire suppression of any consciousness of their own positions in the audience. In this sense, d'Aubignac's paradox (distance makes possible absorption) rehearses a century in advance Diderot's antitheatrical position in regard to painting.[11] And just as Diderot's embrace of the inviolability of the painted narrative can best be read as a reaction against the earlier eighteenth-century rococo excess in theatricality, so too d'Aubignac's rejection of any reflexivity in the spectator's gaze represents a revolt against the seventeenth-century baroque tendency toward the self-conscious play we associate with Calderón or Bernini, where the representation openly declares its position before the spectator and where the border between the beholder and the beheld is playfully traversed.

Though d'Aubignac's anxious voice hardly cries alone in the wilderness, it is still quite clear that the intransigence of his theoretical positions implicitly places him in opposition to the prevailing trends of his own epoch.[12] Indeed, d'Aubignac's arguments are situated in the middle of a resolute movement—starting in the 1630s and culminating in the 1660s—in which comic authors increasingly model characters on their audience and model the fictional setting on the world outside, and even inside, the theater. Of course, there is little doubt that when d'Aubignac criticizes some of Plautus's excesses (condemning, for example, Jupiter's parodic aside to the audience in *Amphitryon* [48]), the theorist expresses a general concern with the inviolability of dramatic illusion, a concern shared by his contemporaries. Likewise, his condemnation of libelous personal depictions is a commonplace of the epoch. However, d'Aubignac pushes his precept prescribing the separation of the fiction from its frame of production well beyond this common ground and thereby parts company with his contemporaries.

In reality, the separation of the fictional "story" from the frame of its "representation" is not an absolute precept for the period, but rather a matter of constant negotiation. The fact is that the period's viewers—and readers—could manage the intermingling of the two levels without de-

---

11. Such is the thesis of Michael Fried's brilliant analysis of Diderot's art criticism. He thus summarizes Diderot's "paradox": "it was only by negating the beholder's presence that this [absorption] could be achieved: only by establishing the fiction of his absence or non-existence could his actual placement before the enthrallment by the painting be secured" (103).

12. Though d'Aubignac limits his reproaches to Greek and Latin comedy (48–51), it is clear that his remarks are aimed, as is the book in general, at the prevailing practices of his day.

stroying their faith in the depiction. The written accounts we have seen, which describe the eye roaming freely from the stage to the audience, are not simply an accidental consequence of contingencies such as the organization of the theater space, the loud behavior of certain spectators, or the lack of special costumes to distinguish actors. They are instead the result of a general aesthetic movement, of the conscious attempt of comic authors to meet the demand of a public that wishes to see its world represented. Far from depicting comic settings that have, as d'Aubignac desires, "nothing in common" with the setting of the theater and its audience, the comic genres of the period offer depictions that have everything in common with their public.

While comedies in foreign settings still flourished through the first half of the century (with Rotrou or Scarron, for example), the early plays of Corneille provide a solid model for the contemporary Parisian setting, one in which the characters on stage explicitly share a common world with the audience. When Corneille adapted a tragedy such as *Le Cid* or a "comédie héroïque" like *Don Sanche D'Aragon* from Spanish originals, he of course kept the Spanish setting for reasons of historical justification and tragic distance. When, however, he imported a comedy of character and manners from Spain, *Le Menteur* (1644), the playwright radically transformed the play for a contemporary Parisian setting, leaving no trace of foreign manners: "I have entirely uprooted the characters in order to dress them up in French style" [j'ai entièrement dépaysé les sujets pour les habiller à la française] (337). Indeed, from his very first comedy, the 1629 *Mélite,* Corneille made a point of placing his characters in the world shared by his audience.[13] Marc Fumaroli has qualified this movement toward the modern Parisian setting as a dramaturgy of "la pastorale urbaine": Corneille transfers romantic dialogues associated with the shepherd's distant fields to a new setting in the streets of Paris—the streets that run just outside the theater ("Corneille" 383).

This proximity allows the author not only to refer to those streets and their buildings (as do the very titles *La Galerie du Palais* [1632–33] and *La Place Royale* [1634–35]), but also to refer to the contemporary theater itself. Thus in the bookshop scene in *La Galerie du Palais,* the characters discuss current plays and even allude to the author Corneille himself: "Your taste," says one character, "is, I'm sure, for Normandy," referring to the playwright's native region [Ton goût, je m'en assure, est pour la Normandie]

13. Although considered by Corneille as an innovation, the realistic contemporary urban setting in fact has traditions in the early-seventeenth-century novel (Sorel) and theater (Troterel, Baro, and Coste). See Gabriel Conesa on Corneille's "innovation toute relative" (*Corneille* 27–30).

(I.vii.146). This self-reference is rendered perfectly credible in the world represented, due to the fact the characters are, given the nature of current customs, well abreast of current theater affairs. The play is explicit on this point: "The fashion now is for plays" [La mode est à present des pièces du théâtre] (I.vi.138). The characters on stage are thus explicitly designated as members of the theater public that watch them.

Does the resulting confusion between the concerns of the audience and those of the characters risk, as d'Aubignac suggests, breaking the dramatic illusion? Modern scholars have, I believe, often too readily embraced this logic. For example, T. J. Reiss, in a masterful study of the rise of dramatic illusion in the baroque era, essentially adopts d'Aubignac's perspective and defines such references to the theater in Corneille and Scudéry as rendering the action "essentially unreal" (118). Another scholar has recently examined Corneille's self-reflexivity as a series of signs pointing out to the audience the artificial "theatricality" of the stage—deeming that such references are designed to remind the audience precisely of the means of representation, to break belief in the characters' fictional status and to transform "these ceremonious puppets back into sophisticated Parisian actors and actresses" (Tretheway 94). I would argue, on the contrary, that the self-reference in question here, a parody of Corneille's own *Horace* uttered by one of the characters in *Le Menteur,* is entirely justified by the rules of verisimilitude and thus does nothing to disrupt dramatic illusion. For if the current rage is indeed for theater, then there is no reason why a typical representative of the fashionable world should not parody a line of a play she has just read or just seen performed. Such a reference need not be part of the privileged world of a professional actress. Corneille represents his public, and his public knows its Corneille; he therefore represents a public that knows, and manipulates, Corneille's plays. The theater public wants to see itself on the stage: such is the principle of the comedy-mirror. It follows that the theater public wants to see itself *as a theater public:* to see its own attitudes toward one of its principal pastimes. Given this state of things, I would number such references to the theater as part of Corneille's general project of anchoring the play in reality. In this sense, what might seem to be literary "self-commentary" in fact acts, quite contrary to the arguments noted, as a marker of contemporary reality, a marker that should be placed alongside references to money or to fashionable Parisian clothing, all of which are intended to break the wall between stage and audience.[14]

14. Conesa presents a taxonomy of such elements designed, as he notes, "à effacer la barrière existant entre la scène et la salle" (*Corneille* 45).

By portraying his characters as spectators of his own plays, Corneille applies to the theater what is in fact a technique of realism, a technique already developed in the realm of the novel a quarter of a century earlier by Cervantes. Cervantes depicts a contemporary world for which novel reading forms an essential characteristic, quite as theatergoing does for Corneille's world. It is only natural then that the novel-consuming characters of the second part of the book will have read the first part of *Don Quixote,* which had been speedily committed "to the Press" after the hero's earlier adventures (pt. 2, bk. 3, ch. 3). The character as contemporary reader is indeed the hallmark of what is often called the "realistic novel" of the seventeenth century, a genre then called in France "le roman comique."[15] Inspired in part by Cervantes, Sorel in *Le Berger Extravagant* (1627) seeks to represent his readers with what was perceived as radical fidelity, holding up what Erica Harth has called an "unadorned mirror" to his public (64). One of this mirror's techniques of reflection is to ask readers to see their own attitudes toward novel reading, attitudes that dominate their own self-representation—and that do so even to the point of madness, as Sorel's title suggests. As the century progresses, social traits associated with reading lose some of the hyperbolic quality (alienation and insanity) associated with Cervantes and Sorel and evolve toward the level of the mundane foibles *(le ridicule)* of the comedy of manners. This movement can be traced from Sorel's bucolic madness through the less spectacular extravagance of *préciosité* in *La Prétieuse,* or from the literary follies depicted in Desmarets de Saint-Sorlin's 1637 *Les Visionnaires* to the more subtle literary mannerisms found in the salons of Furetière's 1666 *Le Roman bourgeois.*[16]

Such examples make clear that there is a shift in reflexive strategies in the mid seventeenth century: the reader is no longer asked to consider the metaphysical and ontological aspects of representation, but instead its purely social and pragmatic ones; literary cultivation no longer breeds existential madness, but instead nourishes mere superficial affectations; the reader's relation to the reality of the universe is in no longer in question, but instead his relation to other mundane readers. Thus, while the consistent link between realism and reflexivity remains unbroken, the nature of the reflexivity evolves. The analogy between reality and art shifts from one

15. Speaking of the new antiheroic novel of the seventeenth century, A. Adam comments "Ne les appelons pas romans réalistes, comme les historiens ont pris la mauvaise habitude de le faire. . . . Les hommes du XVIIe siècle les appelaient des romans comiques" (*Romanciers* 16–17).

16. For the theatrical depiction of contemporary literary life in comedies of the early to mid seventeenth century, see Lancaster (pt. 3, vol. 1, 254–55, 337–38), Fumaroli ("Rhétorique" 470–72), and Van Dyck.

between the cosmic order and the theater (the famous topos of *theatrum mundi*) to one between the social order and theater (society as a *comedy of manners*). This is where Molière steps in with his own depiction of the literary and theatrical public, leading the audience's gaze to wander from the stage to itself and back again, all the time viewing one single comedy of representation and recognition.

Nine

✧

THE SECOND COMEDY

Molière's *oeuvre* presents an astonishing number of stage portraits of theater spectators, whether in the form of verbal satires (*Les Précieuses ridicules, Les Fâcheux, La Critique de L'Ecole des femmes,* and *L'Impromptu de Versailles)* or in plays within plays (notably in *L'Impromptu, Le Malade imaginaire,* and *Le Bourgeois gentilhomme*).[1] His first comedy of contemporary manners, *Les Précieuses ridicules,* adapts the theme of the *character as reader* in the post-baroque manner we have seen. Unlike those afflicted with a kind of literary madness in *Le Berger extravagant* (adapted to the stage six years before *Les Précieuses,* in 1653, by Thomas Corneille), Molière's characters are not urbanites seeking some imaginary pastoral-literary utopia, but instead provincials seeking the very *real* realm of literary production, Paris.[2] Their activity as readers drives them not to a delirious enactment of fantasies based on their reading, but instead to attempt mundane—

---

1. I concentrate here on the verbal satires, as they provide the most interesting commentaries on the problem of self-recognition. For Molière's variants on the play within the play theme, see Forestier, *Le Théâtre dans le théâtre.*

2. Two other comedies portrayed literary madness in the decades before *Les Précieuses:* Desmarets de Saint-Sorlin's 1637 *Les Visionnaires* and Cyrano de Bergerac's 1646 *Le Pédant joué.* Both plays were known and imitated by Molière (*OC* 2: 893, 2: 976). Neither, however, presents their literature-crazed characters as concerned (little less obsessed) with present-day Paris and its literary world, but instead as fantastic dreamers and manipulators of poetic and rhetorical conventions. As for depictions of the Paris literary world, certain precedents can be found in Saint-Evremond's 1638 *La Comédie des Académistes* (which depicts the literary quarrels of the newly named academicians) or Bertaut's 1653 *Jugement de Job et Uranie* (which presents the quarrel between the poets Voiture and Benserade), though neither of these plays depicts what we might call the literary manners of the public. Both typify what Fumaroli has called "une symbiose de la vie littéraire naissante et de la vie théâtrale sur le point de naître" ("Rhétorique", 471), a symbiosis fully realized later in Molière's work.

though illusory—social climbing in fashionable Paris, the world of the producers, consumers, and critics of their books.[3]

In doing so, Molière draws on two literary pastoral traditions: he merges the pastoral burlesque of the mad shepherd with the "urban pastoral" of Corneille's Parisian comedies. Of course, Molière radically reworks this second tradition. Unlike Corneille, whose comedies exhibit what has been called a "réalisme aimable" or a "réalisme discret,"[4] Molière devises a much less indulgent representation of his Parisian public. Nevertheless, Molière continues, at least in one respect, the work of Corneille: he firmly defines his characters as contemporary theatergoers. But Molière goes substantially further than Corneille in collapsing the divide between the world of the audience and that of the stage characters.

Les Précieuses ridicules takes the first step. Here the characters are not just depicted in general as theatergoers, who talk about this form of amusement among other pastimes of the fashionable world they pretend to inhabit; Mascarille not only comments on the current theater, he goes on to *detail his behavior as an audience member*. When he offers to take Cathos and Magdelon to the theater, he thoroughly describes his conduct as spectator:

> Mais je vous demande d'applaudir comme il faut, quand nous serons là; car je me suis engagé de faire valoir la pièce, et l'auteur m'en est venu prier encore ce matin. C'est la coutume ici qu'à nous autres gens de condition les auteurs viennent lire leurs pièces nouvelles, pour nous engager à les trouver belles et leur donner de la réputation; et je vous laisse à penser si, quand nous disons quelque chose, le parterre ose nous contredire! (1: 278; sc. 9)

> But I must ask you to applaud as one should, when we are there; for I have promised to make the play succeed, and the author came to beg me to do so again this morning. It's the custom here that the authors come to read their new plays to we people of quality, in order to get us to appreciate them and give them a good reputation; and I think you can imagine if, when we say something, the lowly parterre would dare to contradict us!

Mascarille's remark on the "custom" of wooing important tastemakers is more than just a general reference to contemporary playwrights, such as

---

3. David Shaw places the "vulgarity of the social climber" (32) of the two *précieuses* in opposition to their literary pretensions. He argues that Magdelon "is not really concerned with culture or taste as such. . . . Her only interest in frequenting witty people is because 'ce sont eux qui donnent le branle à la réputation'"(32). It seems difficult, however, to separate literary glamour from social prestige in *Les Précieuses*. Indeed, one of the distinguishing marks of the play is that the two are indissoluble, allowing Molière to mix literary burlesque with social satire.

4. Appellations credited respectively to R. Garapon and G. Couton, qtd. in Conesa, *Corneille* 47.

Corneille, who performed such readings.[5] It is also a remark applicable to Molière's comedy itself, the one that Mascarille's spectators are watching. Donneau de Visé accuses Molière of having made "visits" among *les gens de qualité* in order to win over possible admirerers; we can add that Molière also indulged in these advance readings, according to contemporary accounts.[6] Mascarille might well be picturing himself as one of Molière's key supporters.

Another element links Mascarille as audience member to Molière's own audience: he imagines himself as a competent playwright, a characteristic that he shares to a greater or lesser degree with Molière's public, as we have seen. He assumes the two literary women are also writers:

MASCARILLE: Je ne sais si je me trompe, mais vous avez toute la mine d'avoir fait quelque comédie.
MAGDELON: Eh! il pourrait être quelque chose de ce que vous dites.
MASCARILLE: Ah! ma foi, il faudra que nous la voyions. Entre nous, j'en ai composé une que je veux faire représenter. (1: 278; sc. 9)

MASCARILLE: I may be mistaken, but you look like you might have written a little play.
MAGDELON: Ah! There might be something to what you said.
MASCARILLE: Aha! We must look at it. Between us, I have written one that I want to have performed.

It is, however, not as a writer of *mémoires* for Molière's comedies that Mascarille appears, but as a writer of a tragedy—or more likely of a heroic tragi-comedy.[7] This becomes apparent when Mascarille insists that his play is meant to be staged by the "grands comédiens," since only they can pronounce with all the resonance necessary his grandiloquent verses. This reference places us in another theater, that of the competing Hôtel de Bourgogne, where the actors were known by the appellation Mascarille employs. We can assume that in the brief depiction of their acting style that follows, Molière, who plays the role of Mascarille, perfectly mimics their well-known particularities, as he will do again in *L'Impromptu de Versailles* (sc. 1).

The audience attending *Les Précieuses,* then, sees in the stage fiction ("l'Histoire véritable") the very real elements associated with the means of

---

5. Mélèse cites numerous cases of advance salon "readings" of plays, including those by Pierre and Thomas Corneille, Racine, Quinault, and Donneau de Visé (234–36).
6. Bray, *Molière,* 131–34; Mélèse 235.
7. Mascarille uses here the word "comédie" in its general sense as any piece of dramatic literature, rather than in its limited sense as a comic play.

"Representation," such as the mannerisms of rival actors and also its own specific behavior as an audience. Marscarille's remarks elaborate the idea that the audience is a spectacle unto itself. When he describes the loud applause and cheers produced by the upper class spectators in the audience, he asserts that those seated in the cheap seats of the parterre are watching closely the reaction of these elite few and following their example: "I think you can imagine if, when we say something, the lowly parterre would dare to contradict us!" Mascarille sees himself as a viewer being viewed as much as the actors are viewed. Furthermore, he is quite content with the sight he must offer as a spectator; he assumes that other audience members are admiring his behavior as a model. Or rather let us say that he *imagines* that the audience is admiring him. Of course the "real" Mascarille—the valet in the parterre as opposed to the marquis he is imitating here—has never been the object of public esteem. However, his spectator fantasy serves to win over the admiration of his present audience, the two impressionable *précieuses*,[8] by adding an important trait to his portrayal of an *homme d'esprit*. When Mascarille attempts to imitate the manners of the people of quality, he turns to their behavior as audience members. For him, comportment in the theater defines character and class. The valet Mascarille in the parterre has certainly watched the behavior of these elite spectators as much as he has watched the plays themselves: just as he can ape the manners of the *amant tendre* of the stage fiction, so too he can copy the gestures and shouts of the noblemen (or rather of the ridiculous *petit marquis*) in the audience.

As with Mascarille, so too with Molière. When, with *Les Fâcheux,* Molière undertook for the first time the imitation of "people of quality"—and not just the depiction of their mimicking valets and provincial parrots—he began his three-act satire of this class with an example of its behavior as theater spectators. Such is the subject of the play's long (106-line) opening monologue. Eraste, the persecuted hero of the play, relates his suffering at the hands of a fatuous aristocrat who once sat next to him on a theater's stage and made a continual nuisance of himself by interrupting the stage action with his exclamations. Eraste's satiric monologue is often cited as an example of Molière chastising certain audience members for bad behavior, somewhat like an irritated schoolteacher telling a rowdy pupil to quiet down.[9] There is of course no reason to doubt that Molière is satirizing here

8. Cathos and Magdelon have probably never entered a Parisian theater. "Nous avons été jusqu'ici dans un jeûne effroyable de divertissement," laments Magdelon as the characters open a discussion on the theater (1: 278; sc. 9).

9. See, for example, Descotes 100 and Mélèse 211. Both see Molière as voicing his audience's aggravation with such behavior.

a popular subject of discontent among spectators. But Molière's decision to tackle his new subject matter—the foibles of court society—by depicting his characters as theater spectators has considerably greater significance than that suggested by these readings. The scene offers an important perspective on the comedy itself and the way it is viewed by its audience; it has ramifications that go well beyond the anecdotal level concerning an occasional public irritation. By comparing the spectacle provided by a spectator with that provided by comic characters on stage, Molière reinforces the realism of the *dramatis personae* by defining them as members of the theater public. He also highlights the position of both characters and audience before the public gaze: together they face the public's observation and judgments, and they define themselves by their reaction to this gaze.

If we look at the text, we see first that Eraste's portrait of the loud spectator bears a number of resemblances to Mascarille's fantasy of himself as spectator. The nameless figure, whom we can call (as the title suggests) "the bore," claims, like Mascarille, to have been party to a private reading; he also sees himself as an admirable critic and voices his opinions loudly to the audience. The references to contemporary theater are, though, considerably heightened in *Les Fâcheux*. The bore names one of the authors who have read for him: "Corneille comes to read me everything he does" [Corneille me vient lire tout ce qu'il fait] (I.i.54). We are here dangerously close to the world of the Old Comedy: a current personality has been named, a personality (playwright) that can only attract the public's attention to the theater space itself. The barrier between the world of the fictional story and that of the theater audience disintegrates even more when Eraste locates precisely where the bore is seated in the theater: on the stage. This allows for an explicit comparison between the *comedy represented by the actors* and the *comedy enacted by the audience member* on stage.[10] Eraste makes the most of this comparaison when he rails at the bore's entry on stage:

Les acteurs commençaient, chacun prêtait silence,
Lorsque d'un air bruyant et plein d'extravagance,
Un homme à grands canons est entré brusquement,
En criant : "Holà ho! un siège promptement!"
Et de son grand fracas surprenant l'assemblée,
Dans le plus bel endroit a la pièce troublée.
Hé! mon Dieu! nos Français, si souvent redressés,
Ne prendront-ils jamais un air de gens sensés,

10. We know the genre of the play enacted on stage is comedy because the "Fâcheux" remarks to Eraste about the performance, "Je le trouve assez drôle" (52).

Ai-je dit, et faut-il sur nos défauts extrêmes
Qu'en théâtre public nous nous jouions nous-mêmes,
Et confirmions ainsi par des éclats de fous
Ce que chez nos voisins on dit partout de nous? (I.i.15–26)

The actors began, and everyone grew quiet,
When, in a loud and extravagant manner,
A man in loud ribbons entered brusquely,
Crying, "Hey there, a seat and quickly!"
And, with a great fracas disturbing the audience,
Interrupted the play in its most beautiful moment.
"Ah, my God! Will our Frenchmen, so often scolded,
Never act like sensible people,"
I said, "and is it necessary that we play
Upon our own faults in public theaters
And prove right by our foolish outbreaks
What all our neighbors say about us?"

The moment of the loud spectator's entry is important. He bustles on stage just when the audience members prepare to immerse themselves in the dramatic illusion, destroying the "silence" that would mute the world of the theater house in order to allow the story depicted to reign sovereign. The bore throws the audience back into the world of the physical space of the actors and public. However, the damage done to the comedy on stage is offset by the new "comedy" that the spectator presents. The comparison between the bore and a comic character is suggested by the text itself, where spectators "play themselves"—and the faults associated with their nation—in the theater. And indeed if a comic character is defined, as Molière insists, as "a ridiculous portrait that one exhibits on the stage" [une peinture ridicule qu'on expose sur les théâtres], then this ridiculous spectator on stage perfectly fits the definition. It is as though there were no real interruption in the comic representation here, so seamlessly does one comedy replace the other.[11]

When Eraste sees the bore, he thinks of whole series of ridiculous actions that he has observed in the past, and that he has categorized as national faults. The "comedy" offered by the spectator allows Eraste to contemplate the comedy offered by his own country and its manners, a comedy that is in fact always in the state of being observed and satirized by others, by France's "neighbors." The bore seated on stage thus becomes a perfect mirror to the parallel comedy of France and its faults, one enacted

11. It is tempting to imagine that the play Eraste views is *Les Précieuses* and that the "plus bel endroit" being interrupted by the bore is the scene where Mascarille describes his own shouts as a spectator. In this case there would be a perfect harmony between the two spectacles.

before the audience of other nations, and he thereby provokes a moral reflection on the general vices of the audience's world.

So it is that a few moments later when the bore increases the audience's aggravation by placing his seat in front of the stage, thoroughly blocking their view of the staged comedy,[12] he is in fact providing in his person a comedy entirely worthy of the name, a true "miroir public" to his society. The comedy slides from the space of dramatic illusion (the action depicted) to its frame of production (the material theater). The audience itself becomes *a second comedy*.

The expression "une seconde comédie" was coined by Molière himself in *La Critique,* wherein Dorante so describes a similarly disruptive spectator seated on a Parisian stage. Dorante's lines form a natural pendant to Eraste's monologue. He makes his remark in reply to the scorn his interlocutor (the marquis) holds for the cheap seats of the parterre.

> Tu es donc, Marquis, de ces messieurs du bel air, qui ne veulent pas que le parterre ait du sens commun, et qui seraient fâchés d'avoir ri avec lui, fût-ce de la meilleure chose du monde? Je vis l'autre jour sur le théâtre un de nos amis, qui se rendit ridicule par là. Il écouta toute la pièce avec un sérieux le plus sombre du monde; et tout ce qui égayait les autres ridait son front. A tout les éclats de rire, il haussait les épaules, et regardait le parterre en pitié; et quelquefois aussi le regardant avec dépit, il lui disait tout haut: "Ris donc, parterre, ris donc." Ce fut une séconde comédie, que le chagrin de notre ami. Il la donna en galant homme à toute l'assemblée, et chacun demeura d'accord qu'on ne pouvait pas mieux jouer qu'il fit. (1: 653; sc. 5)

> So, Marquis, you are one of those refined gentlemen who do not believe that the parterre has common sense and who would be embarrassed to laugh with them, even if it was one of the best plays in the world? I saw the other day seated on stage one of our friends, who made himself ridiculous in just that way. He listened to the whole play with the most sombre seriousness in the world; and everything that amused the others made him furrow his brow. With each outbreak of laughter, he shrugged his shoulders and looked at the parterre with pity; and sometimes while looking down spitefully, he said aloud: "So laugh, parterre, so laugh!" Our friend's anger was truly a second comedy. He played it gallantly to the whole audience, and everyone agreed that one could not perform better than he did.

Just as in *Les Fâcheux,* the portrait of the specific spectator is representative of more general faults. Dorante undertakes this description of an audience member with the goal of illustrating the ridiculous qualities that he has

---

12. "Bien que dans les côtés il pût être à son aise, / Au milieu du devant il a planté sa chaise, / Et de son large dos morguant les spectateurs, / Aux trois quarts du parterre a caché les acteurs" (31–34).

observed in his interlocutor. He begins by placing the marquis into the neat social category of affected noblemen ("les messieurs du bel air"). Dorante then offers the case study of another example of this type: the spectator he has seen at the theater. By what method does Dorante group together under the same type his interlocutor in the salon with the spectator he has observed? The type is of course defined by a visible sign of character shared by the marquis and the spectator: it is what "renders them ridiculous." Both the marquis and the spectator offer the spectacle of *le ridicule*. As we know from the 1667 "Lettre sur la comédie de l'Imposteur," *le ridicule* is defined precisely as the "forme extérieure" and "recognizable appearance" [dehors reconnaissable] of a moral fault—and, more specifically, that of unreasonable or innappropriate behavior (*OC* I: 1174).[13] It is the visible, *recognizable* expression of character; it is what allows Dorante to recognize the similarity between his interlocutor and the spectator he has observed. Furthermore, *le ridicule* is the privileged subject of comedy, due to its spectacular nature, its brilliance as representation. These visible marks of character provide the spectacle in the various fields of observation suggested in Dorante's remarks: first in the salon, where the marquis renders himself ridiculous with his remarks disdaining the parterre; then in the theater space itself, where the marquis's counterpart, the scornful spectator seated on stage, is a spectacle to the public and its laughter; and finally, the "ridiculous" spectator is compared to the spectacle offered by comedy itself, which presents "ridiculous portraits" such as that inspired by overly refined noblemen.

In these two passages from *Les Fâcheux* and *La Critique,* then, the spectator serves to bridge the worlds of the *social comedy* (whether it be that of the French in general or "les messieurs du bel air" in particular) and the *staged comedy.* The spectator acts as a perfect intermediary between the public and its stage portrayal, between the model and its portrait. By nature a perfectly real member of the public, the spectator is nevertheless on view before the inverted gaze of the audience, and offers the advantage of being the real thing—the original of the copies on stage. The spectator is thus the nexus of social person and *dramatis persona.*

If indeed the comic character is designed to be mistaken for its model in the public (as Boileau insists), then the spectator provides a kind of fluid transition as the eye passes from the portrait to the model, from the stage mirror to the world reflected therein. For in between the stage and the

---

13. Though the author of the "Lettre" is unknown, Couton summarizes the general scholarly consensus that Molière probably aided the author and perhaps even collaborated on the text—of which the ideas and language must have been "approuvé de Molière" (*OC* I: 1405).

world outside the theater inevitably stands the audience. When Molière posits his characters as theater spectators, he asks his audience to compare his characters with those seated before them—or next to them. Thus the marquis speaking in *La Critique* is, Dorante tells us, exactly like a marquis in the audience of one of Molière's plays. The characters of the stage comedy and the "second comedy" are the same. The action slides from "l'Histoire veritable" to "le Spectacle" and vice versa. The eye roams freely from one to the other.[14] And as the eye roams, it finds its pleasure in comparing the two spectacles, just as Roger de Piles suggests the beholder does before a painted portrait. So it is that a character in another polemical comedy of the Quarrel of *L'Ecole des femmes*, Chevalier's *Les Amours de Calotin*, speaks of seeing Molière in the audience of a play that satirizes him, *Le Portrait du Peintre*. The following passage demonstrates the delight in gazing on the portrait and the model at the same time. The spectators' eyes shift here from the "Molière" portrayed on stage to the Molière in the audience, like Athens's "vile masses" comparing the two Socrateses.

> Comme de notre Peintre on faisoit le Portrait,
> Et que l'on le croyoit tirer là trait pour trait,
> Tu sçauras que luy-mesme en cette conjoncture
> Estoit present alors que l'on fit sa peinture;
> De sorte que *ce fut un charme sans égal,*
> *De voir et la copie, et son original.* (I.iii.193–98; emphasis added)

> As they were making a Portrait of our Painter [Molière]
> And the audience thought it saw his every feature perfectly drawn,
> You should know that at this moment he himself
> Was present while he was portrayed,
> In such a way as *it was an unequaled charm*
> *To see the copy and its original.*

Was the pleasure of this "unequaled charm" shared by the target of the satire, Molière? How did he respond to seeing himself staged? Having considered the theatrical practice of spectator recognition in the last two chapters, I now return to the question of its moral effects, to the question we left suspended with Aurélie's shame and Cathos's and Magdelon's wrath.

---

14. Of course, in the case of *Les Fâcheux*, the portrait of the spectator is purely verbal: he is only described in Eraste's oral satire and never appears on stage, unlike the marquis in *La Critique*. It would thus seem excessive to speak of the audience's gaze sliding from the role depicted to the audience members targeted. However, Eraste does dramatize his verbal portrait: he quotes the dialogue and imitates the exact wording of the "Fâcheux." When Eraste mimics the "holà!" of the bore, we can assume that the actor playing Eraste will mimic also the bore's mannerisms. At this moment Eraste is no longer Eraste, but the bore he is quoting and portraying. The audience therefore have on stage both the copy and the original of the spectator.

Ten

◈

THE REPRESENTED RESPOND

The plays of the Quarrel follow Molière's lead in placing the second comedy in the position of the first—that is, in placing spectators on stage as characters. In the years 1662–64 the Paris theater collectively contemplated spectator reaction, and chief among the issues raised was that of self-recognition in the comic portrait. How does the spectator confront the comic mirror? How does the target of the audience's gaze react to its censure, to its laughter? The moral utility of comedy depends on the answer. For if the comic mirror is to correct, one must first recognize one's fault and then resolve to profit from the lesson. The ideal spectator, following Uranie's precepts on "miroirs publics," takes pleasure in the comic portrait, recognizing therein general faults and correcting him or herself to the degree to which the portrait fits a personal trait. Such a spectator, however, is only an ideal. The comedy often provokes other, morally less happy forms of self-recognition.

But before looking at the specific effects of self-recognition, we must consider briefly the nature of personal identity in the French classical age, since to recognize oneself in the theater is by definition to match a depiction to a concept of one's self. As the previous examples of viewer recognition have shown, the sense of identity in play is essentially a social and moral one, rather than an intimate or metaphysical one: Cathos and Magdelon, for example, are identified as moral hybrids of the *précieuse* and the *coquette*; Climène identifies herself as a moral type in opposition to that of a woman of loose conduct. Satire, like French classical society in general, employs two principal modes of classification: (1) fixed social categories (class, gender, region) and (2) character taxonomies that may, or may not, transcend those categories (*honnêteté*, piety, wit). In either case, spectators must define themselves with or against the type portrayed. The two modes, though, do not have equal weight. In the "stock exchange of reputation" constituted by Paris and the court under Louis XIV, it is the second mode of classification that dominates; the visible characteristics associated with manners and morals reign supreme in estimations of individual worth. For under absolutism's drain of independent powers, name, family, and rank are increasingly bereft of real significance—though the aristocracy still of course clings to such marks of distinction. In the end, then, personal identity is defined first and foremost by *character:* not character in the sense of deep personal integrity, but instead character as a molecule of visible features, of personal manners and morals. Such is the definition in one dictionary of the time: character is "the result of several particular marks that distinguish one thing from another in such a way that one can recognize it."[1] One distinguishes oneself from others, then, by the signs that allow others to distinguish (recognize) oneself—or that one wants others to distinguish in oneself. The equation is perfect between identity and reputation, that is, between "self" and "character" as construed by the gaze of one's peers.

The power of this paradigm reigned for about a century: it followed the collapse of the supremacy of rank and family that characterized the pre-absolutist period, and it preceded the romantic reaction against the frivolity of the social notion of self that held sway in the last century and a half of the *ancien régime.* (It is no surprise that first great insurgent of this reaction, Rousseau, took such fierce aim at Molière, accusing him of ignoring any profound sense of personal integrity in his effort to please the public's fascination with reputation and esteem.[2]) The "century" of triumphant reputation is of course a European phenomenon, as the comedy of manners in England, for example, so well demonstrates. However, it is in France that the fascination with socially constructed character reaches it highest pitch, thanks to the political and cultural conditions analyzed in chapter 4. It is difficult to imagine, for example, an English comedy of manners about bourgeois pretenders (like *Les Précieuses ridicules*) in

1. The *Dictionnaire* of Furetière defines *caractère* as "ce qui résulte de plusieurs marques particulières qui distinguent tellement une chose d'une autre qu'on la puisse reconnaître aisément." For an analysis of character and personal identity in the classical age, see Louis Van Delft, *Littérature et anthropologie* 137–48. See also the definition of the French classical "self" offered by Pavel (185–99, 326–35).

2. Such is the gist of Rousseau's attack on Molière in his *Lettre à d'Alembert:* In order to please the public, he attacks not real and profound vices, but instead only "les ridicules," that is, superficial faults as defined by purely social considerations. "Ayant à plaire au public, il a consulté le goût le plus général de ceux qui le composent. . . . Il n'a donc point prétendu former un honnête homme, mais un homme du monde; par conséquent, il n'a point voulu corriger les vices; mais les ridicules" (96).

which money and personal wealth are never mentioned; or the representation of an aristocrat salon like that of *Le Misanthrope,* in which references to rank and title play so small a role. Of course, such references to political or economic features are not absent in Molière's work, as we will see; but even a term of rank like "marquis" becomes, in the expression *petit marquis,* a sign of character and manners (here fatuousness) rather than of titled rank. It is no doubt the intensity and purity of the concern with socially defined character that allows Molière's theater to become the model for the theatrical satire of manners as it is translated into its English forms with Wycherley and Congreve and its Italian variants with Goldoni.

To return now to our question of how the represented respond, it is precisely this definition of personal identity as a "character molecule" that allows an apparently *general* portrait of a moral type to provoke such extremely *personal* recognitions. If one identifies oneself essentially as a certain amalgam of moral and social features, the representation of that amalgam will touch home quite sharply. Now, the uncertain moral effect of these character-driven self-recognitions obsessed not just Molière and his contemporaries; it became in the century after his death perhaps the major subject of commentary on Molière's theater, where supporters' claims that the comedies presented a "school for virtue" were hotly contested by those who doubted their ameliorative effect. The problem receives what is perhaps its most coherent analysis in the first book-length study of Molière's comic aesthetic, Louis Riccoboni's 1736 *Observations sur la comédie et sur le génie de Molière.* In his chapter "De la critique des moeurs," Riccoboni discusses the reasons why seeing one's vices depicted often fails to provoke reformation:

> Le Théatre François, depuis Molière qui en a été le restaurateur, est un champ si fécond en Comédies de caractères, qu'il paroîtroit facile d'y corriger les moeurs, si la différence, qui se trouve entre les vices des hommes, ne devenoit quelquefois un obstacle au dessein des Auteurs. (115)

> The French theater, since Molière, who restored it, is a realm so rich in comedies of character that it would seem simple to correct manners and morals through them, if the differences that distinguish men's vices did not sometimes become an obstacle to the authors' intentions.

What are the "vices" that discourage spectators from profiting from the portrayal of their faults? The first named by Riccoboni is vanity:

> Dans ce grand nombre de vices et de passions qui asservissent les hommes, il y en a dont on ne rougit point, et d'autres dont on fait, pour ainsi dire, un trophée. Tel est, par exemple, ou *Misanthrope;* ou *Joueur;* ou *Glorieux;* ou *Soupçonneux,* qui verra sans fruit représenter ce vice ou la passion qui

le domine. Loin d'en concevoir une utile confusion, il en tirera peut-être vanité. (115)

Among this large number of vices and passions that master men, there are some that do not make them blush, and others that they consider, so to speak, a trophy. Such is, for example, the *Misanthrope* or *Gambler* or the *Vainglorious* or *Jealous,* who would fruitlessly see represented the vice or passion that dominates him. Far from deriving from it [the representation] a useful embarrassment or shame, he might feel a sense of vanity.

Riccoboni then names several other vices that are less easily embraced by personal vanity. In these cases, the spectator cannot but recognize the negative nature of the portrait; however, rather than benefiting from the occasion, the spectator either shuns the unbearable portrait or simply refuses to recognize the similarities.

Un *Hypocrite* . . . un *Avare* . . . un *Médisant,* ne pourront soutenir tranquillement sur le Théâtre la vûe de leurs caractères, ou du moins ils se flatteront qu'ils ne ressemblent point aux portraits qu'on leur présente (116).

A *Hypocrite* . . . a *Miser* . . . a *Malicious Wit* [Médisant], could not stand to see their character on stage, or at least they would flatter themselves into believing that they do not resemble the portraits that are presented them.

Narcissism, which allows one to take pride in some vices (pride, gambling), takes umbrage at others (hypocrisy, greed). In the latter cases, providential self-blindness, Riccoboni suggests, prevents the pain of self-recognition.

We can draw from Riccoboni's analysis three principal dysfunctions of audience viewing, that is, three ways in which spectators see themselves portrayed without moral profit: (1) vanity at the moment of recognition, a narcissistic pleasure in seeing one's faults; (2) misrecognition, seeing another in the portrait of oneself, believing that one does "not resemble the portrait"; and (3) painful recognition, the shunning of the comic mirror, the inability to "stand to see [one's] character on stage." Riccoboni's typology of viewer reaction is a general one concerning the *comédie de caractère* as practiced by Molière and his immediate successors. More specifically, this typology corresponds remarkably well to the portraits of spectators found in the plays of the Quarrel, and I will use it as an organizing principle to look at these scenes.

Vain Recognitions

We have already seen a case where the disapprobation of the audience has been met with arrogant indifference by the target of its censure: Eraste's description of the loud spectator in *Les Fâcheux*. Despite the continual surveillance and disapproval of his behavior by the theater public, the bore makes no reflection on future self-improvement. When he blocks the view of the stage and makes himself the principal spectacle in the theater, he manifests his total indifference to the loud expression of public disapprobation that follows:

> Un bruit s'est élevé, dont un autre eût eu honte;
> Mais lui, ferme et constant, n'en a fait aucun compte. (I.i.35–36)

> A clamour arose, which would have shamed another man,
> But he, firm and uncompromising, paid no attention to it.

Of course, Eraste does not describe here a moment of recognition provoked by theatrical *representation;* the audience is looking directly at the bore in person, and not at his portrayal on stage. Would he be any more susceptible to the disapproval of the spectators watching his portrait in Molière's play than he was to the disapproval of the spectators whom he annoyed in person? Or would he see himself being mocked by Molière without any more *shame* ("honte") than he felt before? Or how about the bore's pendant, the spectator in *La Critique*? The language of vanity describing him is more pronounced. His arrogance before the audience's gaze is explicit as he offers himself "gallantly" as a free public spectacle.

The complacent attitude of these two spectator-spectacles seems to reveal a general attitude among fatuous *petit marquis,* one that Regnard illustrated thirty years later with another spectator on stage, the marquis portrayed in *La Coquette:*

> COLOMBINE: Mais de bonne foi, Monsieur le Marquis, croyez-vous que ce soit pour vous voir peigner votre perruque, prendre du tabac et faire votre carrousel sur le théâtre que le public donne ses quinze sous?
> LE MARQUIS: N'est-ce pas bien de l'honneur pour lui de voir des gens de qualité? Ma foi, quand il n'aurait que ce plaisir-là, cela vaut bien une mauvaise comédie. (*OC* I: 1256).

> COLOMBINE: But in good faith, Marquis, sir, do you believe that it is to see you comb your wig, take tobacco, and circulate around the stage that the public pays its money?
> MARQUIS: Is it not an honor for them to see people of quality? My goodness, if they had but that pleasure alone, it would be as good as a bad play.

Having established a type of spectator that glories in being a spectacle before the audience, I return to the question: would spectators of this type react with the same complacent vanity before a public that views their comic portrait on stage, rather than their physical person in the audience? The distinction here is between the disapproval that the bore heard from the audience at his back and the disapproval that he must feel before the audience's reaction to Molière's portrait of him in *Les Fâcheux*. The distinction is important. The real bore in the audience was the object of simple disapprobation; his portrait in *Les Fâcheux* is the object of ridicule and laughter. And according to Molière, there is a great deal of difference between the two. It is in fact this crucial distinction between censure and laughter that assures the moral efficacy of comedy.

[R]ien ne reprend mieux la plupart des hommes que la peinture de leurs défauts. C'est une grande atteinte aux vices que de les exposer à la risée de tout le monde. On souffre aisément des répréhensions; mais on ne souffre point la raillerie. On veut bien être méchant; mais on ne veut point être ridicule. (1: 885; preface to *Tartuffe*)

Nothing reproaches most men more effectively than a painting of their faults. It is a great strike against vices to be exposed to everyone's laughter. One bears lightly reprehension; but one cannot bear mockery. One might want to be bad; but one never wants to be ridiculous.

Although Molière carefully marks his point, it is significant that he also qualifies it: his observation applies only to "la plupart des hommes." There remain those who happily see themselves mocked on the stage, and who recognize the portrayal of their vices with complacent glee. In a general manner, we have seen this kind of reckless narcissism depicted in Donneau de Visé's *Nouvelles nouvelles,* where the audience is described as going to the theater to see its own vices portrayed in public. We can now note that this pleasure in recognizing one's faults is not, according to the critic, simply a vague admiration for the lifelike portraits their own *mémoires* produce. The pleasure in self-recognition can also be very personal and can provoke outright pride at being privileged by the satirist's aim. Furthermore, according to Donneau de Visé, the pride of the satirized seeks public recognition. The targets of the comic portrait wish not only to recognize themselves in the portrayal; their vanity also demands that their fellow audience members recognize them in particular:

[C]e qui fait voir que les gens de qualité sont non seulement bien aises d'être raillés; mais qu'ils souhaitent que l'on connaisse que c'est d'eux que l'on parle, c'est qu'il s'en trouvait qui faisaient en plein théâtre, lorsque l'on les jouait, les mêmes actions que les comédiens faisaient pour les contrefaire. (1: 1020)

What will show that people of quality are not only comfortable being mocked, but that they furthermore want people to know that one is talking about them, is that there are some of them who, in the middle of the theater, make the same gestures as the actors are making in order to imitate them.

Donneau de Visé, like Molière, uses the concept of mocking (railler) to describe comic representation; yet, far from Molière's insistence that one cannot bear raillery, he claims to the contrary that those targeted cannot get enough of it. It is not sufficient to know personally that the audience's eyes are turned toward one's portrait on stage; it is necessary to turn their eyes toward one's real self in the audience. The spectator temporarily diverts attention from the stage copy to the original—himself—by imitating, ironically enough, the satiric portrait. The goal of this diversion is made obvious by Donneau de Visé. It provides a kind of free publicity for the personality who wishes to cut a figure in the world. For in the social commerce of representation, any representation, even if apparently negative, has its value. As La Rochefoucauld acidly remarked, "One would rather say something bad about oneself than to say nothing at all" [On aime mieux dire du mal de soi-même que de n'en point parler] (m. 138). After all, according to the aphorist, personal faults can be quite advantageous for one's reputation: "We please more often in society by our faults than by our good qualities" [Nous plaisons plus souvent dans le commerce de la vie par nos défauts que par nos bonnes qualités] (m. 90).

Indeed, Molière is so well aware of the satisfaction that can arise from having one's faults pointed out that at least on one occasion he refuses to flatter a contemporary with a satiric portrayal, foreseeing the vanity that such gratifying publicity might cause. Molière speaks here of satirizing his fellow playwright Boursault:

> [Q]uand on le bernerait sur un théâtre, il serait assez heureux pour faire rire le monde. Ce lui serait trop d'honneur que d'être joué devant une auguste assemblée: il ne demanderait pas mieux. (1: 695; *L'Impromptu* sc. 5)

> When he is mocked on stage, he'll be only too happy to make everyone laugh. It would be too great an honor for him to be played [imitated, joué] before an august audience: he could not ask for anything better.

Of course, this is the "demand" that Molière is continually meeting: that of honoring his public by depicting it on stage. If Molière here describes that desire for representation as a fatuous one, it certainly has ramifications for his dramaturgy of depiction in general. Does Molière consciously manipulate the vice of vanity in his audience, provoking and sating it with his comedy-mirror, playing with the public's futile, if not vicious, pleasure in being depicted?

There is, in any case, no doubt that Molière masterfully negotiates his public's desire for lifelike portraits—a desire that can be quite dangerous for the portraitist. For not all self-recognitions in the comic mirror are so indulgent as those experienced by the vain; some are insulted where others are flattered. In this case, a wily playwright can attempt to confound problematic self-recognitions, or at least profit from misrecognitions.

Misrecognitions

L'Impromptu de Versailles presents a scene in which two marquis quarrel over which one is the inspiration for the character of the marquis in *La Critique*. Each marquis recognizes the other in the portrait; neither, of course, recognizes himself. The passage begins when one of the marquis (played by Molière) remarks to the other (played by La Grange) that he doesn't wish to become the subject of one of Molière's satires.

> LA GRANGE: "Je pense, pourtant, Marquis, que c'est toi qu'il joue dans *La Critique*."
> MOLIÈRE: "Moi? je suis ton valet: c'est toi-même en propre personne."
> LA GRANGE: "Ah! ma foi, tu es bon de m'appliquer ton personnage."
> MOLIÈRE: "Parbleu! je trouve plaisant de me donner ce qui t'appartient."
> (1: 686; sc.3)

> LA GRANGE: "I think, however, that it is you that he is playing in *La Critique*."
> MOLIÈRE: "Me? At your service, sir, but it's you yourself in person."
> LA GRANGE: "Oh, my, it is good of you to apply your character to me."
> MOLIÈRE: "Egad, I find it amusing that you'd give to me what belongs to you."

The *petit marquis* by nature seems highly resistant to the punitive effect of the public's ridicule. We have already seen that at certain moments this character type proudly trumpets his role as the model of a comic character, considering it a mark of distinction. We see here that at other moments, when he realizes the insult which is inherent in a satiric depiction, he simply evades self-identification and instead identifies the model of the portrait as another—though this "other" be his moral doppelgänger, like the identical twin marquis of this scene.

This distorted identification—seeing one's double in the comic mirror, and not oneself—is in fact one of the mechanisms that allows an audience to bear, even enjoy, satiric comedy. Indeed Boileau largely defines New Comedy by its ability to confound specific self-recognition. In *L'Art poétique* Boileau proposes a definition of New Comedy that is considerably less strict than d'Aubignac's; Boileau does not oppose setting the comic fiction in the contemporary world of its audience. On the other hand, Boileau does insist that the comic poet avoid *direct* references to current personalities; he is not permitted "to mark the names and faces" of his characters. This blurring of focus permits the playwright to present a mirror to the public that cannily obscures any troublesome sense of personal identification:

> Chacun, peint avec art dans ce nouveau miroir,
> S'y vit avec plaisir, ou crut ne s'y point voir:
> L'avare, des premiers, rit du tableau fidèle
> D'un avare souvent tracé sur son modèle;
> Et mille fois un fat, finement exprimé,
> Méconnut le portrait sur lui-même formé. (III.354–58)

> Each person, painted artfully in this new mirror,
> Saw himself with pleasure, or believed he did not see himself:
> The miser was among the first to laugh at the faithful painting
> Of a miser often traced from his own model;
> And a thousand times a fop, finely depicted,
> Misrecognized the portrait made after himself.

Boileau's language is quite ambiguous here. While he suggests that the comic portrait is a general one of character traits and manners (the portrait is of "un avare" as a type), he also suggests that the playwright works from specific "models," whose form the author simply "traces," rather than reworks for general effect. If we follow Boileau's logic, we arrive at a conception of New Comedy that could be defined as follows: New Comedy is simply Old Comedy obfuscated. The comedy remains an exact copy of its public and even imitates particular individuals, but it carefully blurs the contours of the portrait in order to avoid immediate identification of the model. The satire is still largely immediate, especially in this world where character defines identity, but is executed with prophylactic anonymity. Indeed, it appears that Boileau's ideal playwright manipulates the moral faults of the audience in order to avoid any problematic self-identification. The phrase "Each person, painted artfully in this new mirror, / Saw himself with pleasure, or believed he did not see himself" suggests two public vices that the playwright exploits: fatuity and blindness. Thus those who take pride in being the target of ridicule, like Donneau de Visé's marquis reenacting their role before the audience, do so with the complicity of the playwright, who profits from their complacency, the better to mock them. In the second case, the blindness of the two marquis in *L'Impromptu* is a perfect example of Boileau's "fop" who fails to recognize ("méconnaître") his own portrait and takes it for his double, his twin fop in the public. Their error is the comedy's shield.

The two marquis' reaction thus poses no threat to Molière's success; they are both pleased to go to his comedies to see their peers mocked, so long as they themselves are not. So long as the marquis are self-blinded, Molière is quite safe; a little vision on their part, however, would be a dangerous thing. This is the problem that is presented in the next scene of *L'Impromptu,* where the two marquis ask Molière's friend (played by Brécourt) to whom the role in *La Critique* really "belongs" [appartient]; they will not leave until they know which of them is the unique model for the portrait. Molière, in the guise of his spokesman Brécourt, is placed here in a most delicate position, one that curiously recalls another scene Molière staged a few years later: that of Dom Juan faced with two lovers demanding which one is the sole object of his affections. Like Dom Juan, Molière (speaking through Brécourt) must name the unique target of attentions—in this case, of his satiric, rather than amorous, attentions. Of course, there is an important difference: the marquis, unlike Dom Juan's lovers, desire to see their opponent designated, and not themselves. But Molière's satiric attentions, just like Dom Juan's desires, are no doubt equally shared by the two contenders. And like Dom Juan, Molière cannot please one without displeasing the other and so must adroitly circumvent the issue.

He meets the occasion by making his strongest statement on the general nature of his comic portraits, one that denies any resemblance with contemporary personalities. While Molière uses a language quite similar to Boileau's in claiming to have never "*marked* anyone" [*marqué* qui que ce soit], he also uses language that seems to contradict his usual stance on fidelity in portraiture:

> Il disait que . . . tous les personnages qu'il représente sont des personnages en l'air, et des fantômes proprement, qu'il habille à sa fantaisie . . . et que si quelque chose était capable de le dégoûter de faire des comédies, c'était les ressemblances qu'on y voulait toujours trouver. (1: 687; sc. 4)

> He [Molière] said that . . . all the characters that he represented are pulled from thin air and are, properly speaking, phantoms, that he dresses up according to his fantasy . . . and that if something was capable of making playwrighting distasteful to him, it was the resemblances [to real persons] that people always wanted to find in his comedies.

This passage presents a disturbing contrast with Dorante's defense of Molière in *La Critique;* in that passage, resemblance is valorized as the essence of comic representation: "one wants these portraits to resemble." Furthermore, in a radical reversal of position, Molière here presents himself as an *inventor* who creates characters through his imagination ("fantaisie") rather than through observation and imitation. In *La Critique,* imagination and "phantom" characters were associated with the belittled tragic poet, who creates "portraits of fancy, where one does not look for likeness" [des portraits à plaisir, où l'on ne cherche point de ressemblance] and who simply follows the flight of "a soaring imagination" [une imagination qui se donne l'essor]. Here, bizarrely, Molière embraces this heretofore maligned form of arbitrary portrayal.

Can Molière's contradictory language be explained by a shift in attitude in the few months that separate the performances of *La Critique* (June 1663) and *L'Impromptu* (October 1663)? The answer must be no. For in *L'Impromptu* itself, indeed in the very next scene, Brécourt defends Molière by valorizing once again resemblance in portraiture as the essence of comedy. Brécourt here speaks of Molière's critics:

> Et quant à tous les gens [que ces critiques] ont tâché d'animer contre lui, sur ce qu'il fait, dit-on, *des portraits trop ressemblants* . . . je ne vois rien de plus ridicule et de plus mal repris; et *je n'avais pas cru jusqu'ici que ce fût un sujet de blâme pour un comédien que de peindre trop bien les hommes.* (1: 693; sc. 5; emphasis added)

> And as for all the people [that these critics] have attempted to rouse against him, charging that he makes portraits that are too like [ressemblants] . . . I can think of nothing more ridiculous and wrongly censured; and *I did not believe up until now that it was a subject of blame for a man of theater to paint men too well.*

There is a certain ambiguity in the idea of resemblance and the identification it engenders, which Molière fully manipulates to his advantage. It can certainly be argued that Molière is working with a fairly straightforward and yet basically implicit distinction between individual resemblance and general resemblance, that is, between personal identification and collective identification—this latter being an identification where not one individual, but every appropriate individual sees him or herself. Such a synthesis of the two forms of identification is more than plausible given the equation of moral character and personal identity that we have established. Yet if this is the case, then Brécourt's response should be that both the quarreling aristocrats serve as a model for the marquis. Such a statement would certainly be true. We know from Molière's description of La Grange's role as a marquis in *L'Impromptu* that he is characterized by "le bel air" (1: 685; sc. 3). Now, the marquis in *La Critique* is compared precisely to "messieurs du bel air." The marquis that La Grange plays is therefore a model, as a character type, for the marquis of *La Critique*. And so is of course the marquis played by Molière. The honest answer to their quarrel, therefore, is not that neither is the model for the marquis, but that *both* are.

If Molière avoids the troublesome identification in this case, he does so because he faces a very real threat. Brécourt makes this threat clear in his response to the two marquis. Molière's critics "apply" the playwright's portraits to specific individuals in order to stir up indignation in those targeted: his enemies are trying to provoke "affaires" of honor in which powerful persons will challenge the playwright.

> [P]ourquoi vouloir, je vous prie, appliquer tous ses gestes et toutes ses paroles, et chercher à lui faire des affaires en disant hautement: "Il joue un tel," lorsque ce sont des choses qui peuvent convenir à cent personnes? (1: 687; sc. 4)

> [P]lease tell me why you want to apply [to real persons] all his gestures and all his words and try to bring him into scandals [affaires] by saying loudly: "He is playing so and so," when it is a matter of things that could fit a hundred different persons?

The threat of such scandals haunts not only Molière, but all authors who hold up a moral mirror to their eager but susceptible audience. Such perils lead a character portraitist like La Bruyère to comment on his works with an ambiguity, even a disingenuousness, that easily rivals Molière's. The author of *Les Caractères* proudly asserts that his depictions are "painted from life," thereby consciously exciting his audience's desire to find "keys" that will reveal the real models for his portraits; and yet, when faced with the opposition that such cruel resemblances provoke, he paradoxically asserts that the portraits have in fact no models in life and are drawn from abstract generalities.[3] Indeed, even a painter of the most universal vices, La Rochef-

---

3. When La Bruyère claims in the preface to *Les Caractères* that his portraits are "d'après nature," he uses an expression that he knows to be highly charged and that will be used against him by his critics. For example, in 1693 Charpentier criticizes La Bruyère for using living models: "Théophraste a traité la chose d'un air plus philosophique: il n'a envisagé que l'universel; vous êtes plus descendu dans le particulier. Vous avez fait vos portraits d'après nature; lui n'a fait les siens que sur une idée générale. Vos portraits ressemblent à de certaines personnes, et souvent on les devine" (qtd. in Garapon, *Les Caractères* 62). It is in response to such expected charges that La Bruyère, while still maintaining his claim to paint after life, also insists in the preface that his depiction is not simply of contemporary life and that his project is to "peindre les hommes en général." For a general synthesis of the problems faced by moralists in their negotiations with their readers, see Jaouën.

oucauld, is driven to the curious claim that readers should apply his un-flattering maxims to all their peers, and yet somehow never recognize their own selves in his moral *réflexions*. Of course La Rochefoucauld's claim that each reader "is the unique exception" [est seul excepté] to the moral truth is by nature absurd, since the universal application of the claim to each reader would render the "truth" applicable to no one and thus untrue.[4] But faced with the problem of scandalous resemblances, moralists such as La Bruyère and La Rochefoucauld must join Molière in the kind of contradic-tory negotiations with their public that we have seen—whether we qualify their apologies as profoundly insincere or self-consciously ironic. And the recourse to such manipulative strategies will, I think, appear quite justified once we consider specifically the very real dangers posed by indignant self-recognition.

Wrathful Recognition

Significantly, one such scandal *(affaire)* concerns the model for the marquis in *La Critique*—precisely the subject of Brécourt's response to the two quarreling marquis of *L'Impromptu*. According to an anecdote relayed in the 1725 edition of Molière's works, le duc de La Feuillade believed himself to be the model for the marquis's role; he was particularly insulted by the character's inane repetition of the expression "tarte à la crème," which serves the marquis as his principal argument in the play. The duke then approached Molière and freely took his revenge against the playwright, who was helpless against the caprice of a "grand seigneur." The insulted aristocrat took the playwright by the head and, "telling him, *Tarte à la crème, Molière, tarte à la crème,* rubbed his [Molière's] face against his but-tons, which, as they were hard and very sharp, left his face bloody."[5] Whether this tale of revenge be apocryphal or not, it well illustrates the virulent reactions that direct satire can provoke, and it lends a sharpened edge to a subtitle such as *La Vengeance des Marquis,* which menacingly accompanied Donneau de Visé's *Responce à l'Impromptu de Versailles.*

4. La Rochefoucauld makes the assertion (in the guise of the editor) in the 1665 *Avis au lecteur:* "[L]e meilleur parti que le lecteur ait à prendre est de se mettre d'abord dans l'esprit qu'il n'y a aucune de ces maximes qui le regarde en particulier, et qu'il en est seul excepté, bien qu'elles paraissent généra-les; après cela, je lui réponds qu'il sera le premier à y souscrire" (268). On the ramifications of this claim, see Jaouën (79–118) and Norman, "La Rochefoucauld."

5. "[E]n lui disant *Tarte à la crème, Molière, tarte à la crème,* il lui frotta le visage contre ses boutons qui, étant fort durs et fort tranchants, lui mirent le visage en sang." In the "Vie de Molière" of the 1725 La Haye edition of the *Oeuvres de Molière* (xxv, xxvii), qtd. in *OC* 1: 1290. Couton argues that even if this particular anecdote (though supported by other evidence) should be apocryphal, Molière did suffer threats from the satire in the play. "Injures, menaces, peut-être brutalités effectives, on voit que la querelle de *L'Ecole des femmes* avait échauffé les esprits" (1: 1291).

In fact, one of the principal strategies of Molière's critics in the Quarrel is to excite the wrath of those who have been mocked *(bernés)* by Molière. The polemical plays often stress the violence of satire, the force of its scorn. As one of the characters in *Le Portrait du Peintre* asserts: "to satirize is to mock, to scorn" [satiriser, c'est railler, mépriser] (*Querelle* 153; sc. 8). It seems only natural that those whose character is insulted will take revenge. As a poet states in *Zélinde:* "I did not believe until now that those who are in every way the bravest of the court would be so patient as to let themselves be called clowns *(Turlupins)* in full public theater without showing the least resentment" [Je n'avois pas creû, jusques icy, que ceux qui sont en toutes manières les plus braves de la Cour, fussent si patiens que de se souffrir appeler Turlupins, en plein Theatre, sans en temoigner le moindre ressentiment] (41; sc. 6). Furthermore, such brutal satires are not only a personal affront to the marquis, but even more provocative, an insult to the king: "What, to treat so poorly the pillars and ornaments of the State, to have so much scorn for persons who risk their life for the glory of their Prince!" [Quoi, traitter si mal l'appuy et l'ornement de l'Estat! avoir tant de mépris pour des personnes qui ont . . . exposé leur vie pour la gloire de leur Prince!] (Donneau de Visé, "Lettre sur les affaires" 302).

The play from the Quarrel that presents the most detailed depiction of a spectator stung by self-recognition is Chevalier's *Les Amours de Calotin.* The play is set inside the theater space of the Hôtel du Marais and features the conversation of various spectators before the day's performance begins. The first scene presents a discussion between two such audience members, one a baron and the other a marquis, who debate the appropriate response to being ridiculed by Molière. The baron is the very essence of the resentful spectator. He feels his dignity affronted by Molière's satire, and his sense of outrage is so pronounced that he demands vengeance:

> Mais s'il m'en croit, Marquis, loin de nous railler tous,
> Il se taira, s'il veut éviter mon couroux.
> Quoy, si nous nous souffrons traitter de ces manières,
> Nous aurons de sa part bien-tost les étrivieres. (I.i.25–28)

> But if he [Molière] listens to me, Marquis, far from mocking us all,
> He will be quiet, if he wants to avoid my wrath.
> What, if we let ourselves be treated in this way,
> We will soon be lashed by his whip.

The baron's remark reveals once again how personal a collective identification in the comic portrait can be. Though the baron never claims to be a particular victim of Molière's satire (the target is "us all" and not "me")— he nevertheless resents seeing himself in the portrayal. And the affront is so stinging that he can compare it with a whipping ("les étrivières"). He reproaches his fellow spectator, the marquis, with an indulgence toward Molière's satire that borders on self-humiliation:

> Vous aimez la méthode
> De vous souffrir railler toûjours sur chaque mode,
> Qu'un Molière sans cesse en vos habillemens
> Vous fasse les objets de tous ces bernemens,
> . . . .
> Oui, vous aimez cela, car pour vous voir berner,
> Vous n'avez pas assez d'argent pour luy donner. (I.i.55–62)

> You love the routine
> Of watching yourself be mocked in every fashion,
> And that a Molière in your clothing
> Constantly makes you the object of all these jokes,
> . . . .
> Yes, you love it, since to see yourself mocked
> You do not seem to have enough money to give him.

The humiliation remains a general one: in addition to the collective "vous,"[6] the expression "in every fashion" [sur chaque mode], suggests the vast variety of manners and trends that Molière mocks. Nevertheless, the image of Molière staging these portraits in the very clothes ("en vos habille-mens") worn by his models in the audience suggests the directness of Old Comedy. In general, the clothes worn by actors and audience are, as I noted earlier, basically the same, allowing the two spectacles to become identical to the viewer. However, clothing the portrait identically to the model can produce a more individualized bite than this vague similarity of stage costume and audience fashion. Such is the lesson of the anecdote in circulation after the staging of *Les Femmes Savantes,* according to which Molière bought one of abbé Cotin's old outfits to wear while portraying him under the thinly disguised name of Trissotin.[7] Here the baron no doubt refers more generally to Molière's dressing in the role of aristocratic fops: the ribbons and other frivolous accessories of "Marquis Mascarille" or, in a less extravagant vein, the various "Fâcheux" of *Les Fâcheux* or the

---

6. We know "*vous*" to be plural; the baron uses "*tu*" when addressing his interlocutor personally.

7. "[L]e Trissotin de cette même comédie est l'abbé Cotin, jusque-là que Molière fit acheter un de ses habits pour le faire porter à celui qui faisait ce personnage dans sa pièce" (*Menagiana* [1694], qtd. in Mongrédien, *Recueil* 410). Couton suggests that this particular anecdote is probably only an "embel-lissement," even though he lists numerous other proofs that Molière gave his audience of Trissotin's identity as Cotin (2: 978). Once again, it is not so much the *accuracy* of the anecdote as its very *existence*—that is, the existence in the public's imagination of such a sartorial relationship between the staged portrait and its model.

marquis of *La Critique*. Despite the general nature of Molière's travesty (in the etymological sense of the term) of the "messieurs du bel air," the baron seems to feel deeply the insult of being mocked in his own clothes.[8]

The situation cannot but recall that of the two suitors in *Les Précieuses* when they confront the clowning of Mascarille in their suits. La Grange, when asserting that he will not bear mimicry ("vous ne vous rirez pas de nous"), is particularly insulted by the sartorial usurpations that serve as props to the servants' parody of their masters: "It is too much to supplant us, and to supplant us with our own clothing" [C'est trop que de nous supplanter, et de *nous supplanter avec nos propres habits*] (1: 285; sc. 15; emphasis added). The baron feels the same desire to punish Molière as the two masters their servants at the end of *Les Précieuses*. Another element links the position of Mascarille to that of Molière. Just as the two masters of *Les Précieuses* have in fact encouraged their servants to play their roles (such is the plot they devise in the first scene of the play), so too the baron insists that Molière's "masters"—the public—are equally responsible for being mimicked before their eyes: they pay for it freely ("pour vous voir berner, / Vous n'avez pas assez d'argent pour luy donner"). This analogy between Molière and Mascarille is important. It reveals the precarious position of those who please by mocking their master. The hand that pays for the laughter can easily turn to beat the clown. The fragility of the court joker is also that of the satirist.

Such is the danger presented by a resentful spectator such as the baron. On the other end of the spectrum, his interlocutor, the marquis, presents the image of a judicious spectator who takes a measured pleasure in the comedy, not narcissistically seeking a mirror to his vices, but rather a corrective lens for self-improvement. While his discourse in general simply repeats that of Dorante or Uranie from *La Critique*,[9] his commentary on

8. The anonymous 1674 play "L'Ombre de Molière" confirms that the baron's sense of injury is typical of that felt by a significant section of Molière's audience. In this one-act comedy, largely an apology for the playwright, the recently deceased Molière is depicted in Hades, facing the court of Minos and Pluto. These judges hear the complaints of those Molière satirized. Among these plaintiffs are a *précieuse*, a *cocu*, and a *marquis*. The last emphasizes the wrong done to his clothing. The shade of the marquis sees his injury as a collective one; he thus addresses Molière in saying, "Je suis *un de ces marquis . . . que vous tournez en ridicule.*" He then states his case to the judges: "Je demande justice pour mes rubans, mes plumes, ma perruque, ma calèche, et mon fausset, qu'il [Molière] a joués publiquement" (qtd. in Fournel's collection, *Les Contemporains*, sc. 6). This play well illustrates that the indignation felt by certain members of Molière's audience was not extinguished after the polemical eruption of the Quarrel of *L'Ecole des femmes*, but instead continued, at least to some extent, throughout the playwright's career, though it was never again expressed in such a spectacular manner.

9. His description of Molière's satire echos that of the "miroirs publics" passage: "Sçais-tu que la Satyre est la cause qu'on l'aime? / Comme il sçait étaler nos défauts à nos yeux, / Nous pouvons, les voyant, nous en corriger mieux" (I.i.92–94).

the baron's indignation is, in contrast, of keen interest. The essence of the marquis's position is this: the baron is making a spectacle of himself by raging against his portrayal by Molière. Thus, while comparing Molière's satire to thunder, the marquis tells his interlocutor:

> Mais, Baron, tu te vas ériger en folâtre
> Si l'on te voit blâmer ce foudre de Theatre,
> Cet auteur si fertile en Ouvrages puissans. (I.i.79–81)

> But, Baron, you are going to make yourself a public fool
> If you are seen cursing this thunderbolt of the Theater,
> This author so prolific in mighty works.

It is only a short step from being such a "fool" to being a good subject of comedy. Indeed, when the baron promises to take his revenge on Molière by boycotting his theater, the marquis responds that he will thereby only make a mockery of himself—and make some good comic material for Molière's future comedies.

> C'est le moyen d'attirer sa satyre;
> Et s'il vient à sçavoir le dessein que tu fais,
> Tu te feras joüer plus qu'on ne fut jamais.
> Evite, si tu peux, d'en faire la folie,
> Si tu ne veux sur toy voir une Comedie:
> Je suis certain qu'apres tu t'en repentirois. (I.i.40–45)

> It's the sure means to attract his satire;
> And if he comes to know about your project,
> You will see yourself satirized [joué] more than anyone yet.
> Avoid, if you can, such foolishness,
> If you do not want to see a comedy about yourself:
> I am sure that afterward you would regret it.

The baron's attempt to avoid seeing himself satirized on stage will only guarantee more of the same. Resistance to being mocked is a fitting subject of mockery. It is a comic fault; it transforms the spectator into a comic character.

The author Chevalier follows this logic with an audacious step. If anger at being depicted renders one a comic character, then comic characters must be angry at being depicted. Such would be the case, that is, if comic characters were really spectators as well as *dramatis personae*. But Molière's characters are in general posited as typical members of the public. Why not, then, present Molière's characters as such, as simple spectators in the theater audience? Chevalier does so, portraying in his play as "real" spectators a number of fictional characters from Molière's comedies, such as "Monsieur de la Souche" (Arnolphe's adopted name in *L'Ecole des Femmes*) and the "Marquis Mascarille," as well as the Baron de la Crasse, the eponymous hero of Poisson's 1662 play. These fictional characters quite naturally take their seats next to the other spectators, who are quite eager to see these public laughingstocks in person. When the baron hears who his neighbors will be, he prepares for the delight of the "second comedy" that his fellow audience members will provide: "Prepare yourself, my mouth, for a good laugh. / . . . We are going to see quite a performance" [Pour rire tout son sou, prepare-toy, ma bouche. / . . . Nous allons voir beau jeu] (I.iv.284-85).

Chevalier presents these characters—Mascarille, Arnolphe, and the Baron de la Crasse—as all sharing the same abhorrence to their satiric depiction on stage. Though their lines are few (their presence being limited to two short scenes), they all repeat their repugnance at being mocked. Mascarille thus complains that "Molière satirizes too much" (I.v.308), lamenting that there is no escaping the ridicule of the public: "in every place the satire follows us / We do not dare show ourselves, or even open our mouth" [en tous lieux la Satyre nous suit / Nous n'osons nous montrer, ny méme ouvrir la bouche] (II.i.324–25). After Monsieur de la Souche quits the theater in scorn, the Baron de la Crasse sums up their collective curse on comic representation with these parting words: "A curse on the dogs / Authors, actors are truly good-for-nothings" [Peste soit la canaille, / Autheurs, Comédiens, sont des vrais rien quï vaille] (II.i.329–30).

The response of those who resent being targeted by the comic author is not always as passive as these boycott attempts by the indignant. A more aggressive reaction is to mock the mocker, to satirize the satirist. The title of Boursault's *Le Portrait du Peintre* provides a good verbal emblem for this strategy. The desire of the ridiculed to seek revenge—the very same desire that fueled the action of *Les Précieuses ridicules*—provokes a satiric war in the theaters of Paris. Plays portray spectators mocking the author who has mocked them: we might recall here how the aristocrats of *Zélinde* laugh over the portrait of Molière presented by Argimont. The staging of such a "satire of the satirist" is declared only justice, according to Donneau de Visé: "Those who mock and play everyone must, without complaint, bear being attacked, since they started it, and people are only giving back to them what they gave others." [Ceux qui joüent tout le monde doivent, sans murmurer, souffrir qu'on les attaque, puis qu'ils en fournissent le sujet et que l'on ne fait que leur rendre ce qu'ils prestent aux autres] ("Lettre sur les affaires" 309). The language of Molière's critics accentuates the purely retaliatory nature of their attack: Molière, the "Mocker of Manners [. . .] will be mocked, perfectly mocked" [Daubeur de Moeurs . . . sera daubé, mais finement daubé] (Montfleury, *L'Impromptu de l'Hotel de Condé* 335; sc. 2 and 353; sc. 4).

In this theatrical war, the playwright naturally becomes a spectator to his own portrait. I return here to Molière where we left him at the end of chapter 9, viewing his own image satirized on stage by his rivals. We can now gauge his own response to seeing himself ridiculed in his turn. Will he react with the same susceptibility so often displayed by his fellow play-wrights? For we can assume they were at least as indignant as the spectators we have seen earlier. Though the plays do not entirely dismiss the possibil-ity of an author's vain pleasure at seeing himself ridiculed (as we have seen in Molière's description of Boursault), the very mechanics of attack and counterattack that drive the polemic suggest that the dominant reaction to being satirized is the indignation that fuels the machinery of satire. Indeed, any mask of easy indulgence worn by the satirized authors most often simply hides wrath. *Les Amours de Calotin* describes a staging of *L'Im-promptu de Versailles* in which the forced smiles of Molière's rivals in the audience scarcely hide their spite at being ridiculed by the playwright.

> Il berna les Autheurs et les Comediens
> Et je les voyais là faire fort bon visage,
> Quoy qu'au fond de leur ame ils fussent pleins de rage. (I.iii.170–72)
>
> He [Molière] ridiculed the authors and actors
> And I saw them keep a cool face,
> Even though inside they were full of rage.

The fact is that Molière himself displays some of this same rage when he confronts the satiric pictures drawn of him by his rivals. In *L'Impromptu,* he defines precisely how much of his "personage" he is willing to "furnish" to the satiric stage (as the characters of *La Critique* might say). Speaking of those authors who have painted his unflattering portrait, he allows his indignation to rise to the surface:

> Je leur abandonne de bon coeur mes ouvrages, ma figure, mes gestes, mes paroles, mon ton de voix, et ma façon de réciter, pour en faire et dire tout ce qu'il leur plaira. [. . .] je serais ravi que cela puisse réjouir le monde. Mais en leur abandonnant tout cela, ils me doivent faire la grâce de me laisser le reste et de ne point toucher à des matières de la nature de celles sur lesquelles on m'a dit qu'ils m'attaquaient dans leurs comédies. (1: 695–96; sc. 5)

I will happily abandon to them my works, my appearance, my gestures, my words, my tone of voice, and my way of reciting lines, to do with it everything they wish. [. . .] I would be delighted if all this entertains people. But in letting them have all that, they should do me the favor of leaving me the rest and not touching matters of the nature of those for which they have attacked me, so I hear, in their comedies.

If Molière is referring here to suggestions of cuckoldry, as is often suggested, his ire has apparently already been experienced by spectators to his own plays.[10] As the baron in *Les Amours de Calotin,* speaking of Molière's satires of cuckolds, asserts:

Nous sommes tous Cocus, si nous l'en voulons croire;
Appellez-vous cela des Vers à nostre gloire? (I.i.23–24)

We are all cuckolds, if we are to believe him;
Do you call that verses to our glory?

How will Molière respond when faced with the feeling of indignation he has ignited in his own audience, when confronted himself with "verses" not to his own "glory"? This is the question to be resolved in this passage, which forms the climax of *L'Impromptu.* He could easily respond with further satires of opponents, such as he has already undertaken in *La Critique* and more specifically in *L'Impromptu* with a verbal satire of Boursault, who is named directly in the text. This response is advocated in the speech of Mlle de Brie. Molière should go one step further in the battle of satires: beyond enunciating prudent self-justifications, Molière should brutally portray his critics on stage in a comedy dedicated to his opponent, Boursault: "I swear, I would have satirized [joué] this little mister author, who gets mixed up with writing against people who never thought about him" [Ma foi, j'aurais joué ce petit Monsieur l'auteur, qui se mêle d'écrire contre des gens qui ne songent pas à lui] (1: 695; sc. 5).

Molière, however, immediately dismisses such a riposte. "What a fine entertainment for the court Monsieur Boursault would be!" [Le beau sujet à divertir la cour que Monsieur Boursault!] he exclaims. He denounces the war of polemical portraits and counterportraits as "a silly war" designed by his enemies as a trap to divert his attention from his other comedies, to "distract [him], by this strategy, from other works" [détourner, par cet

10. See for example Couton's note on this passage, asserting that Molière is in no way responding here to denunciations of his "irreligion," but instead exclusively to attacks on his "vie privée" and, in particular, to the suppressed song in *Le Portrait du Peintre,* "la Chanson de la coquille," which derides his wife's sexual conduct (1: 1307).

artifice, des autres ouvrages]. Rage at representation is indeed a trap—one that renders the enraged a comic spectacle and provokes a spiral of satiric revenge. And, indeed, in this scene Molière offers himself as a spectacle. He does so when he follows these remarks with the passage cited above, exposing before the audience his susceptibility regarding his private life. Molière does not fail to draw attention to the histrionic possibilities of his rage; when Mlle de Béjart interrupts him, he responds: "But, really, you will make me go mad" [Mais enfin, vous me feriez devenir fou]. Once again, the "mad" folly of the spectator makes for a comedy; we are reminded of the expression in *Les Amours,* "Avoid, if you can, such foolishness, / If you do not want to see a comedy about yourself." This moment of extravagance is no doubt one of the passages that Chevalier has in mind when he describes Molière's self-mockery in *L'Impromptu:*

> Pour nous montrer combien son adresse est extréme,
> C'est qu'en son personnage il se berna luy-méme,
> Afin que si quelqu'un s'en estoit mutiné,
> On vit que le berneur luy-mesme estoit berné. (I.ii.175–78)

> In order to show us his extreme adroitness,
> It's in his own person that he mocked himself,
> So as to show if someone is upset at him,
> That the mocker himself is mocked.

Molière's "response" to his critics then is complex: he verbally satirizes those who have satirized him, at times he satirizes himself, and finally, he proclaims his withdrawal from the battlefield of satire and countersatire. "That's all the response they'll get from me" [Voilà toute la réponse qu'ils auront de moi] he declares at the end of his last monologue of the play, refusing any further attacks on his opponents. He keeps this last promise. Though two plays quickly follow *L'Impromptu de Versailles,* responding to Molière's satire of authors and actors (Donneau de Visé's *Réponse à L'Impromptu de Versailles* and Montfleury's *L'Impromptu de L'Hôtel de Condé*), Molière refuses to return the fire. The quarrel of the playwrights ends.

But comedy cannot so easily escape the system of reciprocal satire that characterizes the Quarrel. Though the battles between authors die down, the power of comic representation to produce response is inescapable. One portrait provokes another; each satiric judgement engenders its own spectacular response. Though Molière does not respond again to satirized and satirizing poets, he will soon have to respond to satirized *dévots* (as he does in the following year with *Tartuffe*). Whether they be *petits marquis,* poets, or moral censors, those satirized inevitably prolong the spectacle with their own responses of vain pleasure, misrecognition, or affront. It is a spectacle whose dynamics are irresistible to Molière's genius. Indeed the dynamic of representation and recognition stretches well beyond the polemical scenes we have seen thus far: in its broadest incarnation, it determines the very dramatic structure of his new style of satiric comedy.

*Part
Three*

DRAMATURGY
DRAMATURGY

Eleven

❖

FROM ARNOLPHE TO ALCESTE

Arnolphe, like Molière, carries tablets. The hero of *L'Ecole des femmes* observes with a keen eye the follies of husbands throughout the town; he records them and turns them into brilliant little satires, which he recounts with glee. When reproached by his friend Chrysalde for his penchant for ridiculing others, Arnolphe delivers an elegant and witty twenty-line monologue on the "vices of his time" and then deftly justifies his attitude:

> Enfin ce sont partout des sujets de satire;
> Et comme spectateur, ne puis-je pas en rire? (I.iv.43–44)

> Thus everywhere one finds subjects for satire;
> And, as a spectator, can I not jest?

Is then Arnolphe not right to enjoy some delicious new gossip when, two scenes later, the young Horace arrives in town with tales to recount? Is not the ribald account of another ridiculous husband cuckolded just the kind of anecdote to add to Arnolphe's repertory, to "put in [his] tablets" as he says [mettre sur mes tablettes] (I.iv.307)?

Arnolphe does of course "have the right" to observe and mock his peers, as he claims. But what he fails at this moment to understand is that the subject of ridicule promised by Horace will be Arnolphe himself. The young Horace, son of an old friend, does not know that Arnolphe's vanity has led him to adopt the aristocratic title of *de la Souche*. Horace therefore freely recounts his efforts at seducing Agnès, the young charge of this Monsieur de la Souche, to the man he knows only as Arnolphe. Horace furthermore delivers a stinging portrait of Arnolphe (under the title, of course, of de la Souche) to the very object of ridicule. As Horace has not met de la

Souche (a meeting that would render his error impossible), his mocking portrait is based purely on Arnolphe's reputation in the town: "He's rich, people say [about Arnolphe], but foolish, / And he's accounted a ridiculous fellow" [Riche, à ce qu'on m'a dit, mais des plus sensés, non / Et l'on m'en a parlé comme d'un ridicule"] (I.iv.330–31).

As Chrysalde predicted, Arnolphe gets what is coming to him: each satirist must suffer a "return of satire" [revers de satire] (I.i.56). Arnolphe's tongue has mocked all his neighbors; they will naturally seek their revenge. But Arnolphe not only must suffer the sight of himself cruelly depicted by his peers, he must furthermore manage his moment of self-recognition carefully. As we have seen, Horace does not realize that his malicious depiction of "de la Souche" is actually of Arnolphe. In order to save face, then, Arnolphe must keep Horace in ignorance; he must avoid the embarrassment of admitting that he is none other than Monsieur de la Souche himself. In other words, Arnolphe must hide his self-incriminating indignation at self-recognition. Though Arnolphe's pain is revealed to the play's spectators with an anguished aside that escapes Horace's ears, he keeps up a cool demeanor and laughs at the "ridiculous portrait" held up to him by the unwitting Horace.

Unfortunately for Arnolphe, his forced laughter is not mercifully brief. But Arnolphe's loss is the audience's gain. Molière nurses the moment of self-recognition for full effect, creating a scene of comic virtuosity as the tortured Arnolphe dodges Horace's repeated punches. Here is the exchange beginning with Horace's first reference to his beloved Agnès and her governor:

HORACE:	[. . .] C'est Agnès qu'on l'appelle.
ARNOLPHE (à part):	Ah, je crève!
HORACE:	Pour l'homme
	C'est, je crois, de la Zousse, ou Source, qu'on lenomme;
	Je ne me suis pas fort arrêté sur le nom;
	Riche, à ce qu'on m'a dit, mais des plus sensés, non,
	Et l'on m'en a parlé comme d'un ridicule.
	Le connaissez-vous point?
ARNOLPHE (à part):	La fâcheuse pilule!
HORACE:	Eh! vous ne dites mot?
ARNOLPHE:	Eh! oui, je le connois.
HORACE:	C'est un fou, n'est-ce pas?
ARNOLPHE:	Eh! . . .

HORACE:	Qu'en dites-vous? quoi?
	Eh! c'est-à-dire oui. Jaloux à faire rire?
	Sot? je vois qu'il en est ce que l'on m'a pu dire.
	(I.iv.327–36)

HORACE:	[. . .] Her name's Agnès.
ARNOLPHE (ASIDE):	Oh, death!
HORACE:	The man, I hear,
	Is called de la Zousse, or Source, or something
	queer;
	I didn't pay much attention to his name.
	He's rich, people say, but foolish,
	And he's accounted a ridiculous fellow.
	Do you know him?
ARNOLPHE (ASIDE):	Ugh, what a bitter pill to swallow!
HORACE:	I said, do you know him?
ARNOLPHE:	Oh, yes, I know him.
HORACE:	He's a fool, isn't he?
ARNOLPHE:	Oh . . .
HORACE:	What? What did you say?
	He is, I take it. And ridiculously jealous too?
	An ass? I see that all they said is true.

Molière adopts here the conventional comic technique of mistaken identity, *quiproquo,* and exploits it for his dramaturgy of representation and recognition. The repeated hammerings of insulting depictions *(un ridicule, un fou, jaloux à faire rire, sot)* and the painful dissimulations of affront they provoke all result from Molière's ingenious dramatic layering. The secret of this comic dynamism is the playwright's fine weaving of the characters' indirect communications. Both Horace and Arnolphe speak obliquely, whether it be conscious or not. Horace delivers a portrait of a man whose identity is vague ("de la Zousse ou Source"). Furthermore, Horace's depiction is not a direct statement of his own opinion (he has after all never seen the man in question); instead he repeats the talk of the town. In ridiculing Arnolphe, Horace simply acts as the indirect mouthpiece of anonymous public opinion, publishing Arnolphe's (de la Souche's) general reputation. Arnolphe, in turn, is equally indirect: he plays on the ambiguity of expressions such as "I know him," hiding his own identity in order to avoid further embarrassment. His only immediate expressions of feeling are directed away from his interlocutor in the exclamations registered in his asides.

By hiding his identity and maintaining this distorted communication with Horace, Arnolphe not only prolongs his pain (for the audience's pleasure), but he furthermore creates the conditions for future action and, ironically enough, for additional embarrassment. Molière transforms the comic dynamism of indirect depiction and concealed self-recognition into the dramatic principle guiding the play. Arnolphe's goal is to continue to keep Horace in the dark in order to better combat him in the battle for Agnès. Arnolphe believes his double identity will help him: it will allow him to become his rival's confident and thereby to preempt Horace's amorous strategies. Thus he will revenge himself on the young gallant who has unknowingly mocked him to his face. But in fact, each of his preemptive strategies will fail in the course of the play. Indeed they will not only fail, but also be followed by scenes of Horace recounting to Arnolphe his own foolish behavior and forcing Arnolphe to recognize his ridiculousness. This simple schema (Arnolphe attempts to foil Horace, Arnolphe fails, Horace recounts to Arnolphe his ridiculous failure) constitutes the very act structure of the comedy and is repeated three times. Arnolphe is forced each time to laugh with Horace as he mocks Arnolphe's jealous fits and describes his ineptitude (III.iv, IV.v, V.ii). Horace even demands that Arnolphe verbally acknowledge the absurdity of his machinations and laugh at de la Souche as a public buffoon.

HORACE:	Trouvez-vous pas plaisant de voir quel personnage
	A joué mon jaloux dans tout ce badinage?
	Dites.
ARNOLPHE:	Oui, fort plaisant.
HORACE:	Riez-en donc un peu.
	(Arnolphe rit d'un ris forcé.) (III.iv.924–27)

HORACE:	Don't you find it amusing to see the role
	My jealous rival played in this whole affair?
	Tell me.
ARNOLPHE:	Yes, very amusing.
HORACE:	Then laugh a little.
	(Arnolphe forces a laugh.)

At the very moment that Arnolphe painfully recognizes his own absurdity, he must laugh at it just as he laughs at others, as he has always laughed at others. And the very drive to escape that laughter, the very declaration "You will never again laugh at me" [. . .de moi tout à fait vous ne vous rirez point] (IV.i.1038) propels him implacably toward more such scenes where he must view himself mocked by others. But the secret of *L'Ecole* is that each laugh forced from Arnolphe creates another in the audience—an uncoerced laugh of delight at the cruel spectacle of Arnolphe discomfited, that is, of the satirist satirized.

◇

In satirizing the satirist Arnolphe, Molière dramatizes the practice of depiction and recognition not only as it is exercised in the everyday realm of social exchange, but also in the realm of the theater. For while Arnolphe is a typical participant in the social game of representation, he is also, as the "tablets" suggest, a figure for the comic satirist. We have seen this analogy between social and theatrical portrayer at work in *Les Précieuses,* with its wordplay on *pièce,* and in *La Critique,* with its analogy between Uranie and Molière. Such scenes are much more than incidental occurrences in Molière's work; they in fact reflect one of the driving principles of his dramaturgy, whether practiced in his comedies of manners, farces, or even comedy-ballets. Molière's plays are propelled by the very mechanics of depicting and identifying that structure Arnolphe's tale. As such, the plays act as a critique of both the social commerce of representation and the satirical comedy of manners that rehearses its dynamics.

This exploratory sketch of *L'Ecole des femmes* begins to reveal just how profoundly Molière explores these dynamics even before the intense scrutiny applied during the Quarrel that followed the comedy. It is, however, in the few years afterward that Molière crafts his richest inquiry in this realm. *Le Misanthrope,* first performed in 1666 but most likely conceived only months after the end of the Quarrel, represents both the culmination of Molière's satiric project and an intense interrogation of its functioning and utility.[1] By designating his characters (Célimène and Alceste) as satirists and by placing them before the reaction of their peers, Molière presents at the same time his most piercing portrayal of the social commerce of representation and his most rigorous commentary on satiric theater. The consequences of the commentary are critical. Gérard Defaux has brilliantly argued that Molière's critique of satire in *Le Misanthrope* effectively puts an end to his "first manner," that is, the accurate depiction and the moral denunciation of current manners as emblemized by *L'Ecole des femmes,* before he embraces a new style in the second half of his career, one that celebrates the pure pleasure of theatricality. Whether or not one accepts the finality of such a rupture, it cannot be denied that *Le Misanthrope* puts in

---

1. According to Broussette, Molière read to friends the first act of *Le Misanthrope* in the first half of 1664 (*OC* 2: 123), that is, just several months after responding to his critics with *L'Impromptu* in October 1663 and at the time when the last plays of the Quarrel were being first printed (*La Guerre comique* in March 1664 and *Les Amours de Calotin* in February 1664).

question the basic utility of satiric representation.[2] This interrogation is motivated not only by the troubling polemics over *L'Ecole,* but also by the controversy surrounding the banning of *Tartuffe* in 1664. It must be remembered here that, according to Molière, *Tartuffe* was banned not because of any general freethinking positions it embraced, but simply because it satirized a group both more touchy and more powerful than those he had targeted in the past. Unlike the others he satirized, the devout hypocrites could not bear seeing themselves in the moral mirror and furthermore held the power necessary to suppress that mirror. In his preface, Molière quite clearly places the reception of *Tartuffe* in the satiric framework elaborated in the polemics over *L'Ecole:*

> Voici une comédie dont on a fait beaucoup de bruit, qui a été longtemps persécutée; et les gens qu'elle joue ont bien fait voir qu'ils étaient plus puissants en France que tous ceux que j'ai joués jusques ici. Les marquis, les précieuses, les cocus et les médecins ont souffert doucement qu'on les ait représentés, et ils ont fait semblant de se divertir, avec tout le monde, des peintures que l'on a faites d'eux; mais les hypocrites n'ont point entendu raillerie. (1: 883)

> Here is a comedy that has created quite a stir and that has been persecuted for some time; and the people it portrays [joue] have shown themselves to be more powerful in France than all those I have portrayed heretofore. The marquis, the *précieuses,* the cuckolds, and the doctors have all peacefully endured being represented on stage and have pretended to be amused with

---

2. Defaux's thesis (*Molière* 29–30, 157–84) has been challenged quite convincingly by Dandrey (*Molière* 8–10, 272–81). However, even Dandrey, while insisting upon a basic continuity in Molière's aesthetics, still views *Le Misanthrope* as a severe aesthetic self-critique, one that marks an important point in the evolution of his work: "*Le Misanthrope* n'est pas un adieu au genre ou à une conception désormais caduque de la comédie, mais une réflexion lucide et sombre motivée par la rencontre d'un obstacle majeur dans la démarche dramatique du poète" (279).

In general, I agree with Dandrey that Molière's principal moral preoccupation throughout his work is the problem of self-knowledge. This position is of course opposed to that of Defaux, who argues that the breakdown in the comedy of manners after *Tartuffe* and *Le Misanthrope* leaves Molière a sceptic as concerns the corrective power of representation and its ability to form a more lucid self image. Instead, Defaux contends that the later comedies simply celebrate the madness of men. Defaux envisions here a Molière who continues the tradition of comic folly as epitomized by Erasmus and Rabelais. An important question of comic theory is raised here. M. A. Screech has recently argued that these Renaissance humanists wrote at a time in which learned attitudes toward laughter were radically transformed. Due to a reinterpretation of Aristotle's theory of laughter around 1513, the essence of the ridiculous was for a time seen to be madness (*anoia*) rather than ignorance (*agnoia*) or self-ignorance. Screech himself admits that the canonization of madness was a brief one, coming to an end after 1561 (*Laughter* 64). However, the dichotomy between madness and ignorance is hardly an irreconcilable one, as Screech points out: "Some readers fused madness and ignorance together. In the judgment of Socrates, the most ridiculous man is one who is so mad as to be totally ignorant of his own nature; such a man is acting flat contrary to the great injunction on the tympanum of the temple at Delphi" (66). I think that this perfectly describes the madness of Molière's self-ignorant heroes.

everyone else by the portraits that have been made of them; but the hypocrites will not stand to be mocked.

Tartuffe, according to Molière, is distinguished not by any provocative statement on religion, but simply by the power of the indignant self-identification it generates in certain spectators. Such is the lesson of the closing lines of the preface:

> Huit jours après qu'elle eut été défendue, on représenta devant la Cour une pièce intitulée *Scaramouche ermite;* et le roi, en sortant, dit au grand prince que je veux dire: "Je voudrais bien savoir pourquoi les gens qui se scandalisent si fort de la comédie de Molière ne disent mot de celle de *Scaramouche*"; à quoi le prince répondit: "La raison de cela, c'est que la comédie de *Scaramouche* joue le ciel et la religion, dont ces messieurs-là ne se soucient point; mais celle de Molière les joue eux-mêmes; c'est ce qu'ils ne peuvent souffrir." (1: 888)

> Eight days after [*Tartuffe*] was banned, a play called *Scaramouche ermite* was performed before the court; and the king in leaving said to the great prince to whom I have referred: "I would like to know why the people who are so scandalized by Molière's comedy say nothing about that of *Scaramouche*"; to which the prince responded: "The reason is that the comedy of *Scaramouche* mocks [joue] heaven and religion, about which those men don't care a bit; but Molière's comedy mocks them themselves, and that they cannot bear."

Molière's games of representation and recognition have reached an impasse; he has found an audience that is no longer so easily manipulated. The rules of the game established in *La Critique*—the mechanics of self-interest and blindness that cause the mocked to laugh at their own reflection in the public mirror—have collapsed. Unlike Arnolphe and Uranie, the professionals of piety will not force a laugh when satirized, but instead fight back.

Such are the general conditions under which Molière undertakes his portrayal of *Le Misanthrope*'s powerfully aristocratic salon, one where the satiric portraits and judgments of Alceste and Célimène are placed in confrontation with the intransigent reactions they provoke in their own audience of noble peers. As such, the play examines (1) comic creation, by presenting characters who are defined as observers, portrayers, and judges of their peers, and (2) comic reception, by depicting the characters' response to these portraits and judgments and the indignation, vanity, and misrecognitions that result from these identifications.

The results of this intense self-critique are contradictory. On the one hand, *Le Misanthrope* has long been considered the culmination of the author's effort to construct a satiric comedy of manners, the play chosen by Boileau in *L'Art poétique* as the comedy best representing "the masterful portraits" [les doctes peintures] of contemporary life (III.391–400). *Le Misanthrope* perfectly realizes the project of creating a comic public mirror—with its mimetic fidelity and its moral utility—as theorized in *La Critique.* In this light, the play represents the victory of satire. On the other hand, by ridiculing the railings of Alceste and by exposing the perfidy of Célimène's biting portraits—revealing both discourses to be without corrective effect on their interlocutors—*Le Misanthrope* is viewed as a satire of the satirist. As such, the play is in itself a kind of allegorical accusation leveled against the fidelity and utility of the comedy-mirror. This self-interrogation is the evidence for Defaux's assertion regarding the end of Molière's "first manner." In this light, *Le Misanthrope* represents the defeat of satire.

It is clear that any effort to gauge the effective functioning of the comedy-mirror cannot discount the challenge presented by this second reading of *Le Misanthrope.* We are obliged then to weigh with care the troubling consequences of Molière's use of the conventional topos of the "satirist satirized."[3] We can start by exploring the implications of the very expression. Its application to comedy rests on two evident premises: first, that at least one of the *dramatis personae* is a satirist; and second, that the comedy itself is a satire, which satirizes the satiric character. Now, as the playwright of such a comedy is necessarily a satirist, we are logically led to compare the *verbal satires* of the characters with the *dramatic satire* of the author. By comparing the satiric function of the characters with that of the author, we engage in a reflexive reading of the play, where the characters become, by analogy, figures for the author. The play is a kind of self-criticism, the negative outcome of which is open to debate. It is in short a satire of the comedy-mirror.

But this reflexive reading must be complemented by another consequence of the logic inherent in "the satirist satirized." Classical satire is by nature a depiction of a contemporary reality. (Thus we have seen Molière's interchangeable use of the terms "satires," "peintures ridicules," and "miroirs publics" in *La Critique* [sc. 6]).[4] Now, *Le Misanthrope* presents a portrait of contemporary aristocratic society as found in Célimène's salon. Neither Alceste nor Célimène nor Philinte, for all their satiric commentar-

---

3. For a broad view on the power of this theme, including a chapter on *Le Misanthrope,* see Elliott.

4. Jean Marmier has shown that the comparison between satire and the faithful mirror is a typical one in the seventeenth century, a period in which satire followed "la doctrine de la *mimèsis,* triomphante" (35).

ies, are comic playwrights. To interpret them as figures of the author is therefore, as I have already suggested for Arnolphe, to engage in an allegorical reading of the play, one based on the analogy of two forms of depiction—one in comedy, the other in social commerce. However justified this analogy, neither Alceste nor Célimène suggest that they have actually acted as playwrights—for example, by sending their satiric productions in *mémoire* form to Molière, as do Dorante and company. Thus in the case of *Le Misanthrope,* the analogy between the characters and the author remains largely unspoken. If we read the play at face value—that is, as a mimetic satire rather than self-reflexive allegory—the characters are defined simply as figures of the public. The characters' verbal satires are thus representative of an aristocratic salon, one defined by the practices of depiction and recognition previously noted. *Le Misanthrope* is a satire of the social commerce of representation.

As a reflection on both theatrical and social exchange, *Le Misanthrope* offers a complex, and at times perplexing, mechanism of depiction and recognition. The duel between Célimène and Arsinoé in the third act provides an illustration. As a satire of salon conversations, Célimène's portrait of the prude Arsinoé presents the following configuration: one character, representing the malicious wit *(médisante)* social type, depicts another character, representing the prude social type. In terms of recognition, the scene offers the spectacle of one character (Arsinoé) seeing herself in the portrait sketched by the other. However, the moral value and mimetic fidelity of the portrait are placed in great doubt, due to the compromising situation of its enunciation, motivated as it is by Célimène's personal antipathy and laced as it is with irony. The scene thus exposes the underbelly of the social art of description and judgment.

In the larger framework of the exchange between Molière and his audience, Célimène-Arsinoé exchange is a telling scene regarding the moral effects of satiric comedy. Molière, through the voice of Célimène, presents a verbal portrait of the prude much like the ones that he has sketched in other comedies—in the figure of Climène, for example. The recipient of the portrait is now the theater public. The members of the audience recognize in the portrait no longer simply Arsinoé, but also certain other spectators and perhaps even themselves. However, this system of depiction and recognition is equally destabilized: the author's satire of the prude cannot escape the problematic nature of its dramatic enunciation (that is, Célimène's malice and indirection). The moral uncertainty resulting from the shifting voices of satire is, I believe, the hallmark of *Le Misanthrope,* the secret of its continual ability to escape fixed interpretations.

Does this uncertainty spell defeat for the moral purpose of satire, its ability to correct by acting as a privileged mirror of vices? Oddly enough, this defeat would be the result of the kind of multiplication of the mirrors just illustrated, a kind of obscurity arising from a chaotic excess of depictions. When the author satirizes characters, who satirize other characters, who satirize in turn others, the question of an authoritative moral perspective becomes a difficult one.

This, then, is the question posed by *Le Misanthrope:* Can the moral aims of satire survive intact the exposure of its imperfect functioning—whether it be in the social realm of verbal exchange or in the theatrical realm of staged portraits? Chapter 12 sketches the dramatic form that makes this interrogation possible—a theater that features characters as satirists and portraitists, the defining mark of Molière's satiric comedy of manners. After this sketch of Molière's dramaturgy, the following two chapters elaborate the parallel interpretations of the characters' verbal satire. Chapter 13 examines characters' satiric utterances as a reflection on the playwright's craft, as a commentary on the comedy-mirror. Chapter 14 evaluates these utterances as a faithful depiction of current *mores,* as a critical portrayal of the social art of character description. After synthesizing these two readings of the machinery of depiction and recognition, I evaluate in the conclusion the moral consequences of the house of mirrors Molière has built in *Le Misanthrope.*

Twelve

✧

SATIRE AND DRAMATIC FORM

Action Makes Depiction

The chapters thus far have primarily treated comedy as a satiric representation, using terms that leave little place for the specificities of theatrical structure. Yet there are readers who see the plays quite rightly as marvels of dramatic and comic form. Of course, problems of dramatic structure have not entirely escaped discussion. Part 1 addressed some of the tensions that can result between the opposing imperatives of exact representation and effective dramatic construction, grappling with La Bruyère's observation that faithful depictions run the risk of artless insipidity and moral futility. The characters in the last scene of *La Critique* confront the choice between, on the one hand, the conventions of a well-structured plot—a dénouement featuring a marriage or a recognition—and, on the other, a precise reproduction of reality.

La Critique, of course, constitutes something of an exception in Molière's work, due to its lack of dramatic action. How then does Molière integrate depiction and action in his comedies? The question has long occupied audiences and readers. Molière has miraculously sustained a twin reputation. He is canonized as the playwright who brought the satire of current manners to the French stage and who then provided for Europe the model for a comedy of observation based on contemporary reality and character types.[1] At the same time, Molière is considered the master of pure theatricality, a manipulator of dramatic conventions—whether they

---

1. A recent guide to French seventeenth-century literature, for example, qualifies Molière as the master who created "la comédie d'observation, qui prend sa matière dans les événements d'actualité, les faits de moeurs ou les types sociaux" (Tocanne, "L'Efflorescence classique" 250).

be the structures of character conflict or the mechanics of farce, both of which function in complete independence from the vicissitudes of current reality. Those critics who embrace this second perspective provide readings that, while helpful in explicating comic structures, tend, as we will see, to efface the representational power of the comedy.

Reconciling these two readings requires an exploration of the characters' verbal satires and depictions as an engine of dramatic conflict. *Le Misanthrope* presents a particularly important case study for testing such a synthesis, since it features an apparently weak plot structure: there is, for example, no conventional comic dénouement: "ni mariage, ni reconnaissance" as Dorante says in *La Critique.* It is also one of the only plays entirely lacking in the kind of mechanical comic devices found even in a serious *grande comédie* such as *Le Tartuffe,* where Orgon hides under the table and where the wily servant Dorine farcically reunites the young lovers with her physical histrionics.

It is therefore not surprising that the critics contemporary to Molière considered *Le Misanthrope* first and foremost a depiction of current manners. So it is that Donneau de Visé's preface to the first edition claims in essence that satire, rather than dramatic action, is the engine of the play:

> Il n'a point voulu faire une comédie pleine d'incidents, mais une pièce seulement où il pût parler contre les moeurs du siècle. (*OC* 2: 132)

> He [Molière] did not want to create a comedy full of actions, but instead a play wherein he could simply speak out against the manners of the time.

Robinet, in his *Lettres en vers* (June 12, 1666), also places this function of "attacking the manners of our age" [fondant les moeurs de notre âge] at the center of the work (Mongrédien, *Recueil* 266). Likewise, Subligny's *La Muse de la Cour* (June 17, 1666) conceives of the play as a painting wherein the audience will see itself and the ways of its world:

> Il peint si bien les péchés
> Que le diable fait faire à toute la Nature,
> Que ceux qui s'en croiront tachés
> Les haïront sur sa peinture. (*Recueil* 267)

> He [Molière] paints so well the sins
> That the devil has sown throughout nature,
> That those who believe themselves guilty of them
> Will hate them in his portrait.

Though the term "comedy of manners" did not exist at the time, we see in these reactions that the qualification is already implicitly operative in descriptions of Molière's works.[2]

It is precisely against such readings that Bray sought to highlight the fantastic and unrealistic comic structures that Molière inherited from farce. His 1954 *Molière, homme de théâtre,* along with W. G. Moore's 1949 *Molière, A New Criticism,* marked a historic turn away from social and satiric readings of the playwright. Bray's attitude however is not limited to Molière's farces; he provocatively cites *Le Misanthrope* as a play without any relationship to "reality" (270). In a less combatively antisatiric mode, critics in the following decades often simply discount Molière's aesthetics of depiction in order to privilege a dramaturgy of plot construction or psychology. It is in this sense that an influential scholar like Jacques Guicharnaud distinguishes between *Le Misanthrope*'s banal "arsenal satirique" and the real interest of the play: "le drame," constituted by the psychological conflict and the unfolding action (503).

The problem with these readings is that they tend to ignore the text itself when it is obviously satiric. To do so, they seek recourse in subtexts or in motivational interpretations of the dramatic action. Guicharnaud's reading of the sonnet scene offers a good example of the art of subtextual interpolation, designed to place the dramaturgic above the satiric. Oronte's sonnet becomes a simple "pretext," in itself "insignificant," for a quarrel between two rivals, Alceste and Philinte (382). The specificity of the text,

2. Since when Molière and his critics describe the comedies as portraits of contemporary *moeurs* they refer to both social convention and individual character, there is no active distinction between a "comedy of character" and a "comedy of manners"; the taxonomy that separated the two was an eighteenth-century innovation. In Molière's time a critic such as d'Aubignac was concerned primarily with the distinction of Old Comedy and New Comedy. Boileau, in addition to this classical distinction, is concerned with separating the "doctes peintures" of comedy from "bouffon" farce, divorcing *Le Misanthrope* from *Les Fourberies de Scapin* (*L'Art poétique* III.395–400). On the other hand, Boileau, like d'Aubignac, does not distinguish between the comedy of character and that of manners, rhyming as synonyms, for example, "humeurs" and "moeurs" (372–74). Riccoboni, in his 1736 *Observations,* is the first critic to firmly establish "ce nouveau genre de Comédie" that is the "pièce de caractère"—a form he attributes to Molière (26–27). However, he places this form in opposition to the "pièce d'intrigue" and not the comedy of manners, a term that he does not use. Indeed, given the vocation of the "comédie de caractère" as a "critique des moeurs" (111–16), Riccoboni's comedy of character largely fits the definition of a comedy of manners. By the second half of the eighteenth century, however, a more complex categorization of the modern comedy was established. Thus the 1776 *Supplément à L'Encyclopédie*'s article "Comédie" divides the genre into four "espèces": (1) "la comédie de caractère . . . qui s'occupe principalement à développer un caractère particulier"; (2) "la comédie de moeurs," which presents "un tableau frappant et vrai des usages ou du genre de vie particulier, que les hommes d'un certain état ou condition ont généralement adopté"; (3) the comedy of "situation"; and (4) "la comédie d'intrigue" (517–18). The *a posteriori* distinction of comedy of character and comedy of manners is thereafter a canonical one.

a satire of certain literary practices, is lost. The sonnet becomes a sign of social pretense equivalent to sartorial excesses, "like a blond wig or large ribbons," just another weapon in the characters' battle for dominance. Bray goes further by simply neglecting altogether the actual verses in favor of his own résumé of the action. So it is that Bray describes the "mécanisme" of *Le Misanthrope:*

> Alceste vient chercher une explication que les circonstances ou le caractère de Célimène lui refusent. Il lui faut s'y prendre à cinq fois pour arriver à son but. Pourquoi cinq fois? Parce que le poète a besoin de ces contretemps pour agencer sa comédie; mais non point parce que la réalité le veut ainsi. Où faut-il donc chercher la vérité que, selon la critique, Molière a fait monter sur la scène? (270)

> Alceste comes to seek an explanation that either circumstance or Célimène's character makes impossible. He must try five times before arriving at his goal. Why five times? Because the playwright needs these obstacles in order to put together his comedy; but not because reality demands it. Where then should we look for the truth that, according to critics, Molière has put on stage?

To answer Bray's question, it is in the verses of the play that we find, on quite a literal level, the depiction of current "reality." Indeed, right from the opening discussion between Alceste and Philinte, "les moeurs du temps" are at the center not only of the play's thematics, but of its lexicon as well; the expression is in fact uttered twice in their dialogue (107,145). This exposition via a debate on current manners follows an established tradition of Molière's *grandes comédies: L'Ecole des femmes* opens with a discussion about the laxness of husbands and the education of women; *Tartuffe,* with the issue of the legitimacy of rigorous moral judgments; *Dom Juan,* with the problem of intellectual and sexual *libertinage.*[3] What is striking, however, in the case of *Le Misanthrope,* is the universal aspect of the debate: rather than limiting themselves to a specific issue of current mores (cuckoldry, hypocrisy, *libertinage*), Alceste and Philinte present their attitudes toward the rules of social behavior in the most broad terms. A brief survey of the vocabulary of the first scene alone amply reveals the breadth of the debate: in addition to "moeurs du temps," we find, "moeurs d'à présent" (220), "[l]es vices du temps (234), "l'usage" and "les communs usages" (66, 154), "la cour et la ville" (89, 165), "bienséance" (decorum)

---

3. Scherer remarks on the uniqueness in the classical period of Molière's moral introductions ("cette façon de faire dépendre l'exposition de principes généraux"), a technique exemplified in French theater by Hardy and completely outmoded by Molière's time (*Dramaturgie* 52).

(77), as well as the terms "le siècle" (117, 154) and "le monde" (103, 149, 158), both referring here to the prevailing codes of social commerce.

It is clear then that the opening scene presents a satire in dialogue form, where the characters describe and judge current manners. But, of course, it would still be foolish to regard the comedy as nothing but depiction. As a picture of society, a "portrait du siècle," the play is a kind of moving picture, governed also by dramatic action.[4] How does the depiction of manners function in its theatrical framework? On a dramaturgic level, *Le Misanthrope's* setting in a salon of aristocratic equals poses a great opportunity for the satire of manners. Without the bourgeois concerns of money (Alceste, unlike Arnolphe, for example, never considers domestic economy in his opposition to polite society) and without the constraints of generational tyranny (Célimène, unlike Agnès, is a widow free of a guardian), social manners themselves become not only an object of discussion in the play, but more importantly the essential dynamism of the drama. These idle and self-sufficient peers have no need to resort to the kind of feigned actions or concealments that create the comic errors, the revelations and recognitions that structure such *grandes comédies* as *L'Ecole des femmes* or *Tartuffe*. Instead, it is the very difference in attitude toward *les moeurs du siècle* that defines the dramatic conflict. As has been remarked, the characters, "free from any obligation to act . . . each exist in their own proper mode. The conflict between these personal modes determines the structure of the play."[5]

Of course these personal "modes" do not exist in a vacuum: individual manners are defined in relation to group manners. Given that the characters' only occupation is social commerce, it seems quite natural that their discussions turn to questions of decorum *(bienséance),* that is to say, to the adaptation of personal actions and speech to larger social laws. And indeed, from the first scene the roles of Alceste and Célimène are tagged by their attitudes toward current manners: Alceste by his "great anger at the manners of the time" [grand courroux contre les moeurs du temps] (I.i.107) and Célimène by her disposition, which "seems to fit in so well with today's manners" [semble si fort donner dans les moeurs d'à présent] (220). But how does this character conflict advance the action? It is Alceste's mission to have the coquettish Célimène declare her preference—and preferably for him. This declaration will end the suspense concerning Alceste's

4. The expression "portrait du siècle" appears in Donneau de Visé's preface to *Le Misanthrope* (*OC* 2: 132).

5. "Débarrassés de toute obligation d'action . . . [ils] existent chacun sur un mode qui lui est propre. Le conflit entre ces différents modes commande la structure de la pièce" (Guicharnaud 502).

romantic fate, resolve the conflict between the hero and heroine and therefore terminate the action of the comedy. But such a resolution would demand a change in attitude on the part of one of the characters toward polite social commerce, the pleasures of which Célimène cannot abandon and the hypocrisy of which Alceste cannot suffer.

Furthermore, just as social manners and characters' attitudes toward them provoke the dramatic conflict, they in large part govern the unfolding of that conflict as well. Alceste is impeded in his quest of cornering Célimène—and thereby ending the drama—by the very rules of the society. As Célimène points out, decorum hardly permits a woman to declare her preference in a salon among a gathering of her admirers. Such a cruel statement to the losing parties would be anathema to the tyrannical "art of pleasing" [l'art de plaire], which is the capital rule of their world, one that oils the machinery of social exchange.[6] It is in adherence to this law that Célimène justifies her delays. When asked to frankly declare the object of her affections, she hides behind decorum, replying:

> Je trouve que ces mots qui sont désobligeants
> Ne se doivent point dire en présence des gens. (V.ii.1631–32)

> I find that these unpleasant words
> Must not be spoken in people's presence.

Of course, the problem is that Célimène is almost always in the presence of others. And even when she is not, in the *tête-à-tête* of the fourth act, she still has recourse to social custom to delay her declaration:

> Puisque l'honneur du sexe, ennemi de nos feux,
> S'oppose fortement à de pareils aveux . . . (IV.iii.1403–4)

> Since the honor of our sex, enemy of our passions,
> Is so opposed to such open avowals . . .

As Guicharnaud has observed, Célimène, in her attempt to avoid an open declaration, is in perfect accord with the social code she embraces (467).

Such is the properly dramatic role of social manners—and of characters' attitudes toward them.[7] Can we therefore say that their presence serves

6. Jean Mesnard calls *l'art de plaire* "la loi de la vie sociale qui permet de constituer une société harmonieuse" (867).

7. The comedy of manners is of course often characterized by another version of the individual strife with collective norms: that of personal appetites (for sex, prestige, marital alliance, or money) conflicting with prevailing social constraints. This is the model for the English comedy of manners, as epitomized by the schemings of Wycherley's Horner or Congreve's Mirabell. And indeed, such plays pitting personal drives against social *mores* were not unknown in Molière's time: Donneau de Visé's

primarily to advance the action of the play rather than elaborate its satiric portrait of society? Such a thesis is hard to defend when we consider the structure of the first act. If we assert the primacy of the dramatic action, we are confronted with the question of how the playwright can afford an exposition featuring a two-hundred line debate on *les moeurs du siècle* before ever mentioning Célimène, and therewith the specific conflict that will constitute the comedy. This is quite a different expository procedure than that of the *L'Ecole des Femmes,* for example, which also begins with a debate between the hero and the *raisonneur,* but which introduces from its sixth line the specific *dessein* of Arnolphe, which defines the dramatic action. *Le Misanthrope,* on the other hand, offers no clear indication before the second act of the nature of Alceste's dramatic "design" of forcing Célimène's declaration. Indeed the short discussion about Célimène (forty-four lines) in the first scene is quickly interrupted by the entry of Oronte. This interruption brings with it yet another discussion of current manners (this time around fashionable literary tastes and pretensions) and another contemporary character type. Almost another two hundred lines later the act ends, without returning to the subject of Célimène or Alceste's plans. In short, we can doubt whether Oronte's entry constitutes an "interruption" in the action, and instead see it as a positive *progression* of the satire.

Of course that satire is one that pits character against character, creating the dramatic tensions and confirming that action and depiction coexist in *Le Misanthrope,* but with this revision: the plot is structured by the portrait. In answer to La Bruyère's dichotomy, a paradox: Depiction makes action. Such a statement allows the resolution of the problem presented by Donneau de Visé when he tries to understand the popular success of plays so apparently undramatic: "one goes," he argues, "to plays like Elomire's for the people that are believed to be seen depicted rather than for the judicious structuring of the play, for it is well known he does not care

---

1667 *Veuve à la mode,* for example, presents the machinations of a widow affecting bereavement while plotting a new marriage with a rich and attractive suitor. The comedy of manners as practiced by Molière, on the other hand, generally places greater emphasis on the personal values of the characters than it does on their appetites (though admittedly Arnolphe's sexual drive is at moments explicit, as is Harpagon's pathological desire for gold). "Character" is as a whole defined by the individual's stated attitudes toward group manners. In *Les Précieuses,* for example, Cathos and Magdelon embrace the current fashion of *préciosité* and gallantry, as does Mascarille; Gorgibus represents the resistance to these values. Two years later, Molière, inspired by the opening of Terence's *Adelphi* (wherein the lenient Micio confronts the censorious Demea), crafts a more elegant version of this kind of conflict in the opening discussion of the 1661 *L'Ecole des maris,* wherein Ariste and Sganarelle debate current "manières" (line 24), "l'usage" (46) and "la mode" (17, 67), thereby inaugurating one of the hallmarks of Molière's dramaturgy.

about that" [l'on va plutost aux ouvrages qui sont de la nature de ceux
d'Elomire pour les gens que l'on y croit voir joüer que pour la judicieuse
conduitte de la Piece, car l'on sçait bien qu'il ne s'en picque pas] ("Lettre
sur les affaires" 304).

What Donneau de Visé fails to understand is that when Molière takes
care of the satire, the drama takes care of itself.

Médisance and Flattery

The perception that Molière developed satire at the expense of plot continued to thrive into the next century. Voltaire considered *Le Misanthrope* a
play so subtle in its plot [intrigue] that it somehow metamorphoses into
"a flowing portrait . . . from one end to the other in the style of the satires
of Despréaux" [une peinture continuelle . . . d'un bout à l'autre dans le
style des satires de Despréaux].[8] Voltaire's comparison of Molière's satire to
that of Boileau poses an important question as to the techniques of satire
utilized in *Le Misanthrope.* Unlike the *Satires,* the play is obviously not a
monologue in the author's (feigned) voice. We are confronted with the
simple Aristotelian distinction regarding the *manner of imitation,* that between narration (in epic poetry or history) and dramatic action. Now, in
an imitation by means of dramatic action, it is what is enacted, rather than
recounted, which constitutes the depiction and thus the satire. The playwright imitates daily life through the action on stage; characters *betray*
their values by their conduct.

But this kind of dramatic satire hardly explains the play's resemblance
to "le style des satires de Despréaux," a resemblance requiring well-crafted,
and self-conscious, verbal satire rather than the staging of ridiculous actions and typical conversation. This verbal satire is of course produced
through the characters' keen observations and judgments. Just how closely
these character-satirists come to the "satires de Despréaux" is suggested by
the fact that Boileau himself claimed to be a model for Alceste.[9] As for
Célimène, the acuity of her portraits is explicitly recognized in the text of
the play: "You are extraordinary at painting people" [Pour bien peindre les
gens vous êtes admirable], says Clitandre to the portraitist (II.iv.650).
Thus, next to author's *dramatic satire,* we can place characters' *verbal satire,*
their descriptions and judgments of other characters and their social envi-

---

8. "Notice" to *Le Misanthrope, Oeuvres de Molière* (Amsterdam, 1765) 3: 335, qtd. in Collinet 89.
9. For an examination of the Alceste-Boileau comparison, see the Grands Ecrivains edition of
Molière (5: 390–91).

ronment.[10] These two techniques of comic depiction also offer two different paradigms of communication. Author's satire privileges a communication between author and public: characters reveal themselves and what
they think of others in an indirect or unwitting fashion, speaking words
loaded by the author and designed to be properly decoded by the public.[11]
On the other hand, characters' verbal satire and commentary privilege a
communication between the characters on stage, who fully understand
each other, and a complicity between perspicacious speakers and their ap-
preciative interlocutors.

The intense utilization of this kind of verbal satire is no doubt the
defining feature of *Le Misanthrope.* Indeed, the characters engage in verbally "painting" each other and the society from the beginning of the play
to the end. The play is largely structured around a number of centerpieces
of this privileged activity: in act 1, the debate on decorum and sincerity
(sc. 1), followed by Alceste's criticism of current literary tastes and practices
(sc. 2); in act 2, the *scène des portraits* uttered by Célimène and depicting a
gallery of contemporary types (sc. 4); in act 3, Arsinoé's and Célimène's
duel of polemical portraits of one another (sc. 4); and the last scene of the
play, a second *scène des portraits,* constituted by the reading of Célimène's
letters describing each person on stage. With the exception of the fourth
act (dominated by the private discussion of Alceste and Célimène), all of
the key scenes of the play are included in this roster.[12]

The characters not only comment on each other and society, but they
also comment on the social commentary of others. For example, among
the things Célimène criticizes in others' social behavior is an obsession with
criticizing others; such is her censure of the censorious Damis (II.iv.634–
48): so it is that the *médisante* Célimène attacks Arsinoé for spreading

10. This returns to the double sense "satire" held at the time, taken both as a social practice and a
literary convention.

11. This parallels the distinction made by Alvin Eustis between verbal irony and author's irony.
"From the spectator's point of view, all ironic elements may be subsumed under two categories, first,
verbal irony, that is, originating with the character, and second, author's irony. It could be argued that
this is a distinction without a difference, since it is the author who puts verbal irony into the mouths
of his characters. Such however is the nature of the dramatic illusion that the spectator, providing the
characters are sufficiently lifelike, unconsciously considers verbal irony to be those characters' autonomous creation and not the author's." Eustis defines author's satire as the procedures by which "the
author talks through his characters, but over their heads, so to speak, and directly to the public" (15).

12. In using the term "key scene," I refer to Scherer's notion of the "scène à effet." Commenting
on the scene structure of *Le Misanthrope,* Scherer remarks: "pas de spectacle, mais une scène à effet
dans chaque acte: scène d'Alceste et d'Oronte à propos du sonnet (Acte I, sc. 2), scène des portraits
(Acte II, sc. 4), discussion aigre-douce entre Célimène et Arsinoé (Acte III, sc.4), volte-face d'Alceste
devant Célimène quand il vient pour l'accuser et se jette à ses pieds (Acte IV, sc. 3), enfin confusion de
Célimène (Acte V, sc. 4)" (*Dramaturgie* 205).

"médisance" (III.iv.946). Alceste, of course, also criticizes these negative portraits that are nursed by the "humeur satirique" of "médisance" (II.iv.660–62). However, his greatest charge of bile is reserved not for these negative depictions, but instead for the positive descriptions that others make of their peers, for the "useless words" [inutiles paroles] of flattery (I.i.46). For the society presented in *Le Misanthrope* is defined not only by *médisance,* but also by the flattering images of the world. Philinte flatters Oronte, Arsinoé flatters Alceste, and the *petits marquis* make a profession of flattering themselves.

Whether the images be flattering or critical, Alceste's aim is to "break the mirror of the world," which he believes to be dysfunctional, incapable of accurately reflecting a man's worth.[13] What, though, are the defining traits of this "mirror of the world," that is, of the social commerce of representation as Molière dramatizes it in *Le Misanthrope? Médisance* and flattery are the twin representational techniques practiced in Célimène's salon. Molière responds here to the dual obsession of his age. These two strategies for depicting the other are at the center of the major texts on conversation in the seventeenth century, beginning with Faret's treatise on the ideal behavior of the French courtier, the 1630 *L'Honnête homme,* with its chapters on flattery (52), compliments (65), complaisance (70), raillery (81), and "médisans" (100). The 1662 *La Logique ou l'Art de penser* of Port-Royal thoroughly explores the social activity of character judgment in its lengthy chapter "Some Faulty Reasonings Practiced in Civil Life and in Common Intercourse" [Des mauvais raisonnements que l'on commet dans la vie civile, & dans les discours ordinaires] (III. xx. 260–89). Principal among the faults under consideration by Nicole and Arnauld is again this inclination to represent the character of the other in either too flattering or too critical terms. On the one hand, humans naturally tend toward criticism of the other, due to faulty logic and *amour-propre:* "It is a common fault among men to rashly judge the actions and intentions of others" [C'est un défaut très-ordinaire parmi les hommes, de juger témérairement des actions et des intentions des autres] (279). On the other, in order to maintain a pleasant social environment, they fear to criticize and are led toward the opposite vice of "complaisance," a tendency "to praise and approve indifferently everything" [de louer & d'approuver tout indifféremment] (271). These two opposite tendencies toward judging the other intertwine in perverse ways in social exchange. So it is that Méré in his *Discours . . . de la conversation*

13. I cite here Ramon Fernandez's expression, "briser le miroir d'une société," found in his time-tested reading of *Le Misanthrope* (193).

notes that excessive flattery is often repaid by sharp criticism. The one who *pictures others* in a too kind light is in turn *pictured by others* in an unkind light, as insincere or vicious: "As most praise is the result of flattery, people are rarely pleased by it; and malice [médisance] creates the impression that one is simply envious or manipulative" [Et puis comme la pluspart des louanges tiennent de la flatterie, le monde ne s'y plaist que bien rarement; et la médisance donne à penser qu'on est envieux ou malin] (123). In social commerce, one character judgment begets another. One cannot escape the reflection cast by the world: the portraitist will be portrayed, and the flatterer denigrated.

Such are the intricacies of social intercourse depicted in *Le Misanthrope*. As far as their will to appraise their peers and their ways, Alceste and Célimène seem to be perfectly credible specimens of their society. But can we equally qualify as credible and verisimilar the polished style and wit ("de Despréaux") of their portraits and denunciations? This question begs a review of the public's adaptation of literary cultivation as a means toward portraying the other. In the case of *Le Misanthrope,* the public's literary talents take on two forms of social appraisal: satire (or *médisance*) and flattery. Most relevant here is *la poésie mondaine,* the fashionable verse forms of the mid seventeenth century that mediate between the realm of conversation and the realm of poetics. These short writings infuse poetic conventions with current conversational usage and offer themselves as poetic models for the public's social language. Needless to say, two of the principal social functions of these forms embody precisely the negative and positive role of social commentary: *moquerie,* with its tradition in satire and epigrammatic portraits, and *la louange,* with its traditions in encomium and dedicatory verses (Génetiot 139–57).

Finally, the sharpened tools of verbal depiction serve one more purpose, a reflexive one. When Célimène appraises the conversation of her peers, or when Alceste denounces the "worthless words" of flattery, their discourse perfectly exemplifies the strong metalinguistic function of social intercourse in the classical age. Conversation serves not only to criticize or condone general social behavior, but also to criticize or condone social speech itself, to criticize or condone the linguistic manners of others. Thus it is that the period produced so many printed "conversations" on the nature of, yes, conversations. Mlle de Scudéry's *Conversations sur divers sujets* comments beautifully on the function of these metaconversations. At the end of the "transcribed" discussion on the aesthetics of conversation, an interlocutor praises the present exchange as one both exemplary in its form and prescriptive in its content:

Enfin, ajouta Amilcar, sans vous donner la peine de parler davantage de la Conversation, pour en donner des Lois, il ne faut qu'admirer la vôtre, et qu'agir comme vous agissez, pour mériter l'admiration de toute la terre. (41)

"In the end," added Amilcar, "without forcing you to speak further about Conversation and establish its codes, it is only necessary to admire your own, and to act just like you act, in order to merit the admiration of the entire world."

Conversation describes social conduct, therefore it describes and judges others' conversation, while offering itself as a model. Simply put, when people talk about others, they talk about the way others talk and thus offer inevitably their own speech for comparison. Such is the reflexive tendency of the social commerce depicted in *Le Misanthrope*. How Molière exploits this tendency to create both a satire of this commerce and a critique of his own comedy-mirror is the subject of the next two chapters.

Thirteen

☙

IS CÉLIMÈNE MOLIÈRE?
IS LA FLÈCHE?

The Misanthrope and the *Médisante*

What can the relationship between the character-satirists and their social peers tell us about the relationship between Molière and his public? What does the failure of Alceste's moralizing tell us about the moral aims of comedy? What does the reception of Célimène's portraits by her entourage tell us about the audience's reception of Molière's own "tableaux"?

Such self-reflexive questions follow a reading instituted with the very first edition of the play in 1667, one contained in Donneau de Visé's prefatory "Lettre écrite sur la comédie du 'Misanthrope.'"[1] Although the reading of Alceste as a figure for Molière has been frequently debated in the three centuries since the play was performed, the powerful consequences of Donneau de Visé's rich analysis have not been fully plumbed. This is likely due in good part to the simple reason that Donneau de Visé's earlier polemics against Molière lead critics even today to dismiss him as a mercenary figure. But it may also be due to the fact that Donneau de Visé gives as much consideration to Célimène's acid wit as to Alceste's moralizing when he makes comparisons to the playwright; and, whether it be for reasons of moral elevation or of gender identity, critics have nearly always

---

1. Although Molière was reconciled by this time with his old enemy of the Quarrel of *L'Ecole des femmes,* he might have been reluctant to include Donneau de Visé's preface with his work. Couton examines certain anecdotal reports of Molière's opposition to the "Lettre" in his edition (2: 124). Molière's possible reluctance, however, in no way need place in doubt the perspicacity of Donneau de Visé's commentary, despite Couton's insistence on the *Lettre's* "qualité médiocre" (2: 124). All page references are to its reprinting in the Couton edition (2: 131–40).

embraced Alceste rather than Célimène as Molière's alter ego. But by drawing Célimène into the reflexive equation, Donneau de Visé is able to illuminate important differences between the two characters' forms of satire, differences that justify a reappraisal of Molière's work.

Donneau de Visé's asserts that *Le Misanthrope* is more satiric portrait than dramatic action, but what is important to consider now is how the critic envisions the comedy's complex levels of representation:

> Il n'a point voulu faire une comédie pleine d'incidents, mais une pièce seulement où il pût parler contre les moeurs du siècle. C'est ce qui lui a fait prendre pour son héros un misanthrope; et comme misanthrope veut dire ennemi des hommes, on doit demeurer d'accord qu'il ne pouvait choisir un personnage qui vraisemblablement pût mieux parler contre les hommes que leur ennemi. (2: 132)

> He [Molière) did not want to create a comedy full of actions, but instead a play where he could simply speak out against the manners of the time. That is what made him take for his hero a misanthrope; and as misanthrope means the enemy of man, it must be admitted that he could not have chosen a character who would be able to speak more believably *(vraisemblablement)* and effectively against men than their enemy.

Donneau de Visé presents the project of the play—"to speak out against the manners of the time"—as a problem. How can the playwright adapt his satiric discourse to a dramatic form? The solution is to utilize the intermediary of the character as a voice denouncing current manners. This solution admirably maintains verisimilitude due to the misanthropic character of the hero. In brief, the author, instead of portraying current manners in the dramatic action, has chosen to portray a painter of current manners, one whose character justifies his verbal satires.

Donneau de Visé then makes the crucial remark that the strategy of "portraying the painter" is a general dramaturgic principle of the play, which is not limited to the character of Alceste. Célimène equally serves the comic function of portraying current manners:

> [L]a maîtresse du Misanthrope est une jeune veuve, coquette, et tout à fait médisante. Il faut s'écrier ici, et admirer l'adresse de l'auteur: ce n'est pas que le caractère ne soit assez ordinaire, et que plusieurs n'eussent pu s'en servir; mais l'on doit admirer que, dans une pièce où Molière veut parler contre les moeurs du siècle et n'épargner personne, il nous fait voir une médisante avec un ennemi des hommes. Je vous laisse à penser si ces deux personnes ne peuvent pas naturellement parler contre toute la terre, puisque l'un hait les hommes, et que l'autre se plaît à en dire tout le mal qu'elle en sait. (2: 132)

The mistress of the Misanthrope is a young widow, a coquette, and a perfect malicious wit [médisante]. One has to marvel here and admire the adroitness of the author: it is not that the character is not typical enough and that other playwrights might not have used it; what is admirable is that in a play where Molière wanted to speak out against the manners of the time and spare no one, he shows us a *médisante* along with an enemy of men. I leave it to you to think if these two persons are not able to speak out against the whole world, because one hates men and the other takes pleasure in saying all the bad things she knows about them.

The satiric speech of the two principal characters works in tandem to realize the satiric objective of the author:

Le misanthrope seul n'aurait pu parler contre tous les hommes; mais en trouvant le moyen de le faire aider d'une médisante, c'est avoir trouvé, en même temps, celui de mettre, dans une seule pièce, la dernière main au portrait du siècle. (2: 132)

The misanthrope alone would not have been able to speak against all men; but in finding the means to have him helped out by a *médisante,* he [Molière] found, at the same time, the way to put, in a single comedy, the finishing touch to the portrait of the times.

What is interesting in this passage is that characters' satire is presented as an original and genial technique that surpasses the tired conventions of author's satire. The author's satire of a *médisante,* whose behavior and discourse are emblematic of current vices, is a rather banal gimmick that might be thought up by any of a number of playwrights: Donneau de Visé assures us that this type of personage is quite common in real life and obvious material for the stage. The genius of the role of Célimène, on the other hand, lies in the character's doubling of the satiric voice of the author (and of Alceste), which permits the playwright to achieve a perfect "portrait du siècle."[2]

Nevertheless, it is important to note that Molière still exploits the emblematic function of Célimène's conduct for his own dramatic satire. The last scene of the play, where Célimène's wicked epistolary portraits are read aloud, is certainly a satiric enactment of current manners. According to Donneau de Visé, the action "makes one see . . . the real ways of the *coquettes médisantes,* who speak and write continually against those that they

---

2. Indeed, Donneau de Visé himself had promoted the idea of depicting a *médisante* three years earlier in his polemical play *Zélinde*. At the time, however, he had imagined the role simply as one of a portrait of current vices, as a character "bien à la mode" (51; sc. 8) and not as a conscious voice of satire.

see everyday with smiling faces" [fait voir . . . la véritable manière d'agir des coquettes médisantes, qui parlent et écrivent continuellement contre ceux qu'elles voient tous les jours et à qui elles font bonne mine] (2: 138–39). The author's dramatic satire—what he "makes us see" [fait voir] through the action—is thus an active communication with the audience. Furthermore, inasmuch as the author's dramatic satire *satirizes* the verbal satirist (the *médisante* Célimène), it can actually detract from the validity of the latter. To restate: Molière "speaks against current manners," yes. Célimène also speaks against current manners. But Molière, in dramatic form, "speaks" against those, such as Célimène, who "continually speak, and write, against" others.

The use of author's satire against characters' satire is a technique that Molière had, of course, already consciously exploited in *L'Ecole des femmes,* as previously noted. I would add now that in *La Critique,* Molière refers specifically to the technique. When Climène, defending her sex, claims that she cannot bear "this impertinent author [Molière, who] calls us animals," Molière's apologist, Uranie, responds by stating that it is Arnolphe who satirizes thus, and *not* Molière: "Don't you see that it is a ridiculous man that he [Molière] makes speak there?" [Ne voyez-vous pas que c'est un ridicule qu'il fait parler?] (1: 659; sc. 6). This technique of satirizing the verbal satirist is most spectacularly employed in the exposition of *Tartuffe,* where Orgon's mother, Mme Pernelle, delivers a series of biting portraits of each member of the family. The anonymous 1667 "Lettre sur la comédie de l'Imposteur" offers a stunning description of this exposition. On the one hand, this text asserts that Mme Pernelle superbly assumes the playwright's role as character portraitist: "she describes in a marvelous manner" [elle décrit d'une merveilleuse sorte], producing each "portrait with the most natural colors" [portrait avec les couleurs les plus naturelles] (*OC* 1: 1149). On the other hand, Mme Pernelle and her biting portraits are themselves targets of the playwright's mockery: her "words and grimaces," ridiculous as they are, taint her depictions and betray her anger and rigidity. Thus the viewer must decipher her language, enjoying her portraits while at the same time laughing at her outrageous bias: "the spectator erases from each [of these portraits] that part of herself that she put in them, that is to say, the ridiculous austerity of the old days" [le spectateur ôt[e] de chacun . . . ce qu'elle y met du sien, c'est-à-dire l'austérité ridicule du temps passé] (*OC* 1: 1149).[3] The audience thus must separate the author's satire of

3. Nina Ekstein has compared the failings of Mme Pernelle's and Célimène's portraits, concluding that the two cases represent a "powerful critique of the portrait genre" by Molière (150). Ekstein does not, however, examine the consequences of this "critique" in terms of Molière's own art of presenting comic portraits to his public.

Mme Pernelle's bitterness from the character's own satire of her family; it is a question of intelligently pulling information, and laughter, from both.

While this dramatic satire of the verbal satirist operates in *Le Misanthrope,* the level of Alceste's and Célimène's verbal commentary is considerably less "ridiculous" than that of the aged Mme Pernelle or of the *cocu* Arnolphe. Thus, while Donneau de Visé notes that Molière's "voice" may at times counteract Célimène's verbal satire, he most often blends together the author's voice with that of the *coquette médisante.* (In this sense, the most fitting comparison with *Tartuffe* would be the character of Dorine, whose verbal satires reflect Molière's own position in his preface, even though she uses an unpolished servant's language that sharply distinguishes her from the playwright.) The fusion of playwright's and characters' voices permits Donneau de Visé to slide from one to the other when he tries to qualify the source of Célimène's character sketches in the "scène de portraits" (II.iv):

> La conversation est toute aux dépens du prochain; et la coquette médisante fait voir ce qu'elle sait, quand il s'agit de le dauber, et qu'elle est de celles qui déchirent sous main jusques à leurs meilleurs amis.

> Cette conversation fait voir que l'auteur n'est pas épuisé, puis qu'on y parle de vingt caractères de gens, qui sont admirablement bien dépeints en peu de vers chacun; et l'on peut dire que ce sont autant de sujets de comédies que Molière donne libéralement à ceux qui s'en voudront servir. (2: 136)

> The conversation is completely at the expense of others; and the *coquette médisante* lets us see what she knows when it comes to mocking, and that she is one of those who rip apart even their best friends.

> This conversation shows us that author is not exhausted, because one describes here twenty characters, which are admirably depicted in a few verses; and it can be said that they are each subjects for comedies that Molière offers liberally to those who want to make use of them.

"One describes here twenty characters"—the indefinite pronoun "one" allows the portrait to be the work of both the coquette Célimène and the author Molière. Both the *dramatis persona* and the playwright display their satiric prowess: the "admirable depiction" of characters is the combined result of the canny knowledge of Célimène ("the *coquette médisante* lets us see what she knows when it comes to mocking") and the fecund genius of the author ("this conversation shows us that author is not exhausted"). For a moment, Célimène assumes the role of the comic playwright, for her literary "caractères" are in themselves "sujets de comédies" offered up to the industrious plagiarists of the audience. Donneau de Visé has hardly forgotten since the Quarrel that mocking ("dauber"), the chosen sport of Célimène, is also that of Molière, the "Daubeur de moeurs."

Thus we see that the confluence of the satiric voices of characters and author lies at the heart of Donneau de Visé's presentation of the play, but that this union of voices is subject to divorce; the author seems in general to be in complicity with his characters' speech, but at other times he overrides it with his own satire of the speaker.

This comparison between the characters' and author's function becomes more refined when we note the differences between the two principal character-satirists, Célimène and Alceste. Like the author, they both speak against current manners; but the circumstances surrounding their satires—in particular the intentions that produce them—differ sharply. Donneau de Visé states clearly that Alceste is motivated by hatred, Célimène by pleasure: "one hates men and the other takes pleasure in saying all the bad things she knows about them." Donneau de Visé also notes that Célimène indulges in portrait sketches as much for her companions' pleasure as for her own: "she is politic and wants to keep good relations with everyone" [elle est politique et veut ménager tout le monde] (2: 136). Célimène's motivation, her "will to satire," then, is diametrically opposed to that of Alceste, whose aim is to attack his peers, to "alienate all mankind" [de rompre en visière à tout le genre humain] (2: 133). This disagreeableness will make him as good a subject of author's satire as Célimène, since it leads to his ridiculous associability; it is clear that "the spitefulness, the bizarre behavior and the fits of a misanthrope [are] things that make good theater" [les dépits, les bizarreries, et les emportements d'un misanthrope [sont] des choses qui font un grand jeu] (2: 132).

How can we interpret this difference in the two characters' satires? If we compare their tendencies to the stated purpose of the comedy-mirror, we find that Alceste and Célimène each represent one half of the function of comedy: Célimène, the pure pleasure of depiction, and Alceste, the moral instruction carried by the voice of disapproval. As a "divertissante instruction" (2: 140), the comedy of course merges the principles of pleasure and utility. On the one hand, like Célimène, who takes pleasure in raillery, Molière aims above all to please. As the critic remarks of the playwright's goal, Molière "has pleased, [and] his intention being to please, the critics cannot say he has failed" [a plu, [et. . .] son intention étant de plaire, les critiques ne peuvent pas dire qu'il ait mal fait] (2: 131). On the other, as the critic notes, the comedy is designed to reform its audience, to provoke in it "the desire to correct itself": "there is nothing in this comedy that could not be useful, and from which one should not profit" [il n'y a rien dans cette comédie qui ne puisse être utile, et dont l'on ne doive profiter] (2: 140). It is in this function that Alceste doubles for the author:

> [Molière] fait encore parler à son héros d'une partie des moeurs du temps; et ce qui est admirable est que, bien qu'il paraisse en quelque façon ridicule, il dit des choses fort justes. Il est vrai qu'il semble trop exiger; mais il faut demander beaucoup pour obtenir quelque chose; et pour obliger les hommes à se corriger un peu de leurs défauts, il est nécessaire de les leur faire paraître bien grands. (2: 139)

> Molière makes his hero speak about some of the manners of the times; and what is admirable is that, even though he sometimes appears ridiculous, he says very reasonable things. It is true that he is too demanding; but it is necessary to demand a lot in order to obtain something; and to force men to correct themselves a little as to their faults, it is necessary to exaggerate them.

To summarize, Donneau de Visé's analysis provides a rare window on the period's conception of metasatire. The author's satiric voice is doubled by that of his characters, Alceste and Célimène. At the same time, these voices are not to be read as entirely identical. Each of the two characters represents only a half of the overall role of the comic author: Alceste embodies the moral function; Célimène, the rule of pleasing. Furthermore, even though the characters speak in tandem with the author "against current manners," Alceste and Célimène themselves are still the subject of the satire of the author, the subject of the audience's laughter, and the subject of the audience's moral edification through their roles as negative examples.

Donneau de Visé's parallel of the roles of the author and the characters of *Le Misanthrope* marks only the beginning of a long critical tradition of reflexive readings of the play, which have almost all tended to concentrate on Alceste.[4] Readings of Alceste as a self-portrait of Molière flourished in the romantic era and found the fullest modern scholarly development in René Jasinski's *Molière et le Misanthrope,* where the play is promoted as "one of the masterpieces of personal literature"(120). Such biographical readings place greatest emphasis on Molière's own troubled relationship with his young coquettish wife, on his tendency toward melancholy, and

---

4. While this aspect of Célimène's role is generally overlooked, Jules Brody offers some comparisons of Célimène's satiric prowess and that of Molière: "These portraits [of Célimène], like Molière's comedies, achieve an aesthetic triumph over the very evils by which they are occasioned" (572). Elliott also gives attention to the parallel between Célimène and Molière, before ultimately tagging Alceste as the privileged figure for the author.

on his frustrations with the court—subjects distant from our present concerns here.[5] Defaux, however, moves well beyond this biographical perspective and examines the parallels between Alceste and Molière that lie in their *common function* as moral reformers.[6] According to Defaux, given the common moral aims of Alceste and Molière, the failure of the misanthrope and his betrayal by the laughing public represent nothing less than the failure of the moral aims of the comic genre as practiced by Molière: an "interrogation of moral comedy and the norms upon which it rests" [remise en question de la comédie morale et de la norme sur laquelle elle s'appuie] (179). Alceste metamorphoses into an allegorical figure representing the moral aims of the comic author:

> Molière s'accuse comme il a accusé les autres, il ne s'exclut nullement de la comédie humaine, il remet en question, à travers Alceste, ce rôle donquichotesque de censeur des moeurs qu'il s'était trop vite et naïvement attribué, et dont il confesse la dérision en se jouant soi-même. (182)

> Molière accuses himself as he has accused others, and he does not exclude himself from the human comedy; he puts in doubt, through Alceste, the quixotic role of the censor of manners, which he too quickly and naïvely assumed, and whose absurdity he admits by mockingly playing himself.

Defaux's reading is no doubt the richest examination of the reflexive nature of the comedy, of the world in which the characters laugh at each other and where "the comic stage and the social scene are identical" [comédie scénique et comédie sociale sont identiques] (175). However, despite the breadth of the analysis suggested by such statements, Defaux's reading of the reflexive nature of the characters' discourse is still limited to the case of Alceste. Célimène is here reduced to a representative of the laughing public, governed by a drive to protect its social euphoria (168–69).

I pick up Defaux's reading where he leaves off: at Célimène's doorstep. For Molière, like Célimène, was also labeled by his peers "the best *médisant* in the kingdom" as well as the "Portrait Maker."[7] My reading of course focuses—at least initially—less on the moral charge of satire, an aspect associated primarily with Alceste. Instead I concentrate on the issues presented by Célimène's portraiture: on its mimetic sharpness and on its

5. Jasinski does however suggest a parallel between Molière the comic author (instead of general biographic subject) and Alceste, noting the sense of persecution Molière developed from the critical attacks on *L'Ecole des Femmes* and *Tartuffe*.

6. "Molière n'a pas seulement nourri Alceste de ses propres tourments d'homme privé, il a aussi . . . projeté en lui ses dilemmes et ses doutes d'artiste et de poète comique"(179).

7. These quotes are from the Quarrel of *L'Ecole:* "Le Médisant le meilleur du Royaume" (Boursault, *Portrait* sc. 6); "Faiseur de Portraits" (Robinet, *Panegyrique* sc. 6).

specificity. Like Molière, Célimène must negotiate the pleasure that her portraits provoke with the *displeasure* associated with the subjects' self-recognition in the portrait, the displeasure that threatened Molière's success during the polemics over *L'Ecole des femmes* and *Tartuffe,* and the displeasure that brings about Célimène's unhappy end.

We have already seen that Célimène's popularity is largely due to her art in depicting her contemporaries: the praise of her followers is unqualified ("Pour bien peindre les gens vous êtes admirable!" [II.iv.650]). However, her success, like Molière's, in pleasing her admirers also depends on the fact they do not find themselves the target of her sardonic portraits.[8] When, at the play's end, her admirers find that they are equally the subject of her satires, that they are among people painted (one is even reduced to the Moliéresque appellation of "petit marquis"), Célimène is undone. She has, up to the last scene, managed to keep the marquis from seeing their own images in her portraits, much like we have seen Brécourt do when confronted with his own two marquis in *L'Impromptu.* But once *Le Misanthrope*'s marquis learn that they themselves are the targets of the *médisante*'s satiric acid, Célimène is confronted with her own "affairs of honor" provoked by those satirized. As Célimène's letters are read aloud before their victims, the spectator is presented with the scene of the satirized confronting their satires—and their satirist. A scene much like that we have seen in Chevalier's *Les Amours de Calotin,* where the reaction of the satirized spectators to *L'Impromptu* is described:

Il berna les Autheurs et les Comediens
Et je les voyais là faire fort bon visage,
Quoy qu'au fond de leur ame ils fussent pleins de rage. (I.iii.170–72)

He [Molière] ridiculed the authors and actors
And I saw them keep a cool face,
Even though inside they were full of rage.

Of course, Célimène's victims also try to maintain a cool demeanor before their own unflattering portraits, exercising a light irony of good sportsmanship: "It's your turn to play" [A vous le dé, Monsieur], says Clitandre, pointing out the next victim of Célimène's sardonic missives. But the depth of their anger is revealed in their project of revenge. Clitandre promises to Célimène that her cruel portraits will be repaid in kind:

8. As Plantié has pointed out, one of the principal rules of portrait drawing in Célimène's salon is to skewer only the absent (501).

[N]ous allons l'un et l'autre en tous lieux
Montrer de votre coeur le portrait glorieux. (V.iv.1693–94)

We will now go everywhere
To display this glorious self-portrait that you've painted.

In harnessing their revenge to a scheme of "counterportraits" of Célimène, Clitandre and Acaste promise "a return of satire" analogous to the one delivered by Molière's critics. Célimène too will be the victim of a kind of *Portrait du Peintre* produced by those she satirized—in this case one that takes place in the salons, not the theaters, of Paris. Acaste and Clitandre can no doubt justify their revenge upon Célimène with the same words we have seen used by Donneau de Visé against Molière: "Those who mock and play everyone must, without complaint, bear being attacked, since they started it, and people are only giving them back what they gave others" ("Lettre sur les affaires" 309). Being portrayed is the price paid by those who portray (and betray) others—whether in a letter or a comedy—a punishment administered by their former victims. The lesson learned by Molière in the Quarrel of *L'Ecole des Femmes,* and the lesson learned after the angry self-recognition of *Tartuffe*'s powerful spectators, are now pitilessly applied to the heroine of *Le Misanthrope.*[9]

If we now apply this analysis of Célimène to the character of Alceste, our notion of his role will be seriously revised. Like Célimène, Alceste must also negotiate the self-recognitions of those satirized in his moral pronouncements. It might appear that Alceste's prideful honesty would impede him from entering into such belittling negotiations with his interlocutors, but in fact even Alceste cannot ignore the danger of provoking the wrath of his targets. To demonstrate the point we need only look at Alceste's altercation with Oronte.

Oronte wants Alceste's opinion of his poem. This is a highly personal matter, and Oronte makes this perfectly clear. He is exposing himself to public criticism: "m'exposant à vous" (I.ii.303) is his term for the reading. After trying to avoid an open criticism, Alceste launches into a satire of affected amateur poets, a verbal satire quite in Boileau's elegant style, as

---

9. In speaking of the lessons of *Tartuffe,* I see its impact quite differently than Defaux, for whom the play's troubled reception reveals the moral chasm separating Molière from his public: "une rupture entre la sagesse sociale et la sagesse comique" (120). Defaux is obviously right in placing the reception of *Tartuffe* at the center of Molière's critique of satire and its utility. It is, however, quite debatable whether Molière's problems in performing and printing the play concerned moral viewpoints or worldviews. As noted, Molière himself claims that it is not such moral questions that provoked his critics, but instead their self-recognition in the mirror of the comedy, their public humiliation in being portrayed by the Painter.

Voltaire remarked. But far from addressing his interlocutor personally, Alceste pretends to direct his satiric railings to an absent unnamed writer. He even uses the collective first-person plural to generalize his remarks:

[I]l faut qu'un galant homme ait toujours grand empire
Sur les démangeaisons qui nous prennent d'écrire.(345–46)

We gentlemen should always restrain ourselves
When the itch to write overtakes us.

In short, Alceste follows closely the principles of the New Comedy, of the public mirror: his "reflection" concerns only "the manners of the time." This attempt at universality is, properly put, ridiculous. Oronte has exposed himself and explicitly demanded that his interlocutor describe him. This is their contract ("traité") (339). It should be obvious to Alceste that Oronte will apply the satire of a "ridicule et misérable auteur" (372) to himself and will recognize himself in the portrait, given the obvious resemblance.

"Do I write so poorly? Am I like them?" [Est-ce que j'écris mal? Et leur ressemblerais-je?] (361). With these words, Oronte poses the only natural question for the recipient of such a "generalized portrait." Three times Oronte rephrases the question "Do you mean me?" and three time Alceste's responds with the famous obfuscation, "I'm not saying that" [Je ne dis pas cela]. Alceste's repetition—the canonical example of the Bergsonian comic automatism—perfectly enacts the game of hide-and-seek of the satirist before his audience (and victim). In denying that his target is specific, and directly before him, Alceste places himself in an absurd position. The dissimulation is so obvious that he himself is forced to admit the personal nature of his remarks after three short interrogations by Oronte. He then brutally disposes with the third person (and the collective first-person plural) and shifts into the accusatory second person ("You've followed the worst models, / And your style is affected" [Vous vous êtes réglé sur de méchants modèles, / Et vos expressions ne sont point naturelles] (377–78). The failure of Alceste's strategy of indirect satire reminds us that a mirror is a place where one recognizes oneself. To believe otherwise is satiric folly. There is no safe, clean border between direct and indirect satire, between Old and New Comedy.

Alceste's bind is further complicated by the fact that his moral mission of correcting men—and miserable authors—demands that the targets of his railings recognize themselves in his barbs. For if Oronte does not see himself in the portrait of the ridiculous poet, if he does not see the resemblance, how will he know that he writes poorly? On the other hand, if Oronte sees himself "trait pour trait" in Alceste's biting description, he will necessarily take offense, consider his honor wounded, and see himself as a victim of slander. As such he will deny the validity of the portrait and then seek his revenge. In short, he will not take the moral medicine easily either way. If he does not recognize himself, it is the affair of others. If he does, it is an affair of honor, and like *les petits marquis,* he will simply strike back. Which he does. And Alceste's misfortune is here again drama's gain. For Oronte's attempt to reclaim his honor (through a special court) after Alceste's satirizing nicely acts to structure the play, creating the necessary obstacles in Alceste's path toward his goal of cornering Célimène. Once again, characters' representations and recognitions create dramatic conflict and drive the action of the comedy.

After *Le Misanthrope:* The Music Master and the Master of Farce

Neither Alceste nor Célimène find the correct balance of specificity and generality for the mirror they hold up to the world. Finding that balance is the satirist's victory; but the battle between satirist and satirized is a joyful spectacle, whichever side wins, Alceste or Oronte, Célimène or her fatuous admirers. And the fight between the two animates Molière's stage well after the battle of *Le Misanthrope* is over. Whether the moral function of satire emerges victorious from the interrogation of *Le Misanthrope* is a question to which I will return. But first I want to cast a glance over the second half of Molière's career, that which follows *Le Misanthrope,* in order to see the persistent hold exercised by the dynamics of depiction and recognition.

Obviously, those dynamics are most manifest in the comedy of manners, which Molière continued to produce after *Le Misanthrope.* In the last such play of his career, *Les Femmes savantes* (*The Learned Ladies,* 1672), Molière brilliantly reworks the indirect satire of the Alceste-Oronte exchange in a duel between two professional poets, Trissotin and Vadius. Placed in the middle of act 3, this important scene occupies the very center of the comedy. The exchange begins when Vadius asks his colleague to comment upon a poem he has just written, and which he is about to read to the company. Before the reading starts, though, Trissotin interjects with a flourish of outrageous flattery on Vadius's previous works; Vadius replies with equally exaggerated praise for Trissotin's verses. Then, just as Vadius begins reading his poem, Trissotin again interjects, asking his fellow poet if he had seen a certain anonymous sonnet circulating around town. The question, though seemingly innocuous, is in fact entirely self-interested: as one might expect from the vain poet, Trissotin is the author of the anonymous sonnet in question. Trissotin then explicitly verifies that Vadius is in total ignorance as to the sonnet's author, thus assuring that his opinion will be unbiased. Like Oronte, Trissotin wants a "sincere" reflection of his talents; like Oronte, he will find such an assessment deeply wounding:

TRISSOTIN: Vous en savez l'auteur?
VADIUS: Non: mais je sais fort bien
    Qu'à ne le point flatter son sonnet ne vaut rien.
      (III.iii.991–92)

TRISSOTIN: Do you know the author?
VADIUS: No, but I know quite well
    That, if truth be spoken, his sonnet is no good.

Once again, like Oronte, Trissotin attempts to counter a single instance of criticism with the praise he has received from others, from his absent peers; again the strategy fails.

TRISSOTIN: Beaucoup de gens pourtant le trouvent admirable.
VADIUS: Cela n'empêche pas qu'il ne soit misérable. (III.iii.993–94)

TRISSOTIN: Many people, though, find it admirable.
VADIUS: That does not stop it from being miserable.

After another protest by the poet, followed in turn by an equally withering remark on the sonnet, Trissotin ends the charade of anonymity, angrily declaring himself the author of the maligned poem. The former pretense to flattery thus effectively ended, the two enter into an exchange of insults as comically exaggerated as their previous mutual panegyrics. Like the Alceste-Oronte exchange, the scene ends with calls for revenge and the threat of a duel for honor—though this duel will be a farcically literary one in "verse, prose, Greek and Latin" at the booksellers (III.iii.1043).

These two scenes from *Le Misanthrope* and *Les Femmes savantes* both transform a dialogue of ridiculous social decorum into indecorous conflict; both dramatize the breakdown in social exchange brought about by honest appraisal—or by spleenful satire. But there is a crucial difference. Whereas Alceste intentionally obfuscates his criticism, consciously redirecting his criticism to an absent straw man, Vadius's indirect appraisal results from unconscious error. A third exchange would be useful to consider here: that between Arnolphe and Horace. Like Arnolphe, Trissotin must recognize himself in the words of his interlocutor; it is up to the victim here either to clarify the situation (by admitting that he is the maligned party) or to keep his interlocutor in error. The audience is regaled by the spectacle of a man who alone knows he is mocked and who must decide whether to end the error or prolong it out of shame. And like Horace mocking Monsieur de la Souche, Vadius enjoys indulging in some easy verbal sport, lulled by the specious security of scorning an absent target. However, the absent proves to be present. The anonymous poet, or the ridiculous old man, is never completely elsewhere, never entirely other. Vadius, like Horace and Célimène, learns this crucial lesson of satire: there is no security in mocking the absent, because satire cannot be directed with precision. There is no such thing as a safe audience.

The foolish complacency of the satirist is perhaps best captured in one of Molière's last farces, the 1671 *Fourberies de Scapin*. The scene pushes the dramaturgy of misdirected satire and comic self-recognition to an almost parodic intensity. It occurs in act 3, just after the trickster servant Scapin has performed his finest practical joke by alluring his master's old father, Géronte, into a bag, where he is beaten mercilessly. When Géronte emerges from the torture sack, he finds that, just as Scapin exits running, a young woman enters laughing furiously. Géronte immediately accuses the woman of laughing at him; she denies it sincerely:

ZERBINETTE: Ah! ah, ah, ah, la plaisante histoire! et la bonne dupe que ce vieillard!
GÉRONTE: Il n'y a rien de plaisant à cela; et vous n'avez que faire d'en rire.
ZERBINETTE: Quoi? Que voulez-vous dire, Monsieur?
GÉRONTE: Je veux dire que vous ne devez pas vous moquer de moi.
ZERBINETTE: De vous?
GÉRONTE: Oui.
ZERBINETTE: Comment? qui songe à se moquer de vous?
GÉRONTE: Pourquoi venez-vous ici me rire au nez?
ZERBINETTE: Cela ne vous regarde point, et je ris toute seule d'un conte qu'on vient de me faire. (2: 936–37; III.iii)

ZERBINETTE: Ha, ha, ha, what a funny story! What a fool that old man was!
GÉRONTE: There's nothing funny about it, and you have no right to laugh.
ZERBINETTE: What? What do you mean, sir?
GÉRONTE: I mean that you shouldn't mock me.
ZERBINETTE: You?
GÉRONTE: Yes.
ZERBINETTE: What? Who wants to mock you?
GÉRONTE: Why are you laughing in my face?
ZERBINETTE: It has nothing to do with you, and I'm laughing all by myself from a story someone just told me.

The codes of decorum are clearly established here: one cannot laugh "in the face" of people, and Zerbinette has no intention of doing so. However, overcome as she is with amusement at the story she has just heard, she begins to recount it to her listener, an act she justifies by "a natural itch to share every tale that [she] hears" [une démangeaison naturelle à faire part des contes que je sais]. Of course, in accordance with inevitable coincidences of comedy, the butt of her laughter will turn out to be no other than her listener. After denying quite sincerely that she is laughing at the old man, she proceeds to do just that, though she does not know it, because she does not know to whom she is speaking. Zerbinette, who foolishly does not ask the name of her new friend, relates the tale of Géronte's humiliation to Géronte himself. And, as in the case of Horace's unwitting mockery of Arnolphe, the mocker not only indulges in the most insulting language, but also blindly attempts to enlist the satirized in the fun. Molière milks her error for all the effects possible; here she introduces the central character—and laughingstock—of her tale:

> ZERBINETTE: . . . un père qui, quoique riche, est un avaricieux fieffé, le plus vilain homme du monde. Attendez. Ne me saurais-je souvenir de son nom? Haye! Aidez-moi un peu. Ne pouvez-vous me nommer quelqu'un de cette ville qui soit connu pour être avare au dernier point?
> GÉRONTE: Non.
> ZERBINETTE: Il y a à son nom du ron . . . ronte. Or . . . Oronte. Non. Gé . . . Géronte; oui, Géronte, justement; voilà mon vilain, je l'ai trouvé, c'est ce ladre-là que je dis. (2: 937–38; III.iii)

> ZERBINETTE: . . . a father, who, though rich, is a complete miser, the nastiest man in the world. Wait. Can't I remember his name? Oh . . . help me a little. Don't you know someone in this town whom everyone knows to be an outrageous miser?
> GÉRONTE: No.
> ZERBINETTE: His name has a *ronte* in it . . . Or . . . Oronte. No. Gé . . . Géronte; yes, Géronte, that's it; that's my nasty old miser, I found it, that's the tightwad I'm talking about.

This is just the kind of torture that Arnolphe suffered at the hands of Horace, with the young man's insistent questions and attempts at naming his subject ("de la Zousse, ou Source"). When Zerbinette relates the long story of Géronte's humiliation (a tale involving another of Scapin's tricks), we are faced with the same comedy of the mocked before his portrait, with the same theatrical gags. But there is a twist here. It is less the mocked that merits our laughter in this scene than the mocker. As Zerbinette blithely laughs throughout her tale at Géronte's misery, she digs her own grave, for she is one of Scapin's coconspirators against the old man—who, after all, has considerable power. The humor is less in the discomfiture of the scorned than in the folly of the reckless laugher who, "burning with desire to retell" her anecdote and mock an absent (2: 939; III.iv), finds herself before the worst audience possible: the mocked.

Read allegorically, these scenes from *Scapin* and *Les Femmes savantes* suggest that the security of the mocker is never assured; revenge will be extracted by the mocked. Vadius and Zerbinette scorn the absent only to find them present; their fault lies in a kind of satiric hubris. Indeed, Molière's later work abounds in such scenes of satirists undone by their own confidence, unwittingly laughing "in the face" of the powerful target of their scorn, only to curse their own cause. Such is the case of George Dandin, inadvertantly mocked to his face by a servant unaquainted with the master of the house (I.ii), or of Argan, brutally derided by a wife who thinks him dead and who seizes on the occasion to deliver a graphic portrait of her husband's grotesque personal demeanor (*Le Malade imaginaire* III.xii). But can we conclude from such scenes that Molière's own confidence in satiric laughter has entirely collapsed in the aftermath of *Le Misanthrope*? I think not. For while these scenes demonstrate perfectly the comedy of the satirist caught by his own audience, there are other, more skillful masters in mockery in Molière's later plays. Furthermore, these skillful portrayers exercise their arts in scenes typical of the dramatic style of the later works—one with music, the other with physical farce. In particular, scenes from *Le Malade Imaginaire* and *L'Avare* not only offer exemplary models of effectively presenting a mirror to one's own audience, but also elaborate important dramatic variants on the dynamics of depiction and recognition.

Molière's last play, *Le Malade imaginaire* (*The Imaginary Invalid,* 1673), presents his most ingenious metatheatrical construction, a favorite device in his later work, as Georges Forestier has shown. The play in the play is the work of a young suitor, Cléante, seeking to communicate with his beloved, Angélique, despite the tyrannical opposition of her father, the imaginary invalid Argan. In order to do so, he feigns the role of the music master of Angélique and undertakes to perform a little piece with her before an assembled company including not only Argan, but also Argan's choice for his daughter, a pedantic young doctor, Thomas Diafoirus. The "little impromptu opera" takes the highly conventional form of a pastoral romance, but one whose plot perfectly reflects the situation in which the young lovers find themselves: the performance depicts a young shepherd who is prevented from wedding his beloved due to the opposition of a heartless father who has chosen another future son-in-law. Thus every figure in the "little opera" represents in pastoral guise either one of the performers (Cléante or Angélique) or one of the spectators (Argan or Diafoirus). The goal of the performance is simple: to allow the performers to freely exchange their love vows in the only manner open to them, by singing publicly. The danger of the performance is equally simple: the performers must mask the musical performance effectively enough to prevent the audience from recognizing themselves in their pastoral "impromptu." The problem is that the closer the lovers come to attaining their goal, that is, to speaking directly to each other about their current plight, the closer they come to revealing the secret of the play, to revealing that it is nothing but a musical depiction of themselves and their listeners.

I return briefly here to a comparison with Shakespeare's Elsinore. Cléante's aims in having a play performed differ crucially from Hamlet's: Molière's lovers want to stage a perfect, if allegorical, recreation of the situation before them, yes; but, on the other hand, the last thing they want for that recreation to do is to "catch the conscience" of their chief viewer—the father. In order to avoid stirring up an inkling of self-recognition in his viewers, Cléante carefully uses the two most powerful tools at his disposal: generality and conventionality. In terms of generality, he is careful to give the father no name and no distinguishing marks, and yet to make quite clear it is Argan in question. In other words, Cléante avoids Célimène's mistake of attaching names to her portraits in her letters, or Zerbinette's carelessness in not tailoring her story to her audience. In terms of conventionality, he masks the operatic recreation in the most banal of theatrical genres and plots, the tale of a star-crossed shepherd and shepherdess. The very clichés of the lyrics sung make the entire little opera so insipid that accusations of a hidden agenda against the music master would almost seem preposterous: it is clearly just good old-fashioned fun. Cléante thus effectively creates a mirror, the universality and hackneyed gimmickry of which make it nearly impervious to assault from the susceptible.

Nevertheless, Argan comes to suspect the truth and to identify too well his own role in the opera. He thus interrupts the performance with the kind of indignant sense of self-recognition that occurred in the Parisian theater houses. As the pastoral lovers sing their vows to each other in front of the shepherd-father, Argan's frustration with the performance breaks forth:

ARGAN: Et que dit le père à tout cela?

CLÉANTE: Il ne dit rien.

ARGAN: Voilà un sot père que ce père-là, de souffrir toutes ces sottises-là
sans rien dire. . . . Non, non, en voilà assez. Cette comédie-là est de fort
mauvais exemple. (2: 1139; II.v)

ARGAN: And what does the father say to all this?

CLÉANTE: He says nothing.

ARGAN: Then he's a foolish father, to bear all this mischief without saying anything. . . . No, no, that's enough of this. This play sets a very bad
example.

As was the case with reaction to *Tartuffe,* Argan's moral outrage at the
lovers' play (it "sets a very bad example") is provoked first and foremost by
his painful sense of identification with the character on stage, in this case,
with a father whose weakness and paralysis provides a repugnant reflection
on Argan's own character. But despite the premature end to his little opera,
Cléante effectively achieved his aims. He managed to recite publicly a
lengthy plot description that denigrates the "ridiculous" rival and denounces the cruelty of the father; above all, he was able to make the meaning of the representation fully apparent to his privileged audience, Angélique. If Argan finally caught on to the game, he still cannot pin down
Cléante: Cléante can hide behind the generality of the character portrayed
(who remains a generic "father," even in Argan's angry words) and the conventionality of the theatrical entertainment. When told to end the performance, Cléante has the perfect justification for his actions: "I thought I
was entertaining you" [J'ai cru vous divertir]. This, after all, is the defense
that Molière himself takes on so many occasions when faced with wrathful
spectators. And it is an effective one. The angry audience members who
respond, as Argan does, that "such foolish things never entertain" [les sot-
tises ne divertissent point] automatically qualify themselves as simple
cranks, as spectators who are ridiculously susceptible if not pathologically
paranoid.

It should now be apparent that, if in the years after *Le Misanthrope,*
Molière devoted so much energy to developing such amusements as the
comédie-ballet, these theatrical experiments hardly signal a weariness with
his old preoccupations with the dynamics of depiction. This scene from
Le Malade imaginaire proves, quite to the contrary, that Molière instead
employed his increasing preoccupation with music and dance in order to
enrich the dramatic possibilities of representation and recognition. And in
so doing he also found new ways to retread the old apology of every satirist
under fire: "I thought I was entertaining you."

What, though, of the moral effects of recognition? They seem glaringly absent from this scene; Argan remains fundamentally impervious to self-questioning. Can we assume then, as Defaux has argued, that in these later works the corrective power of depiction is absent and that Molière focuses instead on the pure pleasure of laughter? The answer may be found in a scene in which Molière fully dramatizes the moral stakes of satire, and dramatizes them in the most energetic and physical form possible: in pure farce. The scene is from the 1669 *L'Avare*. Harpagon, the eponymous miser of the play, has just accused a servant, La Flèche, of filching; he then begins searching for stolen goods in the pockets of the valet, who, outraged, curses the master. But La Flèche curses Harpagon in the most general terms. And that generality is his protection against the master's wrath.

> LA FLÈCHE: La peste soit de l'avarice et des avaricieux!
> HARPAGON: Comment? que dis-tu?
> LA FLÈCHE: Ce que je dis?
> HARPAGON: Oui: qu'est-ce que tu dis d'avarice et des avaricieux?
> LA FLÈCHE: Je dis que la peste soit de l'avarice et des avaricieux.
> HARPAGON: De qui veux-tu parler?
> LA FLÈCHE: Des avaricieux. (2: 522–23; I.iii)

> LA FLÈCHE: A pox on stinginess and misers!
> HARPAGON: What? What are you saying?
> LA FLÈCHE: What am I saying?
> HARPAGON: Yes, what are you saying about stinginess and misers?
> LA FLÈCHE: I say a pox on stinginess and misers.
> HARPAGON: And who do you mean?
> LA FLÈCHE: Misers.

It is important to remember the farcical vibrancy of this exchange. Harpagon can brutally strike La Flèche at any moment—with his hands, with a stick, or with a lash, depending on the performance; indeed, the physical dynamics of the scene will soon be explicit in the language. The scene is a game played out between the impertinence of a servant and the ire of a master, a game in which only one can win. The rules are quite clear. The servant must not personalize his remarks, and the master must not incriminate himself. Both parties (and the audience) know that La Flèche is speaking of Harpagon. However, as long as he keeps his remarks as a general moral denunciation against an indefensible group—misers—Harpagon cannot punish him, that is to say, he cannot strike him. For if Harpagon were to do so, he would admit identifying himself as a member of the group in question. We return to Uranie's public mirror here: to recognize oneself in the reflection is to confess to the sin reflected. Harpagon there-fore provokes La Flèche, attempting to force the servant to specify his tar-get; after all, once La Flèche names the master, the master may strike him. The wily servant, however, understands that he can goad the master in the most outrageous terms, so long as the mirror remains "public" and not private. La Flèche is such a master of the game that he may joyfully employ the most abusive language, while still not feeling the strike of the stick or the lash. He furthermore invites Harpagon to admit his own incriminating self-recognition, though the master is not so foolish as to do so. Thus the game is played out:

> HARPAGON: Et qui sont-ils ces avaricieux?
> LA FLÈCHE: Des vilains et des ladres.
> HARPAGON: Mais qui est-ce que tu entends par là?
> LA FLÈCHE: De quoi vous mettez-vous en peine?
> HARPAGON: Je me mets en peine de ce qu'il faut.
> LA FLÈCHE: Est-ce que vous croyez que je veux parler de vous?
> HARPAGON: Je crois ce que je crois; mais je veux que tu me dises à qui tu
> parles quand tu dis cela.
> LA FLÈCHE: Je parle . . . je parle à mon bonnet.
> HARPAGON: Et moi, je pourrais bien parler à ta barrette.
> LA FLÈCHE: M'empêcherez-vous de maudire les avaricieux?
> HARPAGON: Non, mais je t'empêcherai de jaser, et d'être insolent. Tais-toi.
> LA FLÈCHE: Je ne nomme personne.
> HARPAGON: Je te rosserai, si tu parles.
> LA FLÈCHE: Qui se sent morveux, qu'il se mouche.
> HARPAGON: Te tairas-tu?
> LA FLÈCHE: Oui, malgré moi. (2: 523; I.ii)

> HARPAGON: And who are these misers?
> LA FLÈCHE: Greedy scoundrels.
> HARPAGON: But whom do you mean by that?
> LA FLÈCHE: What are you worried about?
> HARPAGON: I'm worried about whatever I want to be worried about.
> LA FLÈCHE: Is it that you think I'm talking about you?
> HARPAGON: I think what I think; but I want to know to whom you're
> speaking when you say that.
> LA FLÈCHE: I'm speaking . . . I'm speaking to my hat.
> HARPAGON: And I can speak straight to your skull!
> LA FLÈCHE: Are you forbidding me to curse misers?
> HARPAGON: No, I'm forbidding you to blabber and to be insolent. Be quiet!
> LA FLÈCHE: I name no one.
> HARPAGON: I'll give you a lashing if you speak.

LA FLÈCHE: If the shoe fits . . .
HARPAGON: Will you be quiet?
LA FLÈCHE: Yes, despite myself.

"I name no one," says the master moralist, asserting generality at the same time that he successfully targets his own listener. How much more effective is his response than the "I'm not saying that" [Je ne dis pas cela] employed by Alceste in an identical situation! La Flèche benefits here from a sense of brazen irony ("Is it that you think I'm talking about you?") and playful obfuscation ("I'm speaking to my hat") that makes him a much more fitting alter ego to the sly Molière than Alceste could ever be.

To sum up, La Flèche is a kind of a fantasy figure for the vexed Molière. The valet mocks his target with impunity: he exits laughing, without a lashing. But this fantasy is not so far from reality. Molière, also an entertainer and fool, a servant to the Paris public and the court, can likewise win his game with his targets, even if he must play his cards carefully, as does La Flèche. How can the playwright emerge victoriously? In the case of *L'Avare,* Molière exploits not the pacifying amusements of music and dance (as he does in *Le Bourgeois gentilhomme* or *Le Malade imaginaire*), but instead the time-tested comic gimmicks and plot devices of the play's source, Plautus's *Aulularia.* And by adapting the Roman comedy to the French stage, Molière can effectively lay claim to the kind of moral nonspecificity that serves La Flèche so well. If an original creation like *Les Précieuses ridicules* or *Le Misanthrope* presents itself inevitably as a mirror to current life, the reworking of the ancient comic figure of the miser would seem to suggest no such aim. And yet this scene reminds us that, no matter how generic or universal the depiction, certain audience members will inevitably pose Harpagon's question: "And who are these misers?" The adoption of the most ancient plots and the most stereotypical characters will not impede the spectators' desire for a recognition of the immediate. Instead, the return to Latin sources here simply provides a new arena for the same exchange between the satirist and his public. In this case, that exchange is pared down to its essential elements; it is theatrically concentrated in the duel between the figure of the satirized, Harpagon, who wiggles uncomfortable between incriminating self-identification and the unbearable humiliation of continuing scorn, and his satirist, La Flèche, who, threatened constantly by the suspended stick of the listener's wrath, effectively dodges each thrust with all the wiles of indirect mockery.

To return to the concern of moral effects, there is no doubt that La

Flèche forces Harpagon to confront his own nature via his own sense of self-identification in the servant's scorn. However, any corrective effects resulting from this recognition are entirely absent from the scene, and indeed the play: La Flèche escapes punishment but Harpagon hardly reforms. Where is the lesson learned? Where is the medicine of mockery? To answer, I return to the master of satiric portraiture, Célimène, and examine a scene in which the dynamics of depiction and recognition are dramatized in a much more elaborate framework, one shaped by the a highly refined social art of observation and character assassination.

Fourteen

STAGING SOCIAL COMMERCE

Observing Other Observers

The verbal satires of Alceste, Célimène, and Arsinoé are not simply reflexive signs pointing out the comic author's hand, the equivalent of depicting paint brushes and canvasses in a painting; they are part of a faithful depiction of current manners. In fact, while the play only implicitly associates Célimène's satires with the playwright's, it quite explicitly links Célimène's artful *médisance* to current social practices. As Philinte says of Célimène:

> [L]'humeur coquette et l'esprit médisant
> Semblent si fort donner dans les moeurs d'à présent. (I.i.219–20)

> The coquettish air and malicious wit [esprit médisant]
> Are entirely typical of the manners of today.

Alceste too links Célimène's satires to the tastes of her peers, tastes that he decries in addressing her entourage:

> Son humeur satirique est sans cesse nourrie
> Par le coupable encens de votre flatterie;
> Et son coeur à railler trouverait moins d'appas,
> S'il avait observé qu'on ne l'applaudit pas. (II.iv.661–64)

> Her satiric penchant is continually fed
> By your noxious flattery;
> And she would find it less attractive to mock others,
> If she had not seen that you applaud it.

The reference to applause of course advances the parallel between Célimène's salon and comic theater; but the thrust of Alceste's remarks is to link her satires to a strategy of social success, of pleasing current tastes. Ironically enough, this kind of commentary on the fashionable practice of criticizing the other is also voiced by Célimène herself, despite her incontestable penchant for censuring her peers. Such is the gist of her portrait of Damis:

> Depuis que dans la tête il s'est mis d'être habile,
> Rien ne touche son goût, tant il est difficile;
> Il veut voir des défauts à tout ce qu'on écrit,
> Et pense que louer n'est pas d'un bel esprit. . . .
> . . . Aux conversations même il trouve à reprendre. (II.iv.637–46)

> Since he got it in his head to be so clever
> Nothing suits his taste, he's so demanding;
> He must criticize everything newly written,
> And thinks that a wit never praises anything. . . .
> . . . He's become a critic even of conversations.

Célimène ties Damis's censuring to current customs: he thinks that criticizing others is the only way to merit the social distinction of being a "wit" [un bel esprit], however dubious that distinction may be. Indeed, even Alceste's misanthropic railing can be linked to this social competition for distinction. "I want to be esteemed for my worth" [Je veux qu'on me distingue], he declares (I.i.63). As has been often noted, this statement places Alceste in a hypocritical position.[1] While he claims to disdain humanity in general, it is among his peers he must seek his precious distinction. Of course, this distinction is predicated on the will of the other (the indefinite *"on"*), on his faceless peers who judge him. Ironically, Alceste submits himself here to same social peers that he generally decries, as he does when he laments "today people praise everybody" [on loue aujourd'-hui tout le monde] (III.v.1069). Célimène herself asserts that Alceste's mania for reproving is above all a claim to superiority inherently dependent on social exchange: he "would fear appearing too common / If he was of the same opinion as someone else" [penserait paraître un homme du commun / Si l'on voyait qu'il fût de l'avis de quelqu'un] (II.iv.675–76). Alceste's censuring, like Damis's and Célimène's, is thus motivated by his concern for his "appearance" before his peers, with whom he is locked in

---

1. Lionel Gossman thoroughly examines Alceste's bad faith concerning his relationship to the social world in *Men and Masks:* Alceste "dreams of constituting himself as a one-man society. . . . But Alceste can only dream. He would dearly love to annihilate all those whose existence is the principal obstacle to his own absolute supremacy, but he cannot annihilate them, and he cannot ignore them, *because it is only through them he can hope to experience the superiority he desires for himself"* (85, emphasis added).

a battle for superior merit . . . in the eyes of others. His protests notwith-
standing, Alceste is profoundly engaged in the social dynamics of representation.

Of course, though they are driven by similar motivations, our social
censors have their differences. Damis's and Célimène's "humeur satirique"
is turned primarily to aesthetic questions: others' conversational abilities,
wit, poetic pretensions. On the other hand, Alceste's censuring is turned
to moral questions such as sincerity, fairness, virtue. But Alceste is not
alone here. This role of self-appointed moral critic is notably shared by
another character in the play: Arsinoé. Here again, Célimène offers us a
keen analysis: in a stunning portrait of the prude, she thoroughly unmasks
the social strategy behind Arsinoé's censorious discourse:

> [S]on triste mérite, abandonné de tous,
> Contre le siècle aveugle est toujours en courroux.
> Elle tâche à couvrir d'un faux voile de prude
> Ce que chez elle on voit d'affreuse solitude. (III.iii.859–62)

> Seeing her lonely merits forgotten by everyone,
> She is in a rage against this blind age of ours.
> She tries to cover up, with a mask of prudish virtue,
> What everyone knows to be her loveless solitude.

For Arsinoé, reprimanding the other is principally a matter of self-representation before the world. Her unkind portraits of others' behavior are
designed to portray herself in a positive light, that of a moral beacon.

Taken together, the above commentaries by Philinte, Alceste, and Célimène on others' "satiric penchants" and censoriousness demonstrate how
well the characters understand the underpinnings of the social commerce
of representation. Furthermore, their lucidity is not limited to their analysis of critical tongues. They also understand the motivations behind the
fawning depictions that proliferate in social exchange. Flattery is subjected
to the character's skeptical analysis from the opening lines of the play,
where it is unmasked as social artifice, as "that cowardly habit / Affected
by most fashionable people" [cette lâche méthode / Qu'affecte la plupart
de vos gens à la mode] (I.i.41–42). Whether it be *médisance* or flattery,
conversational depictions are regularly dissected and deflated by their
wary audiences.

However, characters do not always analyze so critically others' observations and judgments; often they simply repeat them. Individuals assume
the voice of the social group at large and echo its representations of other
individuals. In short, Molière's characters consciously ventriloquize the

talk of the town. This reiteration of common opinion is one of the standard strategies of flattery. It consists of portraying the other according to the portrait of them already in circulation in the world. Arsinoé well exploits this echoing of flattery in approaching Alceste:

> Un mérite éclatant se déterre lui-même;
> Du vôtre, en bien des lieux, *on fait un cas extrême;*
> Et vous saurez de moi qu'en deux fort bons endroits
> *Vous fûtes hier loué par des gens* d'un grand poids. (III.v.1065–68; emphasis added)

> Brilliant virtues shine forth on their own;
> And everywhere *people make much of yours;*
> And I will tell you that in two very considerable places
> *You were praised yesterday by people* of important weight.

Citing the "world" is a common strategy of self-representation as well. When Oronte fails to solicit the admiration he expects from Alceste concerning his sonnet, he echoes the very same expression employed by Arsinoé: "It is enough for me that *other people make much of it*" [Il me suffit de voir que *d'autres en font cas*] (I.ii.421; emphasis added). The *petit marquis* Acaste pushes this strategy to the limit. When praising himself, he relies heavily on authoritative citations of the world's view of his person:

> Pour le coeur, dont sur tout nous devons faire cas,
> *On sait,* sans vanité, que je n'en manque pas,
> Et, *l'on m'a vu* pousser, dans le monde, une affaire
> D'une assez vigoureuse et gaillarde manière. (III.i.787–90; emphasis added)

> As for courage, our most precious quality,
> I must say without vanity, *people know* I have it,
> And *I have been seen* handling an affair of honor
> In a most cool and forceful manner.

When Acaste observes himself, he observes the others who observe him; his self-portrait is really a portrait from their imagined perspective, narrated in the first person.

Consider here the larger issue of the theatrical rhetoric of vision and its relation to the dynamics of social interobservation.[2] The use of "voir" (to see) in verbal constructions (of the type "I have been seen") is typical

---

2. For a fine analysis of the rhetoric and psychology of self-vision, see Mitchell Greenberg on *Tartuffe* (113–40). I will return later to Dandrey's important moral perspective on vision in *Molière, ou l'esthétique du ridicule.*

of conversation in the closed world of *mondanité* and an effect widely exploited in Molière's social satires, beginning with *Les Précieuses*. La Grange presents his situation from the perspective of an outside viewer, that of *le monde:* "Has one ever seen . . . two men treated with more scorn than us" [A-t-on jamais vu . . . deux hommes traités avec plus de mépris que nous?], he asks Du Croisy (1: 265–66; sc. 1). Pierre Force has justly qualified Molière's characters' tendency to become "spectators of themselves" as a sign of madness: alienated figures such as Arnolphe and Argan do not understand that they are in reality actors rather than spectators of their own drama.[3] But what is folly in some is a wisdom in others; those who know they are actors in the world also understand that they are being watched by others. That is why the language of observation is not limited to a fatuous Acaste or a self-blind Arnolphe, but also practiced by the clear-sighted La Grange and by the very canny Célimène.

Of course, the repeated use of the periphrastic *voir* is not a particularity of Molière's theater, but in fact a general characteristic of classical French drama. Leo Spitzer has catalogued the utilization of *voir* as one of the defining traits of Racine's stylistic muting, his "piano effect." However, in addition to this attenuating effect, Spitzer notes the more active sense of the use of "voir," one that stresses the social dynamic at play between characters: "Instead of saying 'j'ai fait / il a fait,' Racine often puts 'tu m'as / il m'a vu faire.' The speaker gives his experience or action of the self (or the other), but as it is seen by or reflected in the mind of a hearer. It is an expressive devise, which is admittedly social." (37)

It seems to me that in this respect Molière's theater acts as a parody, even a travesty, of tragic visibility. Jean Starobinski's seminal analysis of sight in French tragedy can help illuminate the comic deformations of Acaste's self-portrait. Starobinski remarks that the tragic hero acts in order to be seen, in order to become himself "an eternally brilliant spectacle" (un éblouissement impérissable") in the eyes of others. The hero

> s'offre triomphant aux yeux de l'univers. Son plus haut bonheur ne consiste isolément ni dans l'acte de *voir,* ni même dans l'énergie du *faire:* il est dans l'acte complexe de *faire voir.* (*Oeil* 18; emphasis in original)

> offers himself to the eyes of the universe. His greatest happiness consists not simply in the act of *seeing* nor in the energy of *making or doing:* it is instead in the complex act of *making seen.*

---

3. This particular comic species "ne reconnaît pas d'abord cette situation: il n'est pas un spectateur, mais un personnage parmi d'autres personnages" (42).

Acaste's own efforts to make himself seen and to see himself being seen are then, at least in part, a derisive burlesque of the visual glory of Cornelian heroism. But at the same time, such a scene is much more than a farcical travesty of tragic rhetoric. Acaste's own version of the heroic ideal of visibility is in fact quite justified, even lucid, in Molière's world, where all eyes are turned toward the other, and toward oneself through others' eyes. An understanding of the period's mechanisms of social interobservation gives new meaning to Starobinsky's view of French classical tragedy: it is a drama where "the gaze supplants theatrical action . . . [and] becomes the essence of theatrical action" [*le regard* supplante la gesticulation théâtrale . . . il devient l'acte par excellence] (19).[4] It seems to me clear that the social dynamic that creates a "comédie d'observation," such as *Le Misanthrope*—one lacking precisely in physical comedy—exercises its power over the contemporary tragic stage as well. But whereas in tragedy one views (and watches the others viewing) personal grandeur, comedy explores the eyes' fascination with superficial merits and ridiculous faults.

The Célimène-Arsinoé Duel

What the world observes, and how it depicts what it observes, is the subject of the scene that occupies the very center of *Le Misanthrope*'s five acts: the duel between Arsinoé and Célimène in act 3. The duel presents the most complex and troubling intertwining of characters' voices and gazes as they intermingle not only with each other but also with the whispers of the world swirling outside their little salon—and beyond the theater stage enclosing it. Indeed, we can hear in Célimène and Arsinoé's dialogue the voices of the theater public and of Molière himself.

Just before Arsinoé enters the stage, Célimène prepares us for the face off with a biting verbal portrait of her visitor. Célimène attributes Arsinoé's

---

4. "Dans le théâtre français classique . . . les gestes tendent à disparaître. Au profit du langage, a-t-on dit. Il faut ajouter: au profit du regard. Si les personnages ne s'étreignent ni ne se frappent sur la scène, en revanche, ils se voient. Les scènes, chez Racine, sont des entrevues. Les personnes du drame se parlent et s'entre-regardent"(74). Though Starobinski refers here to the theater in general, his study is limited to Corneille and Racine. His essay "Sur la flatterie" does, however, suggest what such vision-based reading might offer *Le Misanthrope*. Starobinski here places Alceste in a social context characterized by a "forte composante narcissique" (62), a world where every individual is both "le *sujet* qui juge, et l'*objet* jugé" (63), and where each person seeks to be assured "qu'il est *vu* de tous, et bien vu; que tous *parlent* de lui, et pour en dire du bien" (73; emphasis in original). Starobinski neatly suggests the parallel between the visual mirror of this society (one observes how one is seen by others) and the verbal mirror (one hears how others describe one). Stylistically, this leads to the kinds of periphrasis present in the repetitions of the world's judgment: what one says you are ("Vous fûtes hier loué") and what others see you as ("On voit que . . . ").

censoriousness to a hypocritical desire to mask her bitter lovelessness. According to Célimène, Arsinoé's judgments are motivated purely by personal envy. Ironically enough, though, Célimène's remarks put in serious doubt the impartiality and moral value of her own censure of Arsinoé. When Célimène delivers her portrait with typical brilliance before Acaste and Clitandre, she reveals to the spectator her own personal purpose in censuring: she does so first and foremost to please her present audience of the two *marquis*. If Célimène's efforts at seduction through witty mockery were not enough to deflate the value of her little satire, the arrival of Arsinoé in mid-portrait brutally highlights Célimène's insincerity—though her insincerity is dictated here by the rules of politeness and not by personal perfidy. Célimène quite correctly never satirizes her subjects in person. Thus when Arsinoé appears through the door, Célimène shifts instantly from slander to praise, revealing the depths of her own hypocrisy in the matter of censuring—the very fault for which she has just as she attacked Arsinoé. This hypocrisy is dramatized by the radical shift in tone in mid-verse as Célimène rails against Arsinoé:

> Enfin je n'ai rien vu de si sot à mon gré,
> Elle est impertinente au suprême degré,
> Et . . . [Arsinoé enters]
>   Ah! Quel heureux sort en ce lieu vous amène?
> Madame, sans mentir, j'étais de vous en peine. (III.iii–iv.871–74)

> In short I really don't think I've seen anyone so foolish,
> She is impertinent beyond belief,
> And . . . (*Arsinoé enters*)
>   Ah! What happy fate brings you here?
> Madam, I was truly just speaking of my concern for you.

Célimène, to her great credit, transforms hypocrisy into art. In a single beat, she metamorphoses the duplicity of indirect censure into irony. In this case the irony is exquisite: Célimène manipulates the ambiguity of the word "concern" [peine], in order to affirm—no doubt before her still present audience of Acaste and Clitandre—that she is an artist at suggesting the opposite of what she says. Her irony is further heightened by the expression "truly" [sans mentir]. With this claim, Célimène draws attention to the presence of a clear cleavage in her voice, one typical of all social intercourse. On the one hand, it is understood that her salutation —like all such salutations—is a prefabricated formula of polite language, an automatism of civility. On the other, she recognizes that her voice can serve as an expression of her true sentiments, free of the demands of politeness.

By employing the emphatic "truly," Célimène claims these two voices (polite automatism and sincere feeling) speak in happy unison. Why does she make such a wildly false claim? Perhaps in part she is artfully drawing attention to a bit of honesty in her words. If there is any sincerity in Célimène's expression, it is in the possible pun on the word "concern": that is, on her satiric concern with Arsinoé in the previous conversation, rather than on any friendly concern about her or desire to see her. But above all, the "truly" is a simple act of bravado, of intensifying the irony of her greeting by commenting on its content: the expression is to be read by her audience as a signpost to the extravagance of her untruth. We can imagine the little "audience" for Célimène's bravado, the departing Clitandre and Acaste, delighting in her performance. Indeed, the 1734 edition of *Le Misanthrope* includes the following stage direction after this short exchange, "Clitandre and Acaste exit laughing." Célimène has pulled off her act brilliantly.

But the marquis are not the only audience for Célimène. Célimène performs also for Arsinoé, as does Arsinoé for Célimène. In the following duel they exercise their irony with skill one for another and brandish it openly at times. Arsinoé is the first speaker. Her strategy in irony is the following: She wishes to humiliate Célimène with a biting reproach; yet this kind of direct censure is nearly impossible in the social framework at hand. Therefore, in order to blunt the directness of her discourse, she uses indirect discourse, that is, she repeats what others say. Her irony is in pretending that the voice she carries is the voice of the world, not her own, and that she somehow disagrees with it.

> Je viens, par un avis qui touche votre honneur,
> Témoigner l'amitié que pour vous a mon coeur.
> Hier j'étais chez des gens de vertu singulière,
> Où sur vous du discours on tourna la matière;
> Et là, votre conduite, avec ses grands éclats,
> Madame, eut le malheur qu'on ne la loua pas.
> Cette foule de gens dont vous souffrez visite,
> Votre galanterie, et les bruits qu'elle excite
> Trouvèrent des censeurs plus qu'il n'aurait fallu,
> Et bien plus rigoureux que je n'eusse voulu.
> Vous pouvez bien pensez quel parti je sus prendre:
> Je fis ce que je pus pour vous pouvoir défendre. (III.iv.883–94)

> I have come with some information touching your honor
> To show all the friendship I have for you.
> Yesterday I was at the home of some most virtuous people,

When the subject of conversation came to you,
At which point your extraordinary conduct,
Madam, suffered the misfortune of not being praised.
All these people you receive,
Your coquetry and the rumors it provokes
Were more censured than they should have been,
And my friends were much more severe than I would have liked.
You can well imagine what side I took:
I did all I could to defend you.

Arsinoé's strategy of obscuring the path of communication in order to better attack her victim is part of what we have now seen to be a common technique of moralists, whether they be wily like La Flèche or stern like Alceste. It is of course the comparison to the latter that interests us here. Although Alceste claims to be above such civil insincerity, he too seeks a way of softening his criticism before Oronte. I return here to the second scene of the play, this time to fully weigh the social consequences of Alceste's position in confronting the amateur poet. Like Arsinoé, Alceste, well aware of the dangers of a direct condemnation of a social equal, pretends not to speak directly to his interlocutor. He too, like Arsinoé, does so by citing previous judgments from past conversations. Alceste's strategy differs, though, in one respect from that of Arsinoé. Arsinoé pretends that it is not her voice that criticizes Célimène, but the others' voices. She appropriates a social substitute as *the speaker*. Alceste, on the other hand, hides in no way that it is he who speaks with his full heart; instead, he simply pretends, like La Flèche, it is not his listener that he criticizes. He appropriates a social substitute as *the addressee*. So it is that he avoids censuring Oronte directly:

Monsieur, cette matière est toujours délicate,
Et sur le bel esprit nous aimons qu'on nous flatte.
Mais un jour, à quelqu'un, dont je tairai le nom,
Je disais, en voyant des vers de sa façon,
Qu'il faut qu'un galant homme ait toujours grand empire
Sur les démangeaisons qui nous prennent d'écrire. (I.ii.341–46)

Sir, these matters are most delicate,
And we all want to have our wit and style flattered.
But, the other day, to someone whose name I'll not mention,
I said, when I saw his own verses,
That we gentlemen should always restrain ourselves
When the itch to write overtakes us.

Critics have generally dismissed Arsinoé's and Alceste's references here to other conversations as simple polite fictions permitting delicate criticism.[5] Perhaps these past conversations are indeed pure fictions. But far from being visibly rhetorical fictions, they are above all *credible* fictions. Indeed, in a society so devoted to constantly appraising, and condemning, its members, if these previous conversations didn't take place, they should have. And, in fact, they already have taken place in the preceding action of the play. Arsinoé's "fictional" conversation reproving Célimène recalls the opening discussion of the play where her coquettish behavior is faulted. Philinte has already censured Célimène's "galanterie," and her "humeur coquette." Alceste as well condemns her faults not only in this opening scene, but will do so again in the fourth act. Most striking, though, is the fact that the play ends with the promise of her admirers to spread her "glorieux portrait" throughout the town and court, recreating in the future endless repetitions of the exchange that Arsinoé has cited, where the subject turns cruelly on Célimène's conduct. It is apparent then that even if Arsinoé's specific citation, like Alceste's, should be an invention, in the general perspective of salon society, it is still profoundly accurate. Anything bad about someone has surely already been said: social censure is always repetition.

We can draw two important conclusions from Arsinoé's veiled attack. First, the rhetorical use of indirect discourse demonstrates once again the social dangers of criticizing one's peers, and the character's knowledge of this danger. However, the essential duplicity of social discourse (one attacks the absent, one praises the present) proves a source of rhetorical richness in speech. The art of indirection allows *médisance* to confront its victim; the veiling of the speaker's voice allows battle by subterfuge. Second, the specific choice of the evasive tactic—the citation of a previous conversation—emphasizes the rich layering of social commerce in the play. The voice of the character resonantly echoes an endless series of voices from other social gatherings—those that took place yesterday, those taking place elsewhere now, those that will take place after the scene is finished. The mirrors held by the characters, each reflecting one another, are in fact mirrors of the mirror of the world. The voice of the character is a permutation

---

5. Brody is one of the few critics to remark on this odd similarity in Arsinoé's and Alceste's strategies of attack, but he has limited his analysis to the desire shared by both to stay within the limits of "politesse" by clothing their criticisms "in a conventional fiction" (572–73). In another major analysis of the Arsinoé-Célimène duel, Guicharnaud stretches the "conventional fiction" aspect of Arsinoé's rhetoric to the point of identifying it as a recourse to allegory. The critic evokes her strategy of dissimulation in these terms: "Ce n'est pas Arsinoé qui parle, c'est la Vertu incarnée allégoriquement dans un groupe de sages" (426).

of the voice of the world, of the voices of the characters not seen on stage, of the world that stretches far beyond the stage, beyond the audience into the streets and salons of Paris.

Arsinoé's strategies of indirection accomplish their goal. Célimène is wounded. But she quickly devises her response, one that outdoes even Arsinoé's most arch irony. Célimène's replicates Arsinoé's strategy. But Célimène doubles her framing devices, for she couches her own use of indirect discourse in a parody of Arsinoé's speech:

> Madame, j'ai beaucoup de grâces à vous rendre:
> Un tel avis m'oblige, et loin de le mal prendre,
> J'en prétends reconnaître, à l'instant, la faveur,
> Pour un avis aussi qui touche votre honneur;
> Et comme je vous vois vous montrer mon amie
> En m'apprenant les bruits que de moi l'on publie,
> Je veux suivre, à mon tour, un exemple si doux,
> En vous avertissant de ce qu'on dit de vous.
> En un lieu, l'autre jour, où je faisais visite,
> Je trouvai quelques gens d'un très rare mérite
> Qui, parlant des vrais soins d'une âme qui vit bien,
> Firent tomber sur vous, Madame, l'entretien.
> Là, votre pruderie et vos éclats de zèle
> Ne furent pas cités comme un fort bon modèle. (913–26)

> Madam, I have much to thank you for:
> I'm grateful for this information, and far from taking it poorly,
> I would like to pay back immediately the favor
> With some information also touching your honor.
> And as I see you show your friendship for me
> By instructing me about what people say about me,
> I would like to follow, in turn, such a sweet example,
> By telling you what people say about you.
> At a certain place the other day where I was making a visit,
> I met some most respected people
> Who, when speaking of true and profound virtue,
> Let the conversation fall, madam, on you.
> At which point, your prudery and your showy religious zeal
> Were not cited as a model to follow.

It is at this point that Célimène outstrips Arsinoé's attack and proceeds with a twenty-line portrait of the prude, plumbing the depths of her misery, envy, and hypocrisy. Despite the obvious relish Célimène takes in crafting the portrait, she is careful to maintain the device of the indirect discourse, adding for example an attributive clause in mid-course: "What's the use, *they said,* of these chaste expressions" [A quoi bon, *disaient-ils,* cette mine modeste] (937).

Inside its elaborate frame, we can discover three layers of voices in Célimène's enunciation of the portrait. First, Célimène's own voice is unmistakable: after all, she often simply repeats many of the elements from the description she herself just delivered before Arsinoé's entry. The portrait is very much the work of the master *médisante.* Second, we have the voice of the meritable people whom Célimène claims to be repeating. It may seem that Célimène's use of quotation, given its impromptu appearance and its parodic echoing of Arsinoé's rhetoric, is even more obviously fictional than Arsinoé's.[6] And yet, once again, the play offers evidence that even if this particular conversation did not take place, it should have. The opening discussion introduces the epithet "la prude Arsinoé" in Philinte's mouth, and we can assume that her hypocrisy is common fodder for the talk of the town, just as Célimène's *coquetterie* is.

Finally, there is a third voice present in Célimène's reply: Arsinoé's own, which Célimène sarcastically imitates. Célimène's mimicry of Arsinoé follows two strategies: exact imitation and mocking paraphrase. As for the first, we see for example that Célimène copies Arsinoé word for word in her repetition of "some information also touching your honor" [un avis aussi qui touche votre honneur]. In this case, only the addition of the adverb "also" draws attention to the fact that it is Célimène who is speaking, and not simply an echo of Arsinoé. The real genius of Célimène's irony, however, is to be found in her second strategy—that of a freer form of mockery. Célimène's imitation of Arsinoé can be said to reside more in synonyms and repetitions of rhetorical structures than in a word-for-word reproduction.[7] Célimène, for example, appropriates Arsinoé's strategy of a suggestive understatement, a litotes, in describing the speakers' disapproval, but changes Arsinoé's phrasing: when Célimène says that Arsinoé's mannerisms "were not cited as a model to follow," she considerably reworks Arsinoé's remark regarding Célimène's conduct, which "suffered the misfortune of not being praised." In imitating Arsinoé's rhetorical strategy rather than its lexical clothing, Célimène unmasks the hypocrisy at its heart. Arsinoé's expression "the misfortune of not being praised" pretends to be euphemistic, to attenuate the harshness of the reality. But Célimène, by repeating the strategy of the litotes—and highlighting its structural importance by changing its superficial wording—points out that like all

6. Brody has pointed out this contrast (573).
7. Eustis notes this in his analysis of the scene (55).

litotes, it is actually designed to stress the meaning it pretends to attenuate, in this case simply this: they slaughtered her reputation.

Such is one prong of Célimène's strategy: to unmask Arsinoé's discourse. Célimène uses a destructive irony that exposes Arsinoé's false claim to goodwill and her devious rhetoric. As such, Célimène is basically engaged in a defensive strategy of censuring the censor, or satirizing the satirist. Her mockery disarms Arsinoé's commentary of the authority it wishes to gain by her personal *ethos,* (that is, the positive light in which she casts herself as a speaker) and by the use of witnesses, "les gens de vertu singulière." Stripped of her claims, Arsinoé is revealed as a malicious spirit, eager only to attack her opponent.

However, this defensive strategy presents a problem. By neutralizing Arsinoé's remarks, Célimène risks undercutting her own. If Célimène's analysis of Arsinoé's rhetoric shows that these kinds of negative portraits are basically subjective and vicious in nature, how can Célimène's own cruel portrait of Arsinoé inspire credence? Given that she devotes twenty lines to the character sketch, it would seem foolish to reduce its worth to a neutralization of Arsinoé's comments, to a simple statement of the type: "You have delivered a personally motivated and arbitrary description of me, now here is a personally motivated and arbitrary description of you." In this sense, Célimène's portrait inevitably falls victim to its own ironic framework: we can no longer take it seriously. To solve this problem, I think we must read Célimène's discourse as ironic and literal at the same time. For example, when she claims she is only repeating the words of "some most respected people" [quelques gens d'un très rare mérite], we understand that the hyperbolic adjective is meant as a mockery of Arsinoé's own citation of "some most virtuous people" [des gens de vertu singulière]. Célimène's exaggerated qualification of her (and thus Arsinoé's) sources suggests their fictional nature. It also reminds us that Arsinoé's exaggeration of the virtue of those she is quoting is meant to give their attacks against her opponent more weight than Arsinoé's own supposed (and weak) protestations in Célimène's favor. So much for the caustic implications of Célimène's attribution. If we now change tactics and accept at face value this attribution of the portrait to the "voice of the world," Célimène's speech takes on a new meaning. In replying to Arsinoé's repetition of others' slander with her own unkind quotation, Célimène suggests that though people may attack her, Célimène, in her absence, just as Arsinoé states, this is simply the case for everyone. The same people attack Arsinoé's character as well. Such is the profession of the world—to observe, appraise, and condemn others. Thus Célimène's citation of the world's voice can be taken entirely seriously as a commentary on the implacable severity of social judgments.

Indeed, Arsinoé has herself already remarked on the inescapability of the social mirror, and its unkind reflections: one must remember, she warned, that one is constantly observed, that "people are easily tricked by the appearance of crime; / And it is not enough to be virtuous for yourself" [. . . aux ombres du crime on prête aisément foi, / Et ce n'est pas assez de bien vivre pour soi] (907–8). The problem is that Arsinoé underestimates the keenness of the world's perception, its insight. This explains why Arsinoé's portrait of Célimène concentrates almost exclusively on the world's perception of appearances: the shadows ("ombres") and semblances ("l'air dont vous viviez" and its "méchante face" [900, 901]). Célimène in her reply portrays Arsinoé as precisely someone who is a victim of this misunderstanding of her peers' discernment. Arsinoé wears a certain mask for the world but does not understand how transparent the mask is, how easily its cover may be penetrated. In fact, as Célimène notes, the world is quite an analytic observer and can distinguish appearance and reality: "What's the use, they said, of these chaste expressions / And this virtuous appearance that is belied by all the rest" [A quoi bon, disaient-ils, cette mine modeste, / Et ce sage dehors que dément tout le reste?] (937–38). Thus, Arsinoé's first mistake is to believe that the mirror held up by social commerce is entirely superficial. But more important, she errs in not turning the mirror toward herself. While she "reports" the observations of others, she does not realize she is being observed, or rather how well she is being observed. Of course, later in their discussion, Arsinoé credits the world with a more critical discernment: "The world is not fooled" [Le monde n'est point dupe] (1010), she says of Célimène's claim to innocence. But Arsinoé never understands the world is not a dupe before her own feigned virtue. Célimène clearly states the problem: "one must look at oneself a longtime / Before thinking about condemning others" [. . . on doit se regarder soi-même un fort long temps, / Avant que de songer à condamner les gens] (951–52).

But, as we know, to see oneself in the closed social world of *Le Misanthrope* is to see oneself as others do. And that requires precisely the good offices that Arsinoé has offered Célimène, and Célimène Arsinoé: to repeat the world's judgments, one to another. In the final analysis, Célimène's rephrasing of Arsinoé's rhetoric of goodwill can be read on a literal level, as a true statement of purpose. When Célimène's concludes her portrait by mimicking Arsinoé's four-line protest that her "information" is motivated by a "zeal" for the other's "interests," the general claim is, in fact, entirely sound. Arsinoé of course interprets Célimène's echo of her rhetoric as bitterly caustic. Célimène refutes Arsinoé's interpretation with a universalizing commentary:

> Au contraire, Madame; et si l'on était sage,
> Ces avis mutuels seraient mis en usage:
> On détruirait par là, traitant de bonne foi,
> Ce grand aveuglement où chacun est pour soi.
> Il ne tiendra qu'à vous qu'avec le même zèle
> Nous ne continuions cet office fidèle,
> Et nous prenions grand soin de nous dire, entre nous,
> Ce que nous entendrons, vous de moi, moi de vous. (965–72)

> On the contrary, madam; and if people were wiser
> These mutual exchanges of information would be widely practiced;
> We could thus destroy, in speaking openly,
> That great self-blindness that strikes everyone.
> Whenever you want, with the same zeal,
> Let us continue this honest exchange,
> And do all we can to tell each other
> Everything we hear, you about me, and me about you.

Célimène seems to move beyond the squalor of her quarrel with Arsinoé and offer a kind of moral philosophy of the social commerce of representation: self-blindness can be corrected only through the vision of others, by a kind of self-distancing achieved through the intermediary of other's eyes. This is the pedagogic advantage of the social mirror: it can serve as a school for perspicacity.

And yet just at the moment of pronouncement, the "moral" is also undercut by the irony still lurking in Célimène's expression. The exaggerated righteousness of the word "zeal" recalls once again Arsinoé's hypocritical use of the term (912). As in *Tartuffe, zèle* serves as a cover for perfidy. Viewed ironically, Arsinoé's and Célimène's stated enthusiasm for this friendly service is in reality simply an appetite for slander, for mutual character assassination. There is no doubt that such malice drives Arsinoé. Stung by Célimène's verbal satire in this scene, Arsinoé is led not to self-correction, but instead to revenge. And by exacting her revenge mercilessly, she dooms Célimène to her unhappy end. Arsinoé does so by repaying Célimène twice: first, she discloses to Alceste a letter proving Célimène's infidelity, and second, she turns the wrath of the *marquis* against their formerly beloved satirist, Célimène. Thus the consequences of Célimène's acid portrait and Arsinoé's indignant response propel the play toward its fourth act, in which Alceste confronts Célimène with Arsinoé's evidence, and its final act, in which the *marquis* read Célimène's epistolary satires directly to their humiliated targets, thereby ending her reign in their hearts.

Célimène's admirers can bear being satirized no more than can Arsinoé, and we know the form their revenge will take at the end of the play. We are left then with these last questions. The mechanics of depiction and recognition effectively drive the comedy, yes, but can they engender lucid self-understanding? It is no longer a mystery how this lengthy scene of social observation advances the action of the play. But the moral of the scene does remain a mystery. Given the result of the Célimène-Arsinoé duel, can we have any faith in Célimène's proposed cure to self-blindness, her project of exchanging frank depictions? And if the mirror of social commerce has shown itself so dysfunctional—so brilliantly and energetically dysfunctional—can the mirror of comedy promise more beneficial results?

CONCLUSION

Célimène's commentary on self-blindness has long been considered a statement of Molière's moral vision: it provides the one moment where almost all readers deem Célimène a figure representing the playwright.[1] Ironically enough, though, the realization of Célimène's moral project—the creation of a satiric utopia where malicious citizens enlighten each other by openly exchanging biting depictions—depends on the very social practice of *médisance* that has caused her to be so often dismissed as Molière's spokesperson. We must listen again to Célimène's voice as a double for Molière's—but this time in order to weigh its moral significance. According to Célimène, moral reform can result only from a freer exchange of representations: the indirect satires of the salon, where one never ridicules those present, should no longer skirt their absent targets, but be relayed to them, thereby administering a good dose of correction. Does Molière really embrace such a position? Can this moral medicine, so ineffective in social commerce (as Célimène's final demise painfully demonstrates), work its effects in the comic theater?

The answer lies in Célimène's portrait of Arsinoé, but now with Molière's voice integrated into the dialogue. If any of Célimène's portraits can be said to reflect the playwright's position, it is certainly this depiction. There are a number of reasons for detecting Molière's voice here. Molière loves nothing more than mocking prudes: throughout his works they are

1. Citing the line, Guicharnaud has said "S'il y a une leçon dans la pièce, ce sera bien celle-ci, car chacun passe son temps à expliquer autrui à autrui, sans s'expliquer à soi-même" (431). For other readings of Célimène's lines as a moral of the play see also Hubert (137–38) and Defaux (183).

a favorite target of Molière's "spokespersons."[2] Indeed, the character of "Molière" himself in *L'Impromptu* satirizes a prude in language very similar to that employed by the wicked Célimène (sc. 1). Furthermore, Célimène's portrait of Arsinoé strongly recalls another target of Molière's satire, the hypocrite: the *grimaces* of the latter recalls the former's affected "faces" *(mines);* they are both associated with extremism, with *zèle.* With the play *Tartuffe,* Molière, according to his own words, simply delivers to his audience a full-length portrait of the creature: it is "a comedy that decries hypocrites, and rightly makes one see all the affected grimaces of these people" [une comédie qui décriât les hypocrites, et mît en vue, comme il faut, toutes les grimaces étudiées de ces gens] ("Premier Placet," *OC* 1: 889). In attacking Arsinoé's own hypocrisy, can we not assume that Molière is putting in Célimène's mouth just this kind of corrective satire, designed to "attack by ridiculous portraits the vices of his times" [attaquer par des peintures ridicules les vices de [son] siècle] (1: 889)? Donneau de Visé certainly seems right: Molière is a master ventriloquist speaking through Célimène.[3]

But what of the intended effect of the satiric portrait? What kind of moral correction might Célimène's words produce, not on her interlocutor, but on her ultimate audience, the spectators of the play *Le Misanthrope?* Through Célimène's speech, the play's spectators no doubt appreciate Molière's satiric portrait of the contemporary type of the prude, of which they see originals among themselves. As such, they accept the fidelity and corrective edge of the satire. However, the portrait is placed by the author in the mouth of a coquette who is in personal battle with the "prude." As such, they must discount in part the fidelity and moral utility of the satire. Yet, the portrait is cited as the voice of common opinion of respectable people, such as can be found in the audience. As such, it regains a certain authority. But, finally, it must be admitted that the rhetorical device of quoting such authorities appears to be ironic, to be a pure mockery. As such, the portrait not only loses any pretense to objective fidelity and moral purpose, but indeed actively engages in unmasking such lofty claims.

Célimène's portrait of Arsinoé then reveals all the complexity of the

---

2. See for example the portraits of prudes by Dorante in *La Critique* (sc. 5) and Dorine in *Tartuffe* (I.i.121–40).

3. I would further advance the parallel between author and character by considering the transmission of their portraits: the playwright's means of depiction—ventriloquizing through the depicted conversation of characters—resembles strongly Célimène's (and Arsinoé's) own strategy of indirect censure—ventriloquizing through the reported conversation of social peers. Molière portrays characters through the verbal depictions of other characters; Célimène portrays Arsinoé through the verbal depictions of her peers.

comic mirror. The depiction of Arsinoé is either faithful or slanderous, edifying or debasing, depending on the voice to which one chooses to listen: Molière, Célimène, the voice of the world, or the sarcastic echo of Arsinoé. The coexistence of these sources of satire can only provoke perplexity in the audience. Comedy, like all social representations, offers an image simultaneously faithful and arbitrary, useful and vain. No representation, not even Molière's, can be free from spite, nor as "faithful" as it claims. Just as Célimène's irony draws attention to the malice lurking behind her own depictions, so too the comic artist cannot be fully acquitted of the charge of delighting in cruel ridicule. Célimène teaches us that Boursault is right: "To satirize . . . is to rail, to scorn."

And yet even if we take into account this malicious pleasure, and the distortions it may create, these portraits can nevertheless instruct. But they can only instruct if one first understands the portraitist's viewpoint. This is the true lesson of Molière's drama of the satirist satirized: not to abandon satire, but quite the contrary, to extend its insight into its own limitations of vision, and to the limitations of self-recognition on the part of its subjects. The mechanics of the comic mirror, like those of the social mirror, are hardly transparent. But by exposing itself, satire wins another victory, or at least continues its campaign. Though exposed, satire is not defrocked. Faulty as it may be, its mirror is inescapable. Alceste's "desert" doesn't exist, and no one can escape the appraisals of the world. As Nicole observed, "everyone around us forms our portrait." If Molière's comedy is, as Dandrey has justly remarked, a school for understanding oneself, to be effective it must take into account its own function—and dysfunction—in this formation of a lucid self-image.[4] As a school for perspicacity, the comedy imparts to its audience a glimmering image of itself. But this self-vision can never be more than an approximative one, one derived from a knowledge of the portraitist's perspective and its recipient's vanity and myopia. As a kind of anatomical chart for the circulation of representation, comedy provides just the tools for gauging these imperfect operations.

The social commerce of representation may be doomed to an endless cycle of blind revenge, futile misrecognitions, and narcissistic triumphs. But Molière's comedy acts finally as a mirror in which the spectator apprehends the machinery of depiction and recognition, the machinery that fabricates his or her own identity. It offers no clearer vision of human faults than other means of representation: it simply makes us better aware of our

---

4. Dandrey calls the comedy a site for the "élaboration d'une image de soi" (340). I agree, but do so insisting that the malicious pleasures and the deformations of the satiric lens are inescapable in forming such an image.

system of imagining ourselves. And in so doing it celebrates the satiric dynamics that drive dramatic conflict, that prolong it with brilliant malice and punctuate it with risible recognitions. For even in this faulty mirror, sustained by the gratification of ridicule and the wrath of the wounded, the audience sees its image cast.

Selected Bibliography

Editions of Molière

Oeuvres complètes. Ed. Georges Couton. 2 vols. Paris: Gallimard (Bibliothèque de la Pléiade), 1971.

Théâtre Complet. Ed. Eugène Despois and Paul Mesnard. 13 vols. Paris: Hachette (Les Grands Ecrivains de la France), 1873–1900.

Bibliographies and Collections of Documents

Collinet, Jean-Pierre, ed. *Lectures de Molière.* Paris: Colin, 1974.

Fournel, Victor, ed. *Les Contemporains de Molière, Recueil de comédies, rares ou peu connues, jouées de 1650–1680.* 3 vols. Paris: Didot, 1863.

Mongrédien, Georges, ed. *Comédies et pamphlets sur Molière.* Paris: Nizet, 1986.

———, ed. *La Querelle de l'Ecole des femmes: Comédies de Jean Donneau de Visé, Edme Boursault, Charles Robinet, A. J. Montfleury, Jean Chevalier, Philippe de La Croix.* 2 vols. Paris: Didier (Société des textes français modernes), 1971.

———, ed. *Recueil des textes et des documents du XVIIe siècle relatifs à Molière.* 2 vols. Paris: CNRS, 1965.

Saintonge, Paul. *Thirty Years of Molière Studies, a Bibliography, 1942–1971.* In *Molière and the Commonwealth of Letters: Patrimony and Posterity.* Ed. Roger Johnson et al. Jackson: UP of Mississippi, 1975.

———, and R. W. Christ. *Fifty Years of Molière Studies, a Bibliography.* Baltimore: Johns Hopkins UP, 1942.

Primary Sources

Aristophanes. *Works.* Trans. B. B. Rogers. 3 vols. London: Heinemann (Loeb Classical Library), 1924.

Aristotle. *Poetics.* Trans. W. H. Fyfe. Cambridge: Harvard UP (Loeb Classical Library), 1989.

Arnauld, Antoine, and Pierre Nicole. *La Logique, ou l'Art de penser.* 1662. Paris: PUF, 1965.

Aubignac, François-Hédelin, abbé d'. *La Pratique du théâtre.* 1657. Paris: Champion, 1927.

———. *Conjectures Académiques ou Dissertation sur l'Iliade.* Paris: Fournier, 1715; Ed. V. Magnien. Paris: Hachette, 1925.

Boileau-Despréaux. *Oeuvres.* Paris: Classiques Garnier, 1961.

Boursault, Edme. *Le Portrait du Peintre ou la Contre-Critique de l'Ecole des femmes.* Paris: de Sercy, 1664. Mongrédien, *Querelle* 1: 103–59.

Caillières, François de. *De la Science du monde.* Paris: E. Ganeau, 1717.

Cervantes, Miguel de. *Don Quixote.* Trans. P. Motteux, rev. Ozell. New York: Random, 1930.

Chevalier. *Les Amours de Calotin.* Paris: de Sercy, 1664. Scenes relative to Molière (act 1 and act 2, sc. 1) in Mongrédien, *Querelle* 2: 365–89.

Congreve, William. *The Complete Plays.* Ed. Herbert Davis. Chicago: U of Chicago P, 1967.

Corneille, Pierre. *Oeuvres complètes.* Ed. A. Stegmann. Paris: Seuil, 1963.

Corneille, Thomas. *Le Berger Extravagant.* Rouen: Maurry, 1653; Crit. ed., ed. F. Bar. Geneva: Droz, 1960.

Cureau de la Chambre. *L'art de connaître les hommes.* Paris: Ricolet, 1659.

Dacier, Anne Lefebvre. *Les Comédies de Terence, traduites en français, avec des Remarques.* Paris: Thierry, 1688.

Descartes, René. *Discours de la méthode. Oeuvres et lettres.* Ed. A. Bridoux. Paris: Gallimard (Bibliothèque de la Pléiade), 1953.

Donneau de Visé, Jean. "Lettre sur les affaires du théâtre." *Les Diversités galantes.* Paris: Ribou, 1664. Mongrédien, *Querelle* 2: 299–310.

———. "Lettre sur la comédie du 'Misanthrope.'" In Molière, *Le Misanthrope.* Paris: Ribou, 1667. Molière, *OC* 2: 131–40.

———. *Nouvelles nouvelles divisées en trois parties.* 3 vols. Paris: P. Bienfaict, 1663. Sections relevant to Molière in Molière, *OC* 1: 1013–23.

———. *Réponse à L'Impromptu de Versailles, ou la Vengeance des Marquis.* In *Les Diversités galantes.* Paris: Ribou, 1664. Mongrédien, *Querelle* 2: 256–97.

———. *Trois Comédies: La Mère coquette, La Veuve à la mode, Les Dames vengées.* Ed. Pierre Mélèse. Paris: Droz, 1940.

———. *Zélinde, ou la véritable Critique de l'Ecole des Femmes et la Critique de la Critique.* Paris: de Luyne, 1663. Mongrédien, *Querelle* 1: 13–83.

Encyclopédie, ou Dictionnaire raisonné des Sciences, des Arts, et des Métiers (Supplément à). Ed. Diderot and d'Alembert. Amsterdam: Rey, 1776.

Faret, Nicolas. *L'honnête homme, ou l'art de plaire à la cour.* 1630. Geneva: Slatkine, 1970.

Furetière, Antoine. *Dictionnaire universel.* La Haye, 1690.

———. *Le Roman Bourgeois.* Paris: Barbin, 1666; *Romanciers du XVIIe siècle* 899–1104.

Grimarest, Jean-Léonor Gallois de. *Vie de M. de Molière.* Paris: Le Febvre, 1705; Ed. G. Mongrédien. Paris: Brient, 1955.

La Bruyère, Jean de. *Les Caractères, ou les Moeurs de ce siècle.* Paris: Classiques Garnier, 1990.

La Croix, Philippe de. *La Guerre comique, ou La Défense de L'Ecole des femmes.* Paris: Bienfait, 1664. Mongrédien, *Querelle* 2: 397–463.

La Fontaine, Jean de. *Fables.* Ed. R. Radouant. Paris: Hachette, 1929.

La Mesnardière, Jules Pillet de. *La Poétique.* Paris: de Sommaville, 1639; Rpt. Geneva: Slatkine, 1972.

La Rochefoucauld, François, duc de. *Maximes.* Paris: Garnier Frères, 1967.

Mairet, Jean de. "Préface en forme de discours poétique." *La Silvanire, ou la Morte-vive.* Paris: Targa, 1631. *Théâtre du XVIIe siècle* 1: 479–88.

Marmet, Valcroissant de, Sieur de. *Maximes pour vivre heureusement dans le monde.* Paris: de Sercy, 1662.

Méré, Antoine Gombaud, Chevalier de. *Les discours des agrémens, de l'esprit et de la conversation.* Paris: Les Textes Français (Guillaume Budé), 1930.

Montaigne, Michel de. *Essais.* Ed. A. Micha. 3 vols. Paris: GF Flammarion, 1979.

Montesquieu. *Oeuvres complètes.* Paris: Nagel, 1950. Tome 1: rpt. of *Oeuvres complètes.* Amsterdam, 1758.

Montfleury, Antoine Jacob. *L'Impromptu de l'Hôtel de Condé.* Paris: Pépingué, 1664. Mongrédien, *Querelle* 2: 325–57.

Morvan de Bellegarde. *Réflexions sur le ridicule et sur les moyens de l'éviter.* Paris: Guignard, 1699.

———. *Réflexions sur ce qui peut plaire, ou déplaire dans le commerce du monde.* Paris: Seneuze, 1688.

Nicole, Pierre. *Essais de Morale.* Paris: 1675.

Pascal, Blaise. *Pensées.* Ed. Brunschvicg. Paris: Classiques Garnier, 1958.

Piles, Roger de. *Cours de peinture par principes.* 1708. Paris: Gallimard, 1989.

Plato. *The Dialogues.* Trans. B. Jowett. 4 vols. Oxford: Clarendon, 1953.

Plautus. *Works.* Trans. P. Nixon. 4 vols. London: Heinemann (Loeb Classical Library), 1916.

Pure, Michel, abbé de. *La Prétieuse, ou le Mystère des ruelles.* 4 parts. Paris: de Luyne, 1656, 1657, and 1658; Ed. Emile Magne. Paris: Droz, 1938.

Racine, Jean. *Oeuvres complètes.* Ed. Raymond Picard. Paris: Gallimard (Bibliothèque de la Pléiade), 1950.

Rapin, René. *Réflexions sur la Poétique d'Aristote et sur les ouvrages des poètes anciens et modernes.* Paris: Muguet, 1674.

Riccoboni, Louis. *Observations sur la comédie et sur le génie de Molière.* Paris: Pissot, 1736. Rpt. Marzo, Italy: Forni, 1978.

Robinet, Charles. *Panégyrique de l'Ecole des femmes, ou Conversation comique sur les oeuvres de M. de Molière.* Paris: de Sercy, 1664. Mongrédien, *Querelle* 1: 169–243.

Romanciers du XVIIe siècle. Ed. A. Adam. Paris: Gallimard (Bibliothèque de la Pléiade), 1958.

Rousseau, Jean-Jacques. *Lettre à d'Alembert sur son article Genève.* Amsterdam: M. Michel, 1758; Paris: Garnier-Flammarion, 1967.

Saint-Evremond, Charles de Marguetal de Saint-Denis, Sieur de. *Oeuvres en prose.* Paris: Société des textes français modernes, 1966.

Scudéry, Madeleine de. *Conversations sur divers sujets.* Paris: Barbin, 1680.

Sévigné, Marie de Rabutin-Chantal, Marquise de. *Correspondance.* Ed. R. Duchêne. 3 vols. Paris: Gallimard (Bibliothèque de la Pléiade), 1972–78.

Somaize, Badeau de. *Les Véritables Prétieuses.* Paris: Ribou, 1660. Mongrédien, *Comédies et pamphlets* 31–66.

Sorel, Charles. *De la Connaissance des bons livres, ou Examen de plusieurs autheurs.* 1671. Rpt. Geneva: Slatkine, 1981.

———. *Description de l'isle de portraiture et de la ville des portraits.* Paris: de Sercy, 1659.

Terence. *Works.* Trans. John Sargeaunt. 2 vols. London: Heinemann (Loeb Classical Library), 1912.

Théâtre du XVIIe siècle. Ed. Jacques Scherer and Jacques Truchet. 3 vols. Paris: Gallimard (Bibliothèque de la Pléiade), 1975–92.

Voltaire. *Vie de Molière avec de petits sommaires des ses piéces.* 1739. Paris: Gallimard, 1992.

Wycherley, William. *The Plays.* Ed. Arthur Friedman. Oxford: Clarendon, 1979.

Modern Studies

Abrams, M. H. *The Mirror and the Lamp: Romantic Theory and the Critical Tradition.* Oxford: Oxford UP, 1953.

Adam, Antoine. *Histoire de la littérature française du XVIIe siècle.* 5 vols. Paris: Domat, 1949–56.

———. Introduction. *Romanciers du XVIIe siècle.* 7–57.

Albanese, Ralph. "Dynamisme social et jeu individuel dans *Dom Juan.*" *L'Esprit Créateur* 36.1 (1996): 50–62.

Alpers, Svetlana. *The Art of Describing: Dutch Art in the Seventeenth Century.* Chicago: U of Chicago P, 1983. Rpt. London: Penguin, 1989.

Apostolidès, Jean-Marie. *Le Prince Sacrifié. Théâtre et politique au temps de Louis XIV.* Paris: Les Editions de Minuit, 1985.

Auerbach, Erich. "La Cour et la ville." *Scenes from the Drama of European Literature.* Trans. Ralph Manheim. New York: Meridian, 1959. 133–79.

———. *Mimesis.* Trans. W. R. Trask. Princeton: Princeton UP, 1953.

Baltrušaitis, Jurgis. *Le Miroir: essai sur une légende scientifique: Révélations, science fiction, et fallacies.* Paris: Elmayan, 1978.

Banham, Martin, ed. *The Cambridge Guide to Theater.* Cambridge: Cambridge UP, 1990.

Barthes, Roland. "La Bruyère." *Essais critiques.* Paris: Seuil, 1964.

Baschera, Marco. *Théâtralité dans l'oeuvre de Molière.* Tübingen: Biblio 17 (108), 1998.

Becq, Annie. *Genèse de l'esthétique française moderne, de la raison classique à l'imagination créatrice (1680–1814).* Pisa: Pacini Editore, 1984.

Bénichou, Paul. *Morales du Grand Siècle.* Paris: Gallimard, 1948.

Bergson, Henri. *Le Rire, essai sur la signification du comique.* 1899. 6th ed. Paris: Quadridge/PUF, 1991.

Beugnot, Bernard. "Spécularités classiques." *Destins et enjeux du XVIIe siècle.* Ed. Y.-M. Bercé, et al. Paris: PUF, 1985.

Bonfait, Olivier. "Du masque au visage: le portrait dans le la littérature d'art." In *Visages du Grand Siècle.* 35–48.

Borgerhoff, E.B.O. *The Freedom of French Classicism.* Princeton NJ: Princeton UP: 1950

Bray, Bernard, and Christophe Strosetzky. *Art de la lettre, art de la conversation à l'époque classique en France. Actes du colloque de Wolfenbüttel (1991).* Paris: Klincksieck, 1995.

Bray, René. *La Formation de la doctrine classique en France.* Lausanne: Payot, 1931.

———. *Molière, homme de théâtre.* Paris: Mercure de France, 1954.

Brody, Jules. "*Dom Juan* and *Le Misanthrope,* or the Esthetics of Individualism in Molière." *PMLA* 84 (1969): 559–76.

Bury, Emmanuel. "Comédie et science des moeurs: le modèle de Terence aux XVIe et XVIIe siècles." *Littératures classiques* 27 (1996): 125–36.

———. *Littérature et politesse: l'invention de l'honnête homme, 1580–1750.* Paris: PUF, 1996.

Cairncross, John, ed. *L'Humanité de Molière.* Paris: Nizet, 1988.

Calder, Andrew. *Molière: The Theory and Practice of Comedy.* London: Athlone, 1993.

Carmody, Jim. *Rereading Molière: Mise en Scène from Antoine to Vitez*. Ann Arbor: U of Michigan P: 1993.

Cave, Terence. *Recognitions, a Study in Poetics*. Oxford: Clarendon, 1988.

Chambers, Ross. *La Comédie au château*. Paris: Corti, 1969.

Chartier, Roger. *Forms and Meanings: Texts, Performances and Audiences from Codex to Computers*. Philadelphia: University of Pennsylvania Press, 1995.

———. "George Dandin, ou le social en représentation." *Annales: Histoire, Sciences Sociales* 49.2 (1994): 277–310.

———. *L'Ordre des livres: lecteurs, auteurs, bibliothèques en Europe entre XIVe et XVIIIe siècles*. Aix-en-Provence: ALINEA, 1992.

Compagnon, Antoine. *La seconde main, ou le travail de la citation*. Paris: Seuil, 1979.

Conesa, Gabriel. *Le Dialogue moliéresque*. Paris: PUF, 1981. Paris: SEDES-CDU, 1992.

———. *Pierre Corneille et la naissance du genre comique (1629–1636)*. Paris: SEDES-CDU, 1992.

Coquery, Emmanuel. "Le Portrait Français sous Louis XIV," "Le Portrait vu du Grand Siècle," "Le Portrait en tableau." In *Visage du Grand Siècle*. 15–34; 121–136.

Corvin, Michel. *Molière et ses metteurs en scène d'aujourd'hui*. Lyon: PU de Lyon, 1985.

Dällenbach, Lucien. *Le Récit spéculaire: essai sur la mise en abyme*. Paris: Seuil, 1977.

Dandrey, Patrick. *Le Cas Argan: Molière et la maladie imaginaire*. Paris: Klincksieck, 1993.

———. *"Dom Juan," ou La Critique de la raison comique*. Paris: Champion, 1993.

———. "Molière et ses 'miroirs publics.'" *Prospero* 2 (1992): 37–40.

———. *Molière, ou l'esthétique du ridicule*. Paris: Klincksieck, 1992.

Davidson, H. M. *Audience, Words and Art*. Columbus: Ohio State UP, 1965.

Defaux, Gérard. *Molière ou les métamorphoses du comique*. Lexington KY: French Forum, 1980. Paris: Klincksieck, 1992.

DeJean, Joan. *Ancients against Moderns: Culture Wars and the Making of a Fin de Siècle*. Chicago: U of Chicago P, 1997.

———. *Tender Geographies: Women and the Origins of the Novel in France*. New York: Columbia UP, 1991.

Dens, Jean Pierre. *L'Honnête homme et la critique du goût: esthétique et société au XVIIe siècle*. Lexington KY: French Forum, 1981.

———. "Pour une théorie de la critique mondaine." *Papers on French Seventeenth-Century Literature* 24 (1986): 29–37.

Desan, Philippe. *Naissance de la méthode*. Paris: Nizet, 1987.

Descotes, Maurice. *Le Public de théâtre et son histoire*. Paris: PUF, 1964.

Dock, Stephen Varick. *Costume and Fashion in the Plays of Jean-Baptiste Poquelin Molière: A Seventeenth-Century Perspective*. Geneva: Slatkine, 1992.

Dotoli, Giovanni. *Littérature et société en France au XVIIe siècle*. Fasano, Italy: Schena; Paris: Nizet, 1987.

Duchêne, Roger. "Précieuses ou Galantes ridicules?" In *Thèmes et genres littéraires aux XVIIe et XVIIIe siècles. Mélanges en l'honneur de Jacques Truchet*. Ed. N. Ferrier-Caverivière. Paris: PUF, 1992 (357–65).

Duvignaud, Jean. *Sociologie du théâtre*. Paris: PUF, 1965.

Ekstein, Nina. "*Le Misanthrope* and *Tartuffe:* Two Critical Views of Verbal Portraiture." *Rivista di letteratura moderne e comparate* (April–June 1989): 137–52.

Elias, Norbert. *The Civilizing Process*. Trans. Edmund Jephcott. Oxford: Blackwell, 1994.

Elliott, Robert. *The Power of Satire*. Princeton: Princeton UP, 1966.

Eustis, Alvin. *Molière as Ironic Contemplator*. Paris: Mouton, 1973.

Fernandez, Ramon. *Molière, ou l'essence du génie comique*. Paris: Grasset, 1979. Rpt. of *La Vie de Molière*, Paris: Gallimard, 1929.

Force, Pierre. *Molière ou Le Prix des choses. Morale, économie, et comédie*. Paris: Nathan, 1994.

Forestier, Georges. *Essai de génétique théâtrale: Corneille à l'oeuvre*. Paris: Klincksieck, 1996.

———. *Esthétique de l'identité dans le théâtre français (1550–1680)*. Geneva: Droz, 1988.

———. "Illusion comique et illusion mimétique." *Papers on French Seventeenth-Century Literature* 11.21 (1984): 377–91.

———. "Imitation parfaite et vraisemblance absolue: réflexions sur un paradoxe classique." *Poétique* 82 (1990): 189–202.

———. *Molière*. Paris: Bordas ("collection en toutes lettres"), 1990.

———. "Structure de la comédie française classique." *Littératures classiques* 27 (1996): 243–58.

———. *Le Théâtre dans le théâtre sur la scène française du XVIIe siècle*. Geneva: Droz, 1981.

Foucault, Michel. *Les Mots et les choses*. Paris: Gallimard, 1966.

———. "Qu'est-ce qu'un auteur?" *Bulletin de la Société française de Philosophie* 63.3 (1969): 73–104.

———. *Surveiller et punir. Naissance de la prison*. Paris: Gallimard, 1975.

France, Peter. *Politeness and Its Discontents*. Cambridge: Cambridge UP, 1992.

Fried, Michael. *Absorption and Theatricality: Painting and Beholder in the Age of Diderot*. Chicago: Chicago UP, 1980.

Fumaroli, Marc. *L'Age de l'éloquence*. Geneva: Droz, 1980.

———. La Conversation." *Les Lieux de mémoire: III, Les France*. Ed. Pierre Nora. Paris: Gallimard, 1992.

———. "Corneille." *L'Histoire littéraire de la France: 1600–1660*. Ed. P. Abrahmé. Paris: Editions Sociales, 1975.

———. *Héros et Orateurs: rhétorique et dramaturgie cornéliennes*. Geneva: Droz, 1990.

———. "Rhétorique, dramaturgie, critique littéraire: le recours à l'allégorie dans les querelles littéraires (1578–1630). In *Critique et Création Littéraires en France au XVIIe siècle*. Paris: CNRS, 1977. 453–72.

———. ed. *Le loisir lettré à l'âge classique*. Geneva: Droz, 1996.

Gaines, James F. "Molière and Marx: Prospects for a New Century." *L'Esprit Créateur* 36.1 (1996): 21–31.

———. *Social Structures in Molière's Theater*. Columbus: Ohio State UP, 1984.

Garapon, Robert. *La Fantaisie verbale et le comique dans le théâtre français du Moyen Age à la fin du XVIIe siècle*. Paris: Colin, 1957.

———. *Le dernier Molière: des* Fourberies de Scapin *au* Malade imaginaire. Paris: SEDES-CDU, 1977.

———. "Le langage de la comédie au XVIIe siècle: de la rhétorique à la littérature." In *Le langage littéraire au XVIIe siècle*. Ed. C. Wentzlaff-Eggebert. Tübingen: Gunter Narr, 1991. 13–22.

Génetiot, Alain. *Les Genres lyriques mondains (1630–1660)*. Geneva: Droz, 1990.

Genette, Gérard. "Vraisemblance et motivation." In *Figures II*. Paris, Seuil, 1969.

———. "Complexe de Narcisse" In *Figures I*. Paris, Seuil, 1966.

Gilbert, Huguette. "Molière et la comédie polémique." In Truchet, *Thématique de Molière* 105–16.

Goffman, Erving. *The Presentation of Self in Everyday Life*. New York: Doubleday (Anchor), 1959.

Goldsmith, Elizabeth C. *Exclusive Conversations: The Art of Interaction in Seventeenth-Century France.* Philadelphia, U of Pennsylvania P, 1988.

Gombrich, E. H. *Art and Illusion: A Study in the Psychology of Pictorial Representation.* New York: Pantheon (Bollingen Series), 1960.

————. "The Mask and the Face: The Perception of Physiognomic Likeness in Life and Art." In *Art, Perception, and Reality.* Ed. Gombrich, J. Hochberg, and M. Black. Baltimore: Johns Hopkins UP, 1972.

Gordon, Daniel. *Citizens without Sovereignty: Equality and Sociability in French Thought, 1670–1789.* Princeton, NJ: Princeton UP, 1994.

Gossman, Lionel. *Men and Masks: A Study of Molière.* Baltimore: Johns Hopkins UP, 1963.

Greenberg, Mitchell. *Subjectivity and Subjugation in Seventeenth-Century Drama and Prose: The Family Romance in French Classicism.* Cambridge: Cambridge UP, 1992.

Greenblatt, Stephen. *Shakespearean Negotiations.* Oxford: Clarendon, 1988.

Griffin, Dustin. *Satire: A Critical Reintroduction.* Lexington: The UP of Kentucky, 1994.

Gross, Nathan. *From Gesture to Idea: Esthetics and Ethics in Molière's Comedy.* New York: Columbia UP, 1982.

Guicharnaud, Jacques. *Molière, une aventure théâtrale.* Paris: Gallimard, 1963.

Guichemerre, Roger. *La Comédie classique en France.* Paris: PUF ("Que sais- je"), 1978.

————. "Molière et la farce." *Oeuvres & Critiques* 6.1 (1981): 111–24.

————. "Types sociaux et scènes de moeurs chez les contemporains de Molière. L'Apparition de la comédie de moeurs." *Travaux de littérature* I (1988): 105–21.

Gutwirth, Marcel. *Molière, ou l'invention comique.* Paris: Minard (Lettres modernes), 1966.

————. "Visages d'Alceste." *Oeuvres & Critiques* 6.1 (1981): 77–89.

Habermas, Jürgen. *The Structural Transformation of the Public Sphere: An Inquiry into a Category of Bourgeois Society.* Trans. Thomas Burger and Frederick Lawrence. Cambridge: MIT P, 1991.

Hall, H. Gaston. *Comedy in Context: Essays on Molière.* Jackson: UP of Mississippi, 1984.

Hammond, Nicholas. *Creative Tensions: An Introduction to Seventeenth-Century French Literature.* London: Duckworth, 1997.

Harth, Erica. *Ideology and Culture in Seventeenth-Century France.* Ithaca, NY: Cornell UP, 1983.

Hauser, Arnold. *The Social History of Art.* New York: Vintage, 1958.

Herzel, Roger W. *The Original Casting of Molière's Plays.* Ann Arbor: UMI Research P, 1981.

Highet, Gilbert. *The Anatomy of Satire.* Princeton: Princeton UP, 1962.

Howarth, W. D. *Molière: A Playwright and His Audience.* Cambridge: Cambridge UP, 1982.

Hubert, J. D. *Molière and the Comedy of Intellect.* Berkeley: U of California P, 1962.

Jaouën, Françoise. *De l'art de plaire en petits morceaux: Pascal, La Rochefoucauld, La Bruyère.* Saint-Denis: PU de Vincennes, 1996.

Jasinski, René. *Molière et le Misanthrope.* Paris: Nizet, 1951.

Kibédi Varga, Aron. *Les Poétiques du classicisme.* Paris: Aux Amateurs de Livres, 1990.

————. "Réflexions sur le classicisme français: littérature et société au XVIIe siècle." *Revue d'histoire littéraire en France,* 1996. 6: 1063–68.

Knutson, Harold C. *The Triumph of Wit: Molière and Restoration Comedy.* Columbus: Ohio UP, 1988.

Lancaster, Henry Carrington. *A History of French Dramatic Literature in the Seventeenth Century.* 9 vols. Baltimore: Johns Hopkins UP, 1929–42.

Lanson, Gustave. "Molière et la farce." *Revue de Paris* (May 1901): 129–53. Rpt. in *Essais de méthode, de critique, et d'histoire littéraire.* Ed. H. Peyre. Paris: Hachette, 1965.

Lawrence, Francis L. "Artist, Audience, and Structure in *L'Impromptu de Versailles.*" *Oeuvres & Critiques* 6.1 (1981): 125–32.

Lougee, Carolyn C. *Le Paradis des Femmes: Women, Salons, and Social Stratification in Seventeenth-Century France.* Princeton: Princeton UP, 1976.

Lough, John. *Paris Theater Audiences in the Seventeenth and Eighteenth Centuries.* London: Oxford UP, 1965.

Lyons, John D., and Stephen G. Nichols, Jr., eds. *Mimesis: From Mirror to Method, Augustine to Descartes.* Hanover: UP of New England, 1982.

Magendie, Maurice. *La Politesse mondaine et les théories de l'honnêteté en France au XVIIe siècle de 1600 à 1660.* Paris: PUF, 1925. Rpt. Geneva: Slatkine, 1970.

Marin, Louis. *De la représentation.* Paris: Gallimard, 1994.

———. *Philippe de Champaigne, ou la présence cachée.* Paris: Hazan, 1995.

———. *Le Portrait du roi.* Paris: Ed. de Minuit, 1978.

———. *Le Récit est un piège.* Paris: Les Editions de Minuit, 1978.

———. *To Destroy Painting.* Trans. Mette Hjort. Chicago: U of Chicago P, 1995. (*Détruire la peinture.* Paris: Ed. Galilée, 1977.)

Marmier, Jean. "La Conscience du satirique, d'Horace à Boileau." *Critique et Création Littéraires en France au XVIIe siècle.* Ed. Marc Fumaroli. Paris: CNRS, 1977. 29–38.

Martin, John Rupert. *Baroque.* New York: Harper & Row, 1977.

Maskell, David. *Racine, a Theatrical Reading.* Oxford: Clarendon, 1991.

Melchior-Bonnet, Sabine. *Histoire du miroir.* Paris: Imago, 1994.

Mélèse, Pierre. *Le Théâtre et le public à Paris sous Louis XIV, 1659–1715.* Paris: Droz, 1934.

Meltzer, Françoise. *Hot Properties: The Stakes and Claims of Literary Originality.* Chicago: U of Chicago P, 1994.

———. *Salome and the Dance of Writing: Portraits of Mimesis in Literature.* Chicago: U of Chicago P, 1987.

Merlin, Hélène. "L'épistémè classique ou l'épineuse question de la représentation." *Littératures classiques* 19 (1993): 187–97.

———. *Public et littérature en France au XVIIe siècle.* Paris: Belles Lettres, 1994.

Mesnard, Jean. "*Le Misanthrope:* Mise en question de l'art de plaire." In *La Culture du XVIIe siècle, enquêtes et synthèses.* Paris: PUF, 1992. 521–45.

Michaut, Gustave. *La Jeunesse de Molière. Les Débuts de Molière à Paris. Les Luttes de Molière.* Paris: Hachette, 1922, 1923, 1925.

Moore, W. G. *Molière: A New Criticism.* Oxford: Clarendon Press, 1949.

———. "Raison et structure dans la comédie de Molière." *Revue d'histoire littéraire en France* 5–6 (1972).

Morel, Jacques. "Molière et les honnêtes gens." In *Agréables Mensonges: Essais sur le théâtre français du XVIIe siècle.* Paris: Klincksieck, 1991.

Moriarty, Michael. *Taste and Ideology in Seventeenth-Century France.* Cambridge: Cambridge UP, 1988.

Morrissey, Robert. "*La Pratique du Théâtre* et le langage de l'illusion." *XVIIe siècle* 146 (1985): 17–28.

Mousnier, Roland. *Les Institutions de la France sous la monarchie absolue.* 2 vol. Paris: PUF, 1974.

Norman, Larry. "Dramatic Distance and French Classical Comedy: D'Aubignac's Theory of the Spectacle." *Romance Language Annual* 1997: 91–96.

———. "Entendre la voix comique: l'intervention du poème écrit dans *Mélite, Les Visionnaires,* et *La Comédie des Académistes.*" In *A haute voix: Diction et prononciation entre 1550 et 1640.* Ed. Olivia Rosenthal. Paris: Klincksieck, 1998. 177–189.

———. "La Rochefoucauld et le problème de la reconnaissance de soi." In *La Rochefoucauld/Mithridate/Frères et soeurs.* Tübingen: Biblio 17 (Papers on French Seventeenth-Century Literature) (111), 1998: 21–29.

———. "Molière rhapsode." *Fictions d'auteur.* Ed. S. Rabau. Paris: Champion, forthcoming (2000).

———. "Subversive Ancients: The Past as Other in French Classical Thought." *Seventeenth-Century French Studies* 1999.

Nurse, Peter. "Molière and Satire." *University of Toronto Quarterly* (1967): 113–28.

———. *Molière and the Comic Spirit.* Geneva: Droz, 1991.

Paige, Nicholas. "*George Dandin,* ou les ambiguïtés du social." *RHLF* 95–5: 690–708.

Parish, Richard. "*Molière en travesti:* Transvestite Acting in Molière." In *Molière: Proceedings of the Nottingham Molière Conference.* Ed. S. Bamforth. Nottingham: U of Nottingham, 1994. 53–58.

Pasquier, Pierre. *La Mimèsis dans l'esthétique théâtrale du XVIIe siècle: Histoire d'une réflexion.* Paris: Klincksieck, 1995.

Pavel, Thomas. *L'art de l'éloignement, essai sur l'imagination classique.* Paris: Gallimard, 1996.

Peacock, Noël A. "Translating Molière for the English Stage." *Molière: Proceedings of the Nottingham Molière Conference.* Ed. S. Bamforth. Nottingham: U of Nottingham, 1994. 83–91.

Phillips, Henry. "Molière and Authority." *Molière: Proceedings of the Nottingham Molière Conference.* Ed. S. Bamforth. Nottingham: The University of Nottingham, 1994 (12–19).

Picard, Raymond. *Racine polémiste.* Utrecht, Holland: Pauvert ("Collection Libertés"), 1967.

Picard, Roger. *Les Salons littéraires et la société française, 1610–1789.* New York: Brentano, 1943.

Pizzorusso, Arnaldo. *Eléments d'une poétique littéraire au XVIIe siècle.* Paris: PUF, 1992.

Plantié, Jacqueline. *La Mode du portrait littéraire en France 1641–81.* Paris: Champion, 1994.

Poulaille, Henry. *Corneille sous le masque de Molière.* Paris: Grasset, 1957.

Ravel, Jeffrey S. "Définir le parterre au XVIIe siècle." In *Ordre et contestation au temps des classiques.* Ed. R. Duchêne and P. Ronzeaud. 2 vols. Paris: Biblio 17, 1992. 225–31.

Reiss, T. J. *Toward Dramatic Illusion: Theatrical Technique and Meaning from Hardy to Horace.* New Haven: Yale UP, 1971.

Redford, Bruce. *Venice and the Grand Tour.* New Haven: Yale UP, 1996.

Revel, J. "Les Usages de la civilité." Vol. 3 of *Histoire de la vie privée.* Ed. P. Ariès and G. Duby. Paris: Seuil, 1986. 169–210.

Rey-Flaud, Bernadette. *Molière et la farce.* Geneva: Droz, 1996.

Riggs, Larry W. *Molière and Plurality: Decomposition of the Classicist Self.* New York: Lang, 1989.

———. "Dom Juan: The Subject of Modernity." *L'Esprit Créateur* 36.1 (1996): 7–20.

Rousset, Jean. *L'Intérieur et l'extérieur: Essai sur la poésie et sur le théâtre au XVIIe siècle.* Paris: Corti, 1968.

———. *La littérature de l'âge baroque en France: Circé et le paon.* Paris: Corti, 1954.

Rubin, David Lee. "Image, Argument, and Esthetics in *La Critique de L'Ecole des femmes.*" *Romance Notes* 15, supp. 1 (1973): 98–107.

Scherer, Jacques. *La Dramaturgie classique en France.* Paris: Nizet, 1950.

———. *Structures de Tartuffe.* Paris: SEDES, 1974.

Screech, M. A. *Laughter at the Foot of the Cross.* London: Penguin, 1997.

Seidel, Michael. *Satiric Inheritance from Rabelais to Sterne.* Princeton: Princeton UP, 1979.

Shaw, David. *Molière: Les Précieuses ridicules.* Critical Guides to French Texts. London: Grant & Cutler. 1986.

Showalter, English. *The Evolution of the French Novel, 1641–1782.* Princeton: Princeton UP, 1972.

Siguret, Françoise. *L'Oeil surpris: perception et représentation dans la première moitié du XVIIe siècle.* Paris: Klincksieck, 1993.

Spitzer, Leo. *Essays on Seventeenth-Century French Literature.* Trans. David Bellos. Cambridge: Cambridge UP, 1983.

Stanton, Domna. *The Aristocrat as Art.* New York: Columbia UP, 1980.

———. "*L'Art de plaire* and the semiotics of honnêteté." *Papers on French Seventeenth-Century Literature* 6 (1976–77): 11–22.

Starobinski, Jean. *L'Oeil vivant, essai: Corneille, Racine, Rousseau, Stendhal.* Paris: Gallimard, 1961.

———. "Sur la flatterie." *Le Remède dans le Mal: Critique et légitimation de l'artifice à l'âge des Lumières.* Paris: Gallimard, 1989. 61–90.

Stenzel, Hartmut. "Espace public et naissance d'un esprit critique—Molière et la querelle sur la moralité du théâtre." In *Diversité, c'est ma devise. Festschrift für Jürgen Grimm.* Paris: Biblio 17 (86), 1994.

Strosetzki, Christoph. *Rhétorique de la conversation: sa dimension littéraire et linguistique dans la société française du XVIIe siècle.* Paris: Biblio 17 (20), 1984.

Suleiman, Susan R., and Inge Crosman, ed. *The Reader in the Text: Essays on Audience and Interpretation.* Princeton: Princeton UP, 1980.

Tapié, Victor-L. *Baroque et Classicisme.* Paris: Livre de poche, 1980.

Thuillier, Jacques. Preface to Roger de Piles, *Cours de peinture par principes.* Paris: Gallimard, 1989.

Tobin, Ronald W. *Tarte à la crème: Comedy and Gastronomy in Molière's Theater.* Columbus: Ohio State UP: 1990.

Tocanne, Bernard. "L'Efflorescence classique." In *Précis de littérature française du XVIIe siècle.* Ed. Jean Mesnard. Paris: PUF, 1990. 205–306.

———. *L'Idée de nature en France dans la seconde moitié du XVIIe siècle.* Paris: Klincksieck, 1978.

Todorov, Tzvetan. *Théories du symbole.* Paris: Seuil, 1977.

Trethewey, John. *Corneille: L'Illusion comique and Le Menteur.* Critical Guides to French Texts. London: Grant & Cutler, 1991.

Truchet, Jacques. "Molière ou l'Elégance." In *L'art du théâtre: Mélanges en hommage à Robert Garapon.* Ed. Y. Bellenger, et al. Paris: PUF, 1992. 189–97.

———. ed. *Thématique de Molière.* Paris: SEDES, 1985.

Valéry, Paul. *Oeuvres*. Ed. J. Hytier. 2 vol. Paris: Gallimard (Bibliothèque de la Pléiade), 1957.

Van Delft, Louis. *Littérature et anthropologie: Nature humaine et caractère à l'âge classique*. Paris: PUF, 1993.

———. "Littérature et anthropologie: le *caractère* à l'âge classique." In *Le Statut de la littérature: Mélanges offerts à Paul Bénichou*. Ed. Marc Fumaroli. Geneva: Droz, 1982.

———. *Le Moraliste classique, essai de définition et de typologie*. Geneva: Droz, 1982.

Van Dyck, Jan. *La Comédie, écho de la vie littéraire au XVIIe siècle, 1630–1685*. Leuven, Belgium: Cabay, 1982.

Van Vree, Th. J., ed. *Les Pamphlets et libelles littéraires contre Molière*. Courtrai: Vermaut, 1933.

Vernet, Max. *Molière: Côté jardin, côté cour*. Paris: Nizet, 1991.

Viala, Alain. *Naissance de l'écrivain: sociologie de la littérature à l'âge classique*. Paris: Ed. de Minuit, 1985.

———. Introduction to Paul Pellisson-Fontanier, *L'Esthétique galante: "Discours sur les oeuvres de Monsieur Sarasin."* Toulouse: Société de Littératures Classiques, 1989.

Vincent, Jean-Pierre, et al. *Alceste et l'absolutisme*. Paris: Ed. Galilée, 1977.

Visages du grand siècle: le portrait français sous le règne de Louis XIV, 1660–1715. Paris: Somogy, 1997.

Wadsworth, Philip A. *Molière and the Italian Theatrical Tradition*. N.p.: French Literature Publications, 1977.

Waterson, Karolyn. *Molière et l'autorité: structures sociales, structures comiques*. Lexington KY: French Forum, 1976.

Watt, Ian. *The Rise of the Novel: Studies in Defoe, Richardson, and Felding*. Berkeley: U of C Press, 1967.

Weinberg, B. *A History of Literary Criticism in the Italian Renaissance*. 2 vols. Chicago: U of Chicago P, 1961.

Wouters, Hyppolyte, and Christine de Ville de Goyet. *Molière ou l'auteur imaginaire?* Brussels: Editions Complexe, 1990.

Zoberman, Pierre. "Entendre Raillerie." In *Thèmes et genres littéraires aux XVIIe et XVIIIe siècles. Mélanges en l'honneur de Jacques Truchet*. ed. N. Ferrier-Caverivière. Paris: PUF, 1992.

Index